THE
OMEGA REBELLION

What Every Adventist Needs to Know...Now

RICK HOWARD

Remnant
Publications
Coldwater MI 49036

Published by Remnant Publications, Inc.
649 E. Chicago Road
Coldwater, MI 49036
517-279-1304
www.remnantpublications.com

The author assumes full responsibility for the accuracy
of all facts and quotations as cited in this book.

Scripture quotations marked KJV are taken from
The Holy Bible, King James Version.

Scripture quotations marked NKJV are taken from the
New King James Version. Copyright © 1982 by Thomas
Nelson, Inc. Used by permission. All rights reserved.

Cover designed by David Berthiaume
Copy editing by Debi Tesser
Text designed by Greg Solie • AltamontGraphics.com

ISBN: 978-1-937718-27-5

Dedication

I dedicate this book initially to my wife, Rosalie, who respected a call from our Lord—a call neither of us were prepared to answer: that I write a book. She was willing to lose me for four years, yet stand by me during that same time. She believed in me from the inception when many did not, supported me when I had little support, and loved me when some of those I love rejected me. Without her love and commitment, this book could never have been written.

I thank the late Elder Kenneth Holland, who served God extensively in the publishing field, for the many years of prodding to write about my pre-Christian experience with the supernatural. I thank the many others whom God led to contact me in the early days of this project, when, at times, I was disheartened. They, too, saw the danger and understood the deception; I knew they had to be out there, given that God would not bring a warning message such as this through one person, but would use many as evidence of its divine origin.

I thank Herbert Douglass, a new and very dear friend who has instructed and supported me along the way, sharing wisdom that comes from his many years of selfless service to God.

I thank David, my friend and confidant of more than thirty-five years, who has helped me in ways too vast to explain, including the certainty of this book's publication. Thank you, David, for hearing God with your heart, bowing to your conscience and following the Lord to an extent that any Christian would esteem. You are a true friend and brother.

I've saved the Lord for last—and to Him, dedicate this book, thanking Him for sending us His Spirit, who opens our minds, enabling us to discern truth. Though He is the true Alpha and Omega, He inspired Ellen G. White to use these words to identify the two most dangerous deceptions His remnant would ever encounter; deceptions He warned would, if possible, deceive the very elect (Matthew 24:24).

I thank You, Jesus, for the humbling experience of writing this book, for teaching me priceless lessons of patience, for endurance and, most of all, for revealing to me my helplessness, laying my glory in the dust. Thank You, also, for revealing Your divinely infinite attributes and absolute command of heaven and earth, down to every twist and turn necessary for the publication of this book. Thank You for teaching me to watch and pray before planning and doing, moving only through doors opened by You, and not by me. Thank You, too, for Your love and confirmation revealed by the steady stream of Your intervention.

Introduction to Second Edition

I thank God for the overwhelmingly positive response to the first edition of this book. While preserving the central message of the book, this second edition takes into consideration the helpful suggestions I received from readers and reviewers. In a number of places, I have provided additional material and documentation to buttress the message of the book. May the Lord use this revised and updated edition of *The Omega Rebellion* to alert God's people of the dangers we face, dangers we have shown ourselves susceptible to, for many years.

—Rick Howard
April 2012

Endorsements

"Stay away from non-biblical spiritual disciplines or methods of spiritual formation that are rooted in mysticism such as contemplative prayer, centering prayer, and the emerging church movement in which they are promoted. Look within the Seventh-day Adventist Church ..."

On July 3, 2010, Elder Ted Wilson, the then newly elected president of the General Conference, counseled the church with this most important statement to beware of the very matters that are the subject of this book. Thank you, Lord, for paving the way, after four years of preparation.

—Elder Rick Howard, Author

Dr. Herbert Edgar Douglass

"Out of his personal background in New Age experiences, Pastor Rick Howard has given us an overview of the 'emerging church' tsunami that is sweeping over too many churches today. He has 'been there and done that' in a way that few today even understand until they are swallowed up in the excitement. The emerging church emphasis on spiritual formation leads into a parallel universe where God is sought *within* man's experience and *not above* each person's own introspections and feelings. The author writes for those who are captivated by the allure of 'finding' God in conversations with others on the same path and for those who are trying to get a handle on what the 'emerging church' movement is all about."

G. Edward Reid
Author of *Sunday's Coming*

"Christians feel the desire for a deeper relationship with God. We know that at the end Jesus will say to the lost, 'Depart from Me, I never knew you.' Unfortunately, the devil knows this desire of Christians and is seeking whom he may deceive. We know Satan will try to deceive even the very elect right before the great final outpouring of the Spirit of God. This great deception is happening right now! Rick Howard's book, *The Omega Rebellion*, is a real eye-opener to this phenomenon. To make sure you are not sincerely mistaken as to whose voice you are listening to—read this book. We all know time is short—far too short to make the mistake of falling for the devil's deceptions. Rick Howard's research for this book will benefit all who sincerely want to follow the true voice of God on to His soon-coming kingdom."

Joel Tompkins
Retired President of the Mid-America Union

"Dramatic changes are taking place in the Protestant and Catholic communions! They are mixing mysticism, oriental religions, pantheism, New Age spiritism and coming together to form a worldwide religious movement. Rick Howard exposes and documents these activities and reveals the potential deceptions for Adventists in his book. *The Omega Rebellion* ... needs to be in every SDA home."

Contents

Foreword

Rick Howard has given us something in these pages that few in the world today could have even conceived, never mind given birth to. He lived those troubled years snared by the New Age clutches. He sensed something terribly wrong. His logical mind became a fertile field for the Holy Spirit to begin his journey out of satanic mischief. It is not easy for anyone to break away, but truth has a way of exposing the cracks in the walls of the New Age kingdom. This is one man's journey into the fullness of how God leads willing seekers into truth—about how men and God should truly relate to each other.

These pages share how Rick discovered that the Adventist movement is *sui generis* in Christian history—there is nothing else like it! It differs from a church because we are trying to run out of business. We rose in the middle of the 19th century to prepare people to be translated, not only to help people live ten extra years.

The fascinating part of our history as a movement is that we would never have survived past the early 1900s *if it were not for Ellen White*. We would have become only an interesting footnote in someone's doctoral dissertation or in some history book.

In my opinion, this subject is one of the best examples of Ellen White's authenticity and of her trustworthiness as God's messenger for these last days. Of course, there are many other examples of her remarkable predictions as well as her uncanny insights into biblical truths. But Rick's topic tops them all.

When she first used two words, ALPHA and OMEGA, in the early 1900s, nobody knew what those two words meant. Of course everyone knew that alpha was the first letter in the Greek alphabet and omega was the last. Ever since, however, those two words have become simply mysterious, largely because nothing has really been done to resurrect what Ellen meant in the early 1900s.

In *The Omega Rebellion*, the history of the alpha and its meaning is clarified, but even more importantly, the reader will learn that a comprehensive understanding of the alpha apostasy of more than 100 years ago is crucial to their safety, and that of the church at large. Alpha deceptions confused and overtook almost half of the delegates at the 1903 General Conference Autumn Council! It was showdown time at the O.K. Corral! Why? What was so confusing that our top leaders were deceived?

Reality check: We are all interested in last-day events even as our leaders were in 1903. However, whether it is Sunday laws, papal resurgence, natural disasters, or spiritualism—one word trumps them all. That word is "*deception.*" Jesus and Paul purposely emphasized that word or its equivalent in their last-day scenarios. Why? Because it is always easy to be deceived. That is the whole purpose of deception—to hide its presence, to divert attention from what is really happening.

Matthew 24:4, 5: "Take heed that no one deceives you. For many will come in My name, saying 'I am the Christ,' and will deceive many" (NKJV). (See 24:11, 24.)

First Timothy 4:1: "Now the Spirit expressly says that in latter times some will depart from the faith, giving heed to deceiving spirits and doctrines of demons"(NKJV). (See 3:1-5; 4:3, 4.)

The Great Controversy 593: "At every revival of God's work the prince of evil is aroused to more intense activity; he is now putting forth his utmost efforts for a *final struggle* against Christ and His followers. ... "The last *great delusion* is soon to open before us. Antichrist is to perform his marvelous works in our sight. So closely will the counterfeit resemble the true that it will be impossible to distinguish between them, except by the Holy Scriptures" (emphasis added).

How is it possible that many longstanding, Sabbath-keeping, tithepaying health reformers will be utterly deceived before probation closes? We have been warned that "we who know the truth should be preparing for what is soon to break upon the world as an overwhelming surprise" (*Testimonies for the Church*, vol. 8, 28).

And all the depths of satanic skill and subtlety acquired, all the cruelty developed, during these struggles of the ages, will be brought to bear against God's people in the final conflict. ... At this time the special endowment of divine grace and power is not less needful to the church than in apostolic days. ... In the great final conflict, Satan will employ the same policy, manifest the same spirit, and work for the same end, as in all preceding ages. That which has been, will be, except that the coming struggle will be marked with a terrible intensity such as the world has never witnessed. Satan's deceptions will be more subtle, his assaults *more* determined. If it were possible, he would lead astray the elect. (*The Great Controversy*, ix, xi).

How could it be possible that even Bible-believing Seventh-day Adventists, "even the very elect," will be in real trouble in these last days?

The Omega Rebellion will shed light upon this perplexing question. New Spirituality is most subtle, deceptive, and attractive. In the last 50 years, Western civilization has been largely overtaken by the postmodern mindset that moves beyond the rational and the factual into the experiential and the mystical.

Schools, grade schools and up, teach that truth is in the mind of the beholder. They teach that there are no absolute truths, and they value outcome-based education. What may be right for you may be only opinion for someone else. One of the highest goals of education is to learn how to be tolerant.

Most Protestant leaders are looking for ways to reach this postmodern generation. Many start out by looking for the appropriate methods without changing the message. That hope is a delusion. Many start out with good intentions, but the end product is devastating—maybe short-term excitement, but long-term disaster. The record is everywhere!

Many leaders in this new Protestant movement are well-known in our Adventist academic centers—truly pleasing, captivating speakers with fresh, innovative ways of explaining their experience with God. How did all this happen so fast and almost everywhere? Remember the key word is "*deception*"!

New Spirituality is the most subtle, most persuasive deceit of all of Satan's strategies in the end time, far surpassing the mixed messages of the gallant Reformers, completely catching Protestants in the late 20th century by surprise.

Alan Wolfe writes in *The Transformation of American Religion*: "Religion in the United States is being transformed in radically new directions. ... Talk of hell, damnation, and even sin has been replaced by a nonjudgmental language of understanding and empathy. Gone are the arguments over doctrine and theology ... More Americans than ever proclaim themselves born again in Christ, but the lord to whom they turn rarely gets angry and frequently strengthens self-esteem. ... [As a result] the faithful in the United States are remarkably like everyone else." [1]

What should Adventists *not* do in relating to New Spirituality?

We must not deny that some of our church programs are boring and out of touch with young and old. That many church programs emphasize doctrine more than experiencing a daily walk with Jesus as He walked. That New Spirituality leaders are rightly concerned with finding genuine Christian experience.

The basic components of Satan's master plan of deception and confusion, especially in these last days, are outlined in E. G. White's *The Great Controversy.*

Some of these components are the omega, which caused E. G. White to "tremble," and may be recognized in the following:

> Emotional excitement, a mingling of the true with the false, which is well adapted to mislead. (*The Great Controversy*, 464)

> A masterpiece of Satan's deceptions to keep the minds of men searching and conjecturing in regard to that which God has not made known, and which He does not intend that we shall understand. (Ibid., 523)

> Many claim that it matters not what one believes, if his life is only right. But the life is molded by the faith. If light and truth is within our reach, and we neglect to improve the privilege of hearing and seeing it, we virtually reject it; we are choosing darkness rather than light. (Ibid., 597)

An Adventist weakness from our beginning is that we have had to contend with "good" people who believed that they could determine truth. Many say, "If we stay close to God, He will guide us." Such thinking, ignoring that the Bible is the test of truth, opens the door to being led by impressions and impulses, leading to all kinds of fanaticism. In other words, for them, experience determines theology.

---

1   Alan Wolfe, *The Transformation of American Religion* (New York: Free Press, a division of Simon & Schuster Inc. 2003), 3.

Be not deceived; many will depart from the faith, giving heed to seducing spirits and doctrines of devils. We have before us the alpha of this danger. The omega will be of a most startling nature. (*Selected Messages,* Book 1, 197)

The subject upon which he [Dr. Kellogg] was speaking was life, and the relation of God to all living things. In his presentation he cloaked the matter somewhat, but in reality he was presenting scientific theories which are akin to pantheism, as of the highest value. ... One by my side told me that the evil angels had taken captive the mind of the speaker. (*Manuscript Releases,* vol. 5, 375)

Remember: the common appeal of both alpha and omega is that they will lead to higher spiritual awareness (New Spirituality) and that it will come with the subtle allure of panentheism—God is in everything—a theory "akin to pantheism."

Rick Howard will take us on this amazing journey into the maze of alluring deceptions he himself lived through. And then he will show us how we may detect and avoid the allure that even "the elect" will need special preparation to think clearly.

Herbert Edgar Douglass
August 17, 2010
Lincoln, CA

In a Nutshell

Henry J. M. Nouwen, one of the fathers of modern spiritual formation, and others during the last few centuries have simply revised an ancient mystical method of altering one's consciousness, through the knowledge and control of certain mental processes. They gave these processes the names centering prayer and contemplative prayer, tucking them nicely within the Roman Catholic discipline called spiritual formation, deceiving Christians into believing this is a blessing, promoting the spiritual growth of the Christian and eventually leading to a new experience with God, the experience of coming into His presence.

What makes this deception so treacherous is that Satan has designed and initiated the entire process, and that the mystical place called the silence is the same as the trance of psychics or spirit mediums, occultists, and magicians. (*The Omega Rebellion*, 126, 127)

You should understand clearly that satanic agencies are clothing false theories in an attractive garb, even as Satan in the Garden of Eden concealed his identity from our first parents by speaking through the serpent. You are instilling into human minds that which to you seems to be a very beautiful truth, but which in reality is error. The hypnotic influence of Satan is upon you, and upon all others who turn from the plain word of God to pleasing fables.

Dr. Kellogg, sustained as he is by his associates, walks proudly and boastingly, and feels confirmed in his own will and way, which for years the Lord has been warning him to avoid. His associate physicians may strengthen the faith of men and women in his supposed wonderful enlightenment; but the light emanating from him is not the light shining from the Holy of holies; it is a false light that allures to spiritual death. (*Spalding and Magan Collection*, 332, 3, 1985)

1900: "THE TIME WAS NOT YET"

TODAY: "NEVER LEAVE A SOUL UNWARNED"

Chapter 1
Now and Then

We are about to examine a popular trend in Christianity today, a trend with characteristics that reveal its inherent danger. As we examine this new trend, we will discover that the only factor new about it is its name, and that behind the name is the same old form of an ancient, supernatural, and satanic science: a science that Satan has used to deceive humanity throughout the ages. This book seeks to study the characteristics of the end-time omega as detailed by the pen of inspiration. The application of these characteristics to the deception(s) gaining a foothold in our beloved church are just that: an application. These deceptions are not with certainty the predicted omega apostasy, however plausible, but a circumstance nonetheless to be studied, as was the alpha. Will other deceptions meet the omega criteria? But to be sure, as these components are weighed, it would be highly valuable for God's remnant to understand the earmarks that are its identity.

During the entire history of the great controversy, Satan's greatest success has always been directly related to his ability to control the minds of those he ensnares *without their awareness*. This is the secret of his success. When he can deceive those under his power into believing that God is working for them, when in truth it is he, he has won the day. This is the fundamental characteristic of the omega apostasy and is likely the reason it caused Ellen White to "tremble" when she beheld it: many leaders in God's remnant church were carrying on what they perceived as the work of God, while, in fact, they were being directed by the prince of evil.

The more closely Satan can appear Christ-like in both his behavior and his use of the supernatural, the greater is his ability to deceive. He is delighted to see the world perceiving him as some demonic being, a benefactor of evil and destruction, for then he knows his Christian disguise will be more effective.

We will expose how Satan has used this Christian disguise in the past and is using it once again in his final attempt to overthrow God's people.

The distinction between his past and present attempts are the thousands of years he has had to perfect his deceptions and master the manipulation of the human race; and why God is permitting him control of the powers used in his spiritualistic deceptions.

> Here is a channel wholly devoted to himself and *under his control,* and he can make the world believe what he will. The Book that is to judge him and his followers he puts back in the shade, just where he wants it. (*Early Writings,* 91, emphasis added)

To understand this deception—how it works, why the Lord permits it, who will be deceived, and why they will be deceived—it is essential to understand the intimate relationship that exists between the Lord and His bride, the church, the remnant church.

In our earthly relationships is there ever anything, anywhere, more intimate than husband and wife? Are there any words ever spoken more essential for maintaining their relationship than the words of truth they share? And so in the heavenly, the words of truth, so essential for maintaining a loving relationship between Jesus, the husband, and the church, His bride, is the very function of the Spirit of Prophecy.

Our understanding of why it is that those who will not heed the warnings God has given and who fall prey to the omega rests upon our comprehension of the importance and impact of inspiration, manifested in those words of truth, and the dreadful results of its rejection. It is akin to adultery: the rejection of your Lover's love letter to you, for whom He gave His life, and of Him, who you accepted as your loving eternal Savior.

Think for a moment how it affects Jesus when we ignore the counsel contained in the Spirit of Prophecy. He inspired His messenger to write to His beloved bride expressions of His deepest love, a love beyond our understanding, a love that drove Him to the cross, where He chose not to exist forever if we could not be with Him, if you could not be with Him.

These writings also contain warnings and counsels to His beloved, of how to avoid being destroyed by the enemy. He gave His life for her, and to lose her would result in unspeakable sorrow and pain, so when she ignores His counsel, refusing to heed His warnings, His heart is broken. He is being rejected by those He loves and gave His life for. We need to understand these things.

Over and over, Ellen White warned through inspiration:

So long as they refuse to heed the warnings given them, the spell that is upon them cannot be broken. (*Spaulding and Magan Collection*, 464)

To refuse the divine counsel is to be swept out of the church and into the omega deception. Again, to understand the omega-like characteristics that apply to present-day deceptions is to be placed in a position of safety.

Today, it is called "spiritual formation," a comforting and Christian-sounding term that fittingly suggests the growth and forming of Christian character—exactly what it is intended to imply.

There is a dilemma, however, for hidden within spiritual formation's teachings are certain techniques of prayer, supposedly taught to improve one's spiritual life, that are in reality ancient mind-altering processes. We will see that these methods are a form of hypnotism, resulting in an experience in which one believes they have come into the presence of God, when instead a very real deception has taken place.

This is a mighty claim, but one that the author and many others who have been saved by the grace of God from spiritualism's grasp know to be a valid one. The Lord has allowed many of us to experience the occult before being miraculously delivered into His remnant church. It seems that it was for such a time as this—a time to sound a warning—to expose and define this newly garbed ancient mysticism. Ancient, yes, but mysticism nonetheless.

During the few years this book was being written, there were many undeniable providences of God that brought together those who recognize this deception. From across America, conference and union administrators, professors, physicians, pastors, and laymen were brought in contact with one another in such a way that God's direction was unmistakable. On occasion, in answer to prayer, they contacted this book's author and encouraged him to continue on with the project. Thus, it became a clear and deliberate burden by God's leading to expose and explain those teachings hidden under the innocent-sounding term of spiritual formation.

During this time, others were hard at work doing what the Lord impressed them to do. Some were steeped in research into how this deception was affecting the church on a worldwide basis, while others were candidly and honestly writing letters of warning as some of these deceptions reached their local churches. Each had a burden laid upon them by the Lord, and when all were brought together, His divine guidance was obvious.

Dear church family, aspects of what the new "Emerging Church" has termed spiritual formation are deceptions most sinister and specifically designed to appeal to the Christianity of the day, with profound implications for Seventh-day Adventists and the role they are destined to play in the great controversy.

Here now, let us begin the story of the alpha and the omega.

There is a war raging. Not any of the wars that come and go as worldly powers rise and fall, but that war that has gone on without ceasing since Adam and Eve disobeyed God's one command in the Garden of Eden, the war between the faithful of God and all the forces of evil rebelling against Him. This is the universal war between good and evil being waged on our world and has been the focus of all Creation for thousands of years. It is the war Seventh-day Adventists refer to as The Great Controversy between Christ and Satan.

> There was war in heaven: Michael and his angels fought against the dragon; and the dragon fought and his angels, And prevailed not; neither was their place found any more in heaven. And the great dragon was cast out, that old serpent, called the Devil, and Satan, which deceiveth the whole world: he was cast out into the earth, and his angels were cast out with him. (Revelation 12:7–9 KJV)

This is not a war fought with weapons of man's invention; in this war, consequences are decided by acts of the will, by volition. It is a war in which angelic beings contend over the minds of men. Physical battles are fought for us, with outcomes dependent upon our choices, for God's love demands this dynamic. His love is manifest when we choose to follow His will. The angelic beings who battle with our enemies in the heavenly spheres, advance or retreat, in harmony with our choice to love or not to love, to serve God or not to serve Him. Our only hope for victory in this war is to place ourselves within the tender loving care of our Savior, following His instructions wherever He may lead.

This war engages every human being, Satan with his angelic army, and every heavenly angel the Lord has assigned to assist us. Jesus is our Commander-in-Chief, as is Satan of the forces of evil. No one escapes participating, and we are engaged in battle at every moment in time, recognized or not. Whether we are spiritually lost; pleading for the strength to gain victory; grappling for resources to survive; engaged in hypnotic sinful pleasures; striving for power, money, or merriment, or any other of life's endeavors, we are on the battlefield. We are forever in combat until life ends, choosing sides by our decisions for good or evil, aware of what is happening or not.

We are at war! Ask the apostles and the countless millions who gave their lives for the Lord, called to follow Jesus in His death on the cross, the light of His selfless love shined brightly through their willingness to die for their Savior. In this war, many victories have been gained by the deaths of God's soldiers, confounding the ranks of the enemy to whom death is defeat, not victory. Determined not to yield the conviction of truth and duty, or deny their faith in Jesus, His army of martyrs stood firm unto death.

Ask Peter, hanging upside down on his cross; or Paul, his head severed from his body by the filthy blade of a gruesome guillotine; ask John the Baptist, whose head was delivered on a platter to a sadistic queen. Ask Stephen, his body crushed and broken under the blast of boulders; or the apostle John, who just couldn't be killed, even while submerged in boiling oil that would, under normal circumstances, melt away his flesh, leaving only his bones. Just ask any of them if there is a war going on. Imagine the astonishment and confusion as the apostle John stood before the emperor's throne, the royal carpets being spoiled by dirty oil dripping off John's body—the very oil that was to cook him to oblivion. What was an emperor to do with this disciple who could not be destroyed? It was obvious to all present that this war had supernatural elements.

Satan was intent on taking the life of the last living apostle. John, who often referred to himself as the disciple whom Jesus continued to love, was the last living apostle, and when it came to the apostles, Satan was intent on having a perfect record of murder, but it was not to be. The Lord was not going to allow Satan this victory; never. He still had plans for this aged apostle, plans involving you and me, plans essential for finishing the work in this world. John would peer into the realms of glory as no one ever had before. While an old man in exile on the Isle of Patmos, in the Mediterranean Sea, Jesus appeared to him and opened to his vision heaven itself. This most elaborate vision was to be recorded for all future generations.

The book of Revelation, the final book in the canon of Scripture, would not only reveal the world to come, but would record the climactic struggle in the universal war between good and evil. Peering through the portals of heaven, it would outline history, exposing Satan and his allies as they attempted to overthrow God's church through the ages. The second half of the book would record how God's remnant church, being obedient to their Lord's command and clothed with His righteousness, go to every nation, kindred, tongue, and people with the gospel message. It records the final, climactic battle in this ongoing war between good and evil, the Battle of Armageddon. It records how after His victory and before the very eyes of His saints, He creates a new world; a world that will be their home and where Jesus will reign as King of kings and Lord of lords forever and ever.

The Lord purposed that the book would enable His army to know their exact position on the battlefield, ever able to hear the instructions of their Commander. The faithful would discern the enemy's movements, only acquiescing to his deceptions, or suffering defeat, as a part of the Lord's plan for ultimate victory.

Revelation would not only reveal the future history of the world through to its demise at the second coming of Jesus, the beauty of heaven and our home on the new earth, but would also reveal as never before God's loving character, a perfect balance of mercy and justice, holiness, beauty, and power.

It records how countless martyrs gave their lives as a witness of the selfless love of God, a witness far-reaching in its significance. The earth was enriched by the blood they spilled, a surety for the final generation who, by God's grace, would be restored to the image of God, the image in which we were created. Those martyrs, who surrendered their lives for our sakes, knew we were at war.

Now, friends, it is time for us to awaken to this reality also. We are at war.

The dragon was wroth with the woman, and went to make war with the remnant of her seed, which keep the commandments of God, and have the testimony of Jesus Christ. (Revelation 12:17 KJV)

But this final battle will not be as before; it will far surpass anything the world has ever experienced.

That which has been, will be, except that *the coming struggle will be marked with a terrible intensity such as the world has never witnessed. Satan's deceptions will be more subtle, his assaults more determined.* (*The Great Controversy*, xi, emphasis added)

In this world, Seventh-day Adventists are God's special denominated people. We are the only denominated people who maintain that God's law is a revelation of His character, and the standard by which all created beings in heaven and earth are enjoined to live by. For this reason, the prophetic gift has been restored to us, the remnant church.

> As the third angel's message arose in the world, which is to reveal the Law of God to the church *in its fullness and power*, the prophetic gift was also immediately restored. (*Loma Linda Messages*, 33, emphasis added)

The end of all things is upon us, and we have been called, as were Elijah and John the Baptist, to prepare the way for the coming of the Lord. If there was ever a time when God's people needed to be guided and assisted by the Spirit of Prophecy, it is now. Through this precious gift, coupled with the Holy Scriptures, our Commander-in-Chief instructs and directs His church.

Satan understands how essential this gift is to the church and has had great success through the ages counterfeiting the work of the Holy Spirit. He knows he has but a short time. His final struggle is looming before him, and his end is near. He is frantic—filled with hate and fraught with anxiety; he is desperate to prolong his days. He is enraged at God and those who serve Him and will use all his experience and devious scheming genius to prepare his masterpiece of deception, the "omega" deception: the deception that caused God's messenger to "tremble" when she beheld it.

In this final conflict, we can expect him to use the same deceptions that gave him such success in the past. The question we need to answer is, how will he counterfeit the work of the Holy Spirit today? As mentioned, in His infinite wisdom and for reasons not completely understood, God has given Satan complete control over the powers of spiritualism to cause the world to believe what he wants them to believe.

There can be no mistake when the Scriptures are humbly consulted, that supernatural power of the type considered "spiritualistic" is not something the Christian should expect to acquire, but something to be extremely wary of. Those who venture into that territory, having the truth of Scripture and the messages of warning in the Spirit of Prophecy, are making an intelligent decision to ignore those warnings and disobey God. This is the seed of rebellion, as spoken of in the later chapter entitled "Rebellion," chapter 11.

We know of the many spiritualistic deceptions in the world today, such as those that occur in the practices of the occult and New Age. Psychics and spirit mediums, as well as those who practice witchcraft, are well acquainted with the supernatural. Then there are also counterfeit manifestations of the Holy Spirit among the fallen and so-called "spirit-filled" churches. All these we are aware of, but how will Satan attempt to deceive the "very elect"? How will he deceive the remnant church? The answers, according to God's prophet, lie in the characteristics of the "omega," and we can be sure it will be different from earlier deceptions.

Consider the supernatural manifestations of the "silence," acquired by those who practice the "contemplative/mystical prayer" learned in the thousands of institutes and home missions where spiritual formation is taught. How might they be deceptive for the very elect?

Of all the deceptions we have faced as God's chosen people, none have been so subtle, cunning, or widely accepted by God's people as has spiritual formation. Many in our midst have embraced this practice without discerning its hidden dangers. This unique program of Roman Catholicism, spreading like wildfire through the Christian world as the "Emerging Church," should be understood in the context of both Scripture and the Spirit of Prophecy.

We will briefly outline the history of spiritual formation, showing where this teaching comes from, what it teaches, and how its designer—the Roman Catholic Church—plans to use it to win the entire world to its worship community. We will present how the same church, by its own admission, deems its use by the leaders of nations essential to gathering them all under one central leading authority: a system toward which they are working diligently and covertly.

Chapter 2
Spiritual Formation

Martin Luther and Ignatius Loyola were contemporaries. Both were drawn to God by His Spirit; both were convicted of the sin in their lives, and both sought a way of escape from their guilty consciences through the power of God. Finding God and His power to bring them victory was at the core of their search.

For reasons that will only be revealed in the judgment, they looked for that victory in different places. Martin Luther searched the Holy Scriptures and found the God of Creation, while Loyola searched the world of "spirits" and believed he found God in His creation.

Luther learned that the power, for which he searched to gain Christian victory, was through simple faith in the promises of God found in the Holy Bible. He discovered that he must come to Scripture like a babe, accepting all, as if the God of heaven was standing before him speaking to him personally. Fundamentally speaking, he discovered that the Holy Bible is the unerring Word of God and is the standard of faith and doctrine for every true Christian, containing all the needed instruction for our salvation.

Loyola, on the other hand, chose to suppress his guilty conscience, refusing to think any more of his sins. Instead of searching the Holy Bible, he sought enlightenment through the supernatural world, satisfying his own carnal propensities. He always desired to see God in everything, everywhere, all the time. This was the desire of his heart.

> Inigo, instead of feeling that his remorse was sent to drive him to the foot of the cross, persuaded himself that these inward reproaches proceeded not from God, but from the devil; and he resolved never more to think of his sins, to erase them from his memory, and bury them in eternal oblivion. Luther turned toward Christ, Loyola only fell upon himself.

Visions came erelong to confirm Inigo in the convictions in which he had arrived. ...

Inigo did not seek truth in the Holy Scriptures but imagined in their place immediate communication with the world of spirits. ...

Luther, on taking his doctor's degree, had pledged his oath to Holy Scripture. ... Loyola, at his time, bound himself to dreams and visions; and chimerical apparitions became the principle of his life and his faith.[2]

Loyola longed for supernatural experiences, believing them to be evidence of God's presence and power. Deceived, he turned to the writings of the Roman Catholic mystics and saints, longing for God to reveal Himself in everything, all the time. He desired God's presence on his terms, and Satan made sure he would think he found Him. From these experiences he was profoundly changed and for the rest of his life asserted that God miraculously gave him the enlightenment of a lifetime in just a few moments.

The concept of God as revealed to Loyola in these mystical experiences reveal a God who is pantheistic in nature—His person existing in the things of His creation. Loyola developed what is called today his "Spiritual Exercises," which contain all the teachings from which modern spiritual formation was constructed. From these spiritual exercises comes the most important practice of the "examen," a daily practice of prayer and meditation essential to spiritual formation.

The contemplative in action, according to St. Ignatius Loyola, not only contemplates the active world and sees wonderful things, but also sees in these wonderful things signs of God's presence and activity. The contemplative in action is deeply aware of God's presence even in the midst of a busy life. It is a stance of awareness. Awareness of God.

That leads us to a second goal: *finding God in all things.* By now you've seen how everything can be a way to experience God. ... In all things. And in all people. And we've talked about an easy way to jump-start that awareness, to help you find God in everything:

---

2   J. H. Merle D' Auburgine, *History of the Reformation of the 16th Century* (Grand Rapids, MI: Baker Bookhouse, 1976), 354.

the examen. The contemplative in action seeks God and seeks to find him in action.

That means that he or she sees the world in an *incarnational way*, a third definition. God dwells in real things, real places and real people. Not just "up there" but "all around." …

So tying it altogether you could say this: Contemplatives in action seek *to find God in all things* by looking at the world in an incarnational way, and, in their quest, they realize their desire *freedom and detachment*, which helps them move even closer to God. That's probably a fair summary of Ignatian spirituality.[3]

Loyola's experience was mysticism, and he taught all those enlisted in the Jesuit order, which he founded. Malachi Martin in his classic, *The Jesuits*, speaks of Loyola's passion for mysticism:

Each companion in the Society (of Jesus) was burning and busy to find every trace of God and God's handiwork throughout the cosmos where he, God the Workman, the deus faber of the medieval mystics, was ever at work creating … Of course, I saw God at work in all things—vivifying, beautifying, freshening, and quickening human beings and all of nature into life-nourishing cycles. Throughout, I thus saw God *in all things*.

But more than that, I strove with my spirit and with my whole being to arrive at the summit of love where I could see *all things in God*; see them rather as manifestations of His power and beauty, as rays of light descending from the sun, as streams of water leaping from the spring well. Nothing in creation could escape this viewpoint—the fearful symmetry of the tiger, the ridiculous curl to a piglet's tail, perfumes, colors, tastes, the audible silence settled on mountaintops, the patterns traced by a dancer, the cries of children at play, the songs of birds, the toils of the least of insects.

Seeing all things in God, with their being and their beauty, the scales would fall away from my flesh bound eyes. Quietly, unresistingly,

---

3   James Martin, SJ, *The Jesuit Guide to (Almost) Everything* (New York, NY: First Harper Collins, 2012), 391, 392.

coherently all would be absorbed in Him, for me; and the dust and ashes of their mortality and of my own mortality would be consumed in the stainless luster of His eternal existence and beauty. …

Ignatius [Loyola] presumed that every Jesuit would have this same perpetual preoccupation with finding God in all things.[4]

Friends, the spiritual exercises of Ignatius Loyola, the founder of the Jesuit Order, is the foundation upon which spiritual formation is built. The theology taught in all spiritual formation seminars is that of Ignatius Loyola. The language so often used, the phrases and terminology that describe the mission behind the teaching, is now used by SDA leaders who have been trained in this discipline. It is the language of Roman Catholicism. The basic theology behind what is being taught in the very missions and institutes where Seventh-day Adventists have gone to learn spiritual formation is the theology of Loyola: pantheistic, mystical, and Roman Catholic. It includes contemplative/mystical prayer, leading one into an altered state of consciousness believed to be the "presence of God."

Here is what Inspiration has to say about the Jesuits, the Roman Catholic order founded by Ignatius Loyola.

At this time, the order of the Jesuits was created, the most cruel, unscrupulous, and powerful of all the champions of popery. Cut off from every earthly tie and human interest, dead to the claims of natural affection, reason and conscience wholly silenced, they knew no rule, no tie, but that of their order, and no duty but to extend its power. The gospel of Christ had enabled its adherents to meet danger and endure suffering, undismayed by cold, hunger, toil, and poverty, to uphold the banner of truth in face of the rack, the dungeon, and the stake. To combat these forces, Jesuitism inspired its followers with a fanaticism that enabled them to endure like dangers, and to oppose to the power of truth all the weapons of deception. There was no crime too great for them to commit, no deception too base for them to practice, no disguise too difficult for them to assume. Vowed to perpetual poverty and humility, it was their studied aim to secure wealth and power, to be devoted

---

4   Malachi Martin, *The Jesuits* (New York: Simon & Schuster, Inc., 1987), 206, 207.

to the overthrow of Protestantism, and the re-establishment of the papal supremacy.

When appearing as members of their order, they wore a garb of sanctity, visiting prisons and hospitals, ministering to the sick and the poor, professing to have renounced the world, and bearing the sacred name of Jesus, who went about doing good. But under this blameless exterior the most criminal and deadly purposes were concealed. It was a fundamental principle of the order that the end justifies the means. By this code, lying, theft, perjury, assassination, were not only pardonable but commendable, when they served the interests of the church. Under various disguises the Jesuits worked their way into offices of State, climbing up to be the counselors of kings, and shaping the policy of nations. They became servants, to act as spies upon their masters. They established colleges for the sons of princes and nobles, and schools for the common people; and the children of Protestant parents were drawn into an observance of popish rites. All the outward pomp and display of the Romish worship was brought to bear to confuse the mind, and dazzle and captivate the imagination; and thus the liberty for which the fathers had toiled and bled was betrayed by the sons. The Jesuits rapidly spread themselves over Europe, and wherever they went, there followed a revival of popery.

To give them greater power, a bull was issued re-establishing the Inquisition. Notwithstanding the general abhorrence with which it was regarded, even in Catholic countries, this terrible tribunal was again set up by popish rulers, and atrocities too terrible to bear the light of day were repeated in its secret dungeons. In many countries, thousands upon thousands of the very flower of the nation, the purest and noblest, the most intellectual and highly educated, pious and devoted pastors, industrious and patriotic citizens, brilliant scholars, talented artists, skillful artisans, were slain, or forced to flee to other lands. Such were the means which Rome had invoked to quench the light of the Reformation, to withdraw from men the Bible, and to restore the ignorance and superstition of the Dark Ages. But under God's blessing and the labors of those noble men whom he had raised up to succeed Luther, Protestantism was not overthrown. Not to the favor or arms of princes was it to owe its strength. The smallest countries, the humblest and least powerful nations, became its strongholds. It was little Geneva in the midst of mighty foes plotting her destruction; it was Holland on her sand-banks by the Northern Sea, wrestling against the tyranny of Spain, then the greatest and most opulent of kingdoms; it was bleak, sterile Sweden, that gained victories for the Reformation. (*The Great Controversy,* 1888 ed., 235, 236)

Here is the basic premise of our concern, which we will give evidence for, and the reason this book was written.

Spiritual formation is a satanic deception, structured upon Jesuit pantheistic spirituality. Its planned use is to be the primary tool used by Roman Catholicism to regain control of the world, while concurrently counteracting the worldwide mission of the Seventh-day Adventist Church. Spiritual formation counterfeits the work of the Holy Spirit that directs our minds to Jesus in the heavenly sanctuary. People are deceived by the teaching that they can come into Jesus' presence whenever they desire, communicating with Him through the practice of "centering" and "contemplative prayer," which brings them into the mystical state of the silence. Furthermore, they are taught a false type of pantheism that claims Jesus, in His fullness, can be found in every human being and in all of His creation, everywhere.

The mystical experience of the silence leaves people extremely motivated to evangelize, wanting to vigorously work for God. They sense that God is leading them in every step they take, at every moment in time. This seems to be a universal experience for those who have been to the "mystical silence." They are definitely being led by a spirit, but is it the Holy Spirit? We think not!

It was February 1904, and the time had come for Ellen White to bring finality to the twenty years of pointed warnings and reproofs aimed at Dr. J. H. Kellogg and others who joined with him in an apostasy among the leaders of the remnant church. This apostasy included, but was not exclusive to, the pantheism espoused in Dr. Kellogg's book *The Living Temple*, which contained theories leading to erroneous conclusions concerning the presence and nature of God. The acceptance of these theories by the thought leaders of the church in Battle Creek opened the door to satanic control of their minds.

We need not the mysticism that is in this book. Those who entertain these sophistries will soon find themselves in a position where *the enemy can talk with them*, and lead them away from God. It is represented to me that the writer of this book is on a false track. He has lost sight of the distinguishing truths for this time. *He knows not whither his steps are tending.* (*Selected Messages,* Book 1, 52)

In this chapter, we will do our best to understand what Ellen White intended when she used the words "alpha," and/or "omega," words she used to identify the most dangerous deceptions that would ever confront the Seventh-day Adventist Church.

As we read, I recognized the very sentiments against which I had been bidden to speak in warning during the early days of my public labors. When I first left the State of Maine, it was to go through Vermont and Massachusetts, to bear a testimony against these sentiments. *The Living Temple* contains the *alpha* of these theories. I knew that the *omega* would follow in a little while; and I *trembled* for our people. (*Early Writings,* 53, emphasis added)

By the end of this book, we will attempt to understand just what Ellen White may have meant when she said, *"those who entertain these sophistries will soon find themselves in a position where the enemy can talk with them."* This frightening concept may be applicable to experiences some are having in our ranks currently; matters that are "omega-like" to God's people.

It is important to understand that it was not only Dr. Kellogg's *theology* that needed to be addressed; his use of *psychological techniques of mind controlling mind*, while at the helm of the largest and most influential institution of the church and one of the largest in the world, placed the doctor and the leaders under his influence, in the bull's-eye of Satan's attacks against the church. This arrangement placed *Dr. Kellogg where he could influence the leaders of the church. Satan had already led the doctor astray, and now the leadership of the church was precisely where Satan wanted them to carry out his destructive work.* When leaders can be deceived they are of the greatest use to the arch deceiver. *The deception of the leaders in Kellogg's day, identified as the "alpha," contains many similarities to how the future "omega" deception will operate. This final satanic evil will appear as yet another in a "train of heresies" as the close of probation approaches.*

Under the Lord's direction, Ellen White sent a number of warnings to convey how these dangerous theories were leading our medical workers astray. A sixty-page pamphlet, "Testimonies for the Church Containing

Letters to Physicians and Ministers Instruction to Seventh-day Adventists"
(1904), was published.

For upwards of twenty years, Ellen White agonized in prayer for the
wayward doctor, for whom she had great love and concern. It was her men-
toring and assistance that enabled him to receive the education needed to
fill the position to which the Lord called him. In a letter she wrote to him
in November of 1902, she said:

> I love your soul and I want you to have eternal life. I must tell you
> the truth. And whether you acknowledge it or not, you know that
> what I tell you is truth.

> Shortly before your father died, he called me to him, saying that
> he had something to say to me. "I feel that John is in great danger,"
> he said. "But, Sister White, you will not get discouraged, will you,
> even though he seems to be headstrong? You are the only one who
> can help him. Do not let him go, even though his case appears
> discouraging."

> I promised that I would do as the Spirit of the Lord directed me.
> God's word to me has always been, "You can help him." (*Manu-
> script Releases,* vol. 12, 4)

The emotional pain Ellen White endured as she watched this brilliant
and dedicated son, friend, and physician slip beyond the reach of the Holy
Spirit's influence must have been heart-wrenching. Consider her feelings
while writing these final words of warning to Dr. Kellogg after his continued refusal to heed her inspired counsels:

> I have the tenderest feelings toward Dr. Kellogg. For many years I
> have tried to hold fast to him. God's word to me has always been,
> "You can help him." Sometimes I am awakened in the night, and,
> rising, I walk the room, praying: "O Lord, hold Dr. Kellogg fast. Do
> not let him go. Keep him steadfast. Anoint his eyes with the heav-
> enly eyesalve, that he may see all things clearly." Night after night
> I have lain awake, studying how I could help him. Earnestly and
> often I have prayed that the Lord may not permit him to turn away
> from sanctifying truth. This is the burden that weighs me down,—
> the desire that he shall be kept from making mistakes that would
> hurt his soul and injure the cause of present truth. But for some

time his actions have revealed that a strange spirit is controlling him. The Lord will take this matter in His own hands. I must bear the messages of warning that God gives me to bear, and then leave with the Lord the results. I must now present the matter in all its bearings; for the people of God must not be despoiled. (*Testimonies for the Church Containing Letters to Physicians and Ministers Instruction to SDAs,* 58, 59)

Ellen White loved Dr. Kellogg's soul. The way she hung on to the hope and studied how she might help him gives us insight into the heart of love and concern that the Lord's messenger had for one who was falling away from the truth. It reveals how God filled her heart with the same tender care and forgiveness Jesus has for each and every one of us. It is an encouragement to realize that the Lord chose someone, a person truly converted and sanctified by the Spirit of God, to watch over His children and give them divine counsel.

The way she loved and counseled Dr. Kellogg is an example for us of how to love and care for the misdirected in our church and families. She labored year after year, writing letter after letter, entreating the doctor to turn from the theories that beclouded his mind. She meticulously pointed out every aspect of his mistaken theology and leadership style, promising him the Lord's love and acceptance if he would only surrender, but he would not.

Longsuffering reached its limit. With a tear, the waiting time had to end, and action was necessary to save God's church. She said, "The people of God must not be despoiled;" the gift of salvation must not be stolen from God's children by these false and deceptive theories. The patient waiting for Dr. Kellogg to respond to the pleadings of the Holy Spirit had to come to an end. God's people must be saved. As the Lord's messenger, Ellen White was forever vigilant in her watch-care over the people of God. The Lord revealed to her the changes that might have taken place in the structure of the church if Dr. Kellogg and his associates would have implemented their plans.

The enemy of souls has sought to bring in the supposition that a great reformation was to take place among Seventh-day Adventists, and that this reformation would consist in giving up the doctrines which stand as the pillars of our faith, and engaging in a process of reorganization. Were this reformation to take place, what would result? The principles of truth that God in His wisdom has given to the remnant church would be discarded. Our religion would be changed. The fundamental principles that have sustained the work for the last fifty years would be accounted as error. A new organization would be established. Books of a new order would be written. A system of intellectual philosophy would be introduced. The founders of this system would go into the cities, and do a wonderful work. The Sabbath, of course, would be lightly regarded, as also the God who created it. Nothing would be allowed to stand in the way of the new movement. The leaders would teach that virtue is better than vice, but God being removed, they would place their dependence on human power, which, without God, is worthless. Their foundation would be built on the sand, and storm and tempest would sweep away the structure.

Who has authority to begin such a movement? We have our Bibles. We have our experience, attested to by the miraculous working of the Holy Spirit. We have a truth that admits of no compromise. Shall we not repudiate everything that is not in harmony with this truth? (*Selected Messages,* Book 1, 204, 205)

Here we have an inspired statement of the changes that would have taken place in the church, if the "alpha" apostasy had been successful. Dr. Kellogg's apostasy included controlling minds, the resistance of inspired counsel, self-exaltation, the misuse of church funds, and his insistence in advocating false theories concerning the personality and presence of God. This was, however, just the beginning. She termed this beginning phase the "alpha," implying that forms of this deception will arise again and again, reaching its final mature stage just before the end of time. Many have envisioned the "omega" as something separate and distinct from the "alpha," but that theory does not correspond with the way Ellen White used the terms "alpha and omega." These words were a regular part of her vocabulary and she used them together or separately, in reference to the beginning or the ending, or to the entire cycle of beginning to end, for many subjects. Let's look at a few examples.

[Read] a Book containing the words of Him who is the Alpha and Omega of wisdom. The time spent in a study of these books might better be spent in gaining a knowledge of Him whom to know aright is life eternal. (*Counsels on Health,* 369)

Here she refers to Jesus as the "Alpha and Omega of wisdom."

I think we should consider that problem. If there are those who do not want to send their children to our school, at which preparation is given for the future eternal life, to learn here the alpha of how they should conduct themselves for the omega, the end, then they can take their children and put them where they please. (*Manuscript Releases,* vol. 6, 373)

Here, alpha is in reference to the beginning of education, learning how to conduct themselves in preparation for the "omega, the end," the end of all things.

Here we have the Alpha of Genesis and the Omega of Revelation. The blessing is promised to all those who keep the commandments of God, and who cooperate with him in the proclamation of the third angel's message. (*The Review and Herald,* June 8, 1897)

This is a reference to the beginning and end of Scripture.

"I thank the Lord that the work is begun in Washington. I am glad that the publishing work has been moved from Battle Creek to Washington, and that plans are being laid for the establishment of a sanitarium in Washington. We see the alpha, and we know that Christ is also the Omega."—*Extract from Testimony, written December 2, 1903. (Pamphlet 143, 8)*

The alpha here is the beginning of the publishing work in Washington. It will succeed because Christ is also the "Omega," and will be with the work to the end.

In all that we do or say, in all our expenditure of means, we are to strive with full purpose of heart to fulfill the purpose of him who is the Alpha and Omega of medical missionary work. Beside all waters we are to sow the seeds of truth, winning souls to Christ by tender compassion and unselfish interest. (*The Review and Herald*, May 5, 1904)

Here we learn that Jesus is the "Alpha and Omega of medical missionary work." These are a few examples of her use of alpha and omega, demonstrating her frequent use of these terms.

How did she apply them to the dangerous theories of Dr. Kellogg? A few references follow:

The work of advancement in the proclamation of truth has at such times been greatly hindered (by) specious workings, which are the *alpha of the omega*, which means very much to the people who are in any way connected with parties who have received the warnings of the Lord, but refused to heed them. (*Manuscript Releases*, vol. 11, 211, emphasis added)

Notice "specious workings, which are the "alpha *of* the omega." Here and in other places, she refers to the "alpha" as being part *of* the "omega." Examine the following:

One, and another, and still another are presented to me as having been led to accept the pleasing fables that mean the sanctification of sin. Living Temple contains the *alpha of a train of heresies.*

I was instructed that the ideas they had accepted were but the *alpha of a great deception*. I had to meet similar delusions in Portsmouth and in Boston. (*Manuscript Releases*, vol. 11, 247, emphasis added)

The alpha was simply the *first of a great deception.*

During the General Conference of 1901 the Lord warned me against sentiments that were then held by Brethren Prescott and Waggoner. These sentiments have been as leaven put into meal. Many minds have received them. The ideas of some regarding a great experience supposed to be sanctification have been *the alpha of a train of deception. (The Review and Herald*, May 26, 1904, emphasis added)

Sometimes "alpha" is used concerning false theories "that mean the sanctification of sin," as in the book *The Living Temple*. Other times it refers to deceptions during the early stages of the work in Portsmouth and Boston. Prescott and Waggoner shared sentiments concerning sanctification she labeled the *"alpha of a train of deception."*

Considering the many usages of "alpha and omega" in the context of the end-time threat to the Seventh-day Adventist Church, what emerges is this: Satan is at war with the remnant church and does not cease his deceptive activity; when he is exposed in one deception, he manufactures another. *This compilation of satanic devices against the remnant church, over its entire existence during the "time of the end," is the "omega."* This *"train of deceptions"* has a beginning and will have an end. The deceptions in the *beginning of our work,* in Boston and Portsmouth, leading up to and primarily surrounding Dr. Kellogg's apostasy, especially the pantheism in *The Living Temple*, Ellen White termed the *"alpha of the omega,"* and sometimes just the *"alpha."* She implied that this future *final deception against the church will be "the omega"* of the *"omega,"* or, simply the *"omega."* The following is a summary of facts about the "alpha" and what would have happened had the church not heeded the warning. It is compiled from two chapters on the "alpha and omega," found in *Selected Messages*, volume 1, 193–208.

THE ALPHA

- It would "lead astray the minds of those who are not thoroughly established in the foundational principles of present truth."

- It would "undermine the fundamentals of our faith."

- It is the "teaching and doctrine of devils."

- The Scripture when used to substantiate the doctrine set forth "is Scripture misapplied."

- "The spiritistic theories regarding the personality of God, followed to their logical conclusion, sweep away the whole Christian economy."

- "They make of no effect the truth of heavenly origin and rob the people of God of their past experience, giving them instead, a false science."

- "The principles of truth that God in His wisdom has given to the remnant church would be discarded."

- "Our religion would be changed. The fundamental principles that have sustained the work for the last fifty years would be accounted as error."

- "Books of a new order would be written."

- "Nothing would be allowed to stand in the way of the new movement"

- It will delude those not willing to heed the warning.

- The people deceived who would have brought on the alpha were "hypnotized" by Satan.

- "The omega will follow, and will be received by those who are not willing to heed the warning God has given."

Let us remember that the "alpha" was the alpha *of* the omega, the beginning stages of the same end-time deception that will be perfected just before probation closes. Many, if not all, the characteristics of the alpha may be included in the omega, but we can be assured that the omega will be beyond anything we have imagined up to this point. Why? It is because this made Ellen White tremble for the safety of the church, and she was startled when she beheld it (see *Selected Messages*, Book 1, 203).

Here is a summary of what we can expect to find in the omega deception, from *Selected Messages,* Book 1, 193–208. Notice how the removal of the pillars of our faith is one of the dangers of the omega and how its acceptance would sweep away the entire Christian economy.

THE OMEGA

- The omega "will be of a startling nature."

- It will result in the "control of men's minds."

- It would "rob people of their past experience giving them instead a false science."

- Receiving these theories "will undermine the foundations of our faith," "especially Christ's ministry in the Most Holy Place and the three angels' messages."

- Those who entertain these sophistries will soon find themselves in a position where Satan can "talk with them and lead them away from God."

- The "omega" "introduces that which is naught but speculation in regard to the personality of God and where His presence is."

The spiritual revival that grew into the Seventh-day Adventist Church is identified in Revelation chapter 10 and immediately followed the event characterized by the blowing of the sixth trumpet in August of 1840. That spiritual revival was forecast to arise at the end of the longest time prophecy in the Bible, the 2300 days of Daniel 8:14, and is known in history to this day as "The Great Awakening," the greatest Christian revival since apostolic times. We will study the history of this amazing experience in chapter 5, "Who Are We Anyway? Part II," out of which came the remnant church of Revelation 12:17. "And the dragon was wroth with the woman, and went to make war with the *remnant of her seed*, which keep the commandments of God, and have the testimony of Jesus Christ." Their experience was unique and most trying.

After the Great Disappointment in the fall of 1844, only a few faithful Adventists emerged, a small fellowship of believers who refused to give in to the temptation to abandon ship. They knew it was their Lord and Savior who led them through this most trying experience. They had a close and definite relationship with Him, knowing His voice personally. They had no doubt they were following their Lord as He directed, even though the outcome was not what they expected.

As they persisted to search out the meaning of their experience, pleading with God for better understanding, He opened up their minds to the most profound and thorough understanding of Scripture since apostolic times. As this small dedicated group of faithful Bible students continued searching, Christ's ministry in the heavenly temple was opened to their understanding, explaining the reason for the Great Disappointment. Shortly thereafter, the truth of the Sabbath was presented to them, and as they studied under the guidance of the Holy Spirit they saw how the seventh-day Sabbath had been neglected for almost two thousand years and determined to begin to live according to this newly discovered Bible truth. The Spirit of Prophecy was then revived in the church and verified the new truths that were constantly being revealed as they all continued to study together.

As they searched the Scriptures with the diligence of the Bereans, the Lord unfolded to their eager minds the change in Christ's ministry that took place on October 22, 1844. Jesus entered the final phase of the work of the atonement, entering on that day in to the Most Holy Place of the heavenly sanctuary, providing "a new and living way, which He has consecrated for us, through the veil," where we are to have "boldness to enter into the Holiest by the blood of Jesus" (Hebrews 10:19).

It is our discovery and acceptance of two wonderful truths—that it is the love of Christ that drives us to "keep the commandments of God" (Revelation 14:12), and that we have in our midst the Spirit of Prophecy—which verify that we are God's remnant church. It was and is the absolute rejection of these very truths by every other Protestant and Christian denomination that make them the "daughters of Babylon."

According to the Spirit of Prophecy, the "omega" will lead to the denial of these precious truths, the very beliefs that make us God's chosen people.

Before we continue our study of spiritual formation and the alpha and omega, I would like to share a short history of how the Lord allowed me to wander through the world of the supernatural for reasons I did not understand until the time He called me to write this book. The experience gained during those years was essential in the detection of the omega-like characteristics.

Chapter 3
Early Experiences

Earliest Memories

Looking back, allowing my most powerful memories to arise, I feel the security of sitting in Grandpa's lap, examining the bulging veins on his old, gifted hands. I am listening to the most beautiful piano music and remember how often I would ask him, "Grandpa, what's the name of the song you're playing," and in his thick Hungarian accent he would say, "Oh, der iss no name, I yust play vot I feel." Music was his life. He spent the final twenty years of his career playing French horn in the New York Philharmonic Orchestra under the leadership of the great maestro Arturo Toscanini. I remember being enthralled with the autographed pictures and personal notes from the great conductor. I would spend hours with pictures of foreign cities, newspaper articles, and other memorabilia of Grandpa's travels around the world. I loved to peruse those large 33 rpm book-albums of the world's finest classical music, recorded by the world's finest orchestras, turning over record after record, respectfully handling them as delicately as possible. Those memories are most wonderful.

I can see his tall, thin, bent-over form slowly rise from the piano, slowly walk through the living room, through the kitchen and into the dining room, finally sitting down to begin working with his massive stamp collection. Grandpa would spend hours each day separating stamps from the mail he received from around the world. With his magnifying glass, bowls of water to soak the envelopes, and those little sticky papers used to attach the stamps to the page in the stamp book, he would tell me stories of his travels through each stamp's country of origin. His friends from all over the world were always writing to him. "Who did you know here, Grandpa?" I often asked as I wondered at the beautiful stamps from Europe or the Far East. Each stamp was an incredible work of art and was an adventure through that country.

"Edvard," Grandma would call. "It's time to eat." He would clear the table of stamp paraphernalia, and she would bring out a bowl of that day's mush—soft food—his daily fare.

Grandpa was twenty-something years old, playing in the orchestra at a famous opera house in Prague, Czechoslovakia, when he first laid eyes on Margaret, a child prodigy ballet dancer performing in the opera. It was love at first sight. The only problem was that Margaret was much younger than Edward. She was actually little more than a child. They waited until she was, for that time, an appropriate age; then they married. Right out of a fairy tale!

I spent hours listening to my dad practice his woodwind instruments, mostly on weekends when we were both home together. The saxophone was my favorite. Hour after hour, I heard the scales—up and down, over and over. He would say, "Five hours a day to keep what I have and six to get better." During the week, Dad was usually gone by the time I got home from school. He'd go in to New York City from the Long Island suburbs where we lived to do, at first, *The Steve Allen Show*, and later to tape *The Johnny Carson Show*. For fifteen years he played in *The Tonight Show*'s band, first with Skitch Henderson conducting, then Doc Severenson. I still have one of the first "instant picture" Polaroid cameras made that Steve Allen gave Dad for a Christmas present one year. His career spanned radio, television, and the theater; from the original *Lucky Strike Hit Parade*, through Johnny Carson and Steve Allen, on to Broadway with *Hello Dolly* for the last eight years of his career.

During those early years, home consisted of Grandma, Grandpa, Mom and Dad, and my older sister Gail. I was comfortable and secure. Life was visiting family, white Christmases, Long Island beaches in the summer and sleigh riding in the winter; I had the security of the same home since birth, and neighbors who were also close friends, much like family. Best of all, I enjoyed the rainy days at home with Grandma and Grandpa. Until the heart attacks began—one after another after another. It seems I can remember at least ten heart attacks Grandpa had at home; there was panic, shouting, calling the doctor and anxiously watching out the window for his car to drive up; then, having to wait downstairs until the doctor came down with the rest of the family to know if Grandpa was still alive. Finally, after many heart attacks, he couldn't go on and decided to stop eating until he died. He was gone.

And, there were those feelings. I didn't tell anybody about them; they were feelings I couldn't explain that swept over me and made me stop whatever I was doing. I felt alone, sad, and distant. I was only seven or eight years old when they began, much too young to deal with that level of emotion. They could occur many times each day, or just a few times a week.

They were my little secret and it would be another twenty years before I would understand what was happening.

From Rocket Ships to Rock & Roll, Church Bells Ring

"Hi, Mrs. Holtburg, can David come out and play?" We played Cowboys and Indians, War, and my favorite: Rocket Ship. Thanks to a hurricane that hit Long Island in 1955, I had the "Starship Enterprise" right in my own backyard in the form of a huge willow tree that had fallen, and our imaginations did the rest. I traveled for years on that tree "where no man has gone before." This, coupled with an old empty lot that we christened The Nursery, which had been a nursery of sorts in the past, but was now just a few acres of overgrown land where we would gather every day to play, were the mainstays of my childhood. It was also the place I hid my cigarettes. It's hard to believe: just eight years old, in third grade, and actually needing a cigarette! Every day, I would anxiously await the end of the school day to dash over to The Nursery and have a cigarette. I guess things could have been worse; at least I wasn't drinking—yet.

I was twelve when that vice grabbed hold of me. "Want a drink?" Mary asked. Mary was one of our friends' housekeepers, filling in as bartender for a neighborhood party. *OK, why not,* I thought. One drink, two, three; and then I lost count. I vaguely remember getting sick in the middle of Jericho Turnpike about a mile from home. That set a course that continued all the way through high school. Then it happened—deliverance—deliverance from that terrible cycle of drinking, vomiting, and swearing I would never do it again, then repeating it all over again.

It was a beautiful fall day, and I was visiting my cousin in Queens, New York. "Here, Rick, try one of these on your way home," she said, handing me a little, funny-looking cigarette. You know the kind, with the ends twisted so nothing falls out. I decided to take a look at what was inside before doing the inhale, hold-your-breath-until-you-explode procedure. I found two little seeds and reasoned that they should go back where they belonged, planted in the soil beside my house. Daily watering along with a little Miracle Grow, combined with constant attention and loving care and, there they were: two eight-foot-tall marijuana plants, beckoning me to come to their harvest. Those two little plants supplied me, along with my little group of friends, with a two-years' supply of marijuana. It was the fall of 1963, before the drug revolution hit our area, even before most law officers knew what marijuana looked like.

After experiencing the effects of that first marijuana cigarette, which amounted to feeling happy and laughing as I drove along the Long Island

Expressway to my home, I was convinced that I had discovered a perfect replacement for alcohol and all the evils associated with it. I was definitely a strong advocate for the "cause," the spread of the marijuana message. I didn't feel guilty breaking the law because the cause was a moral one and we were on "the right side." I knew the terrible effects of alcohol firsthand. I had been beaten up, chased by police, caught by police and almost blown off the roof of the sixty-story NBC skyscraper by forty-mph winds. I had crashed cars, stolen cars, started "rumbles" at the Four Seasons Night Club involving hundreds of people, and on and on and on. Why? I believed and was partly correct: it was alcohol!

Marijuana, on the other hand, simply meant fun times eating, laughing, and venturing beyond the "final frontier" with Captain Kirk and his Starship Enterprise. I truly believed that my friends and I were delivered from the horrors of alcohol. This was true, but we were deceived by another kind of horror even more frightening. More on that later.

I never really had much musical talent, but *did* spend most of my 18 years tapping on things. Anything, anywhere, my feet, hands, and fingers were always moving. Stop tapping! Stop tapping! I can still hear everyone pleading. It seemed that I always had some kind of rhythm going inside my head. It seems I should have been an extremely "musically inclined" person, given that my parents and grandparents were musicians of the highest order, but for some reason all this usually inherited talent passed me by. The only thing I possessed was the rhythm.

I had another friend, also named Frank, who played the guitar. Through a mutual friend we met Sal, also a guitarist. They got together for a "jamming" session at my house and became real excited at how well they played together; so excited, they decided to look for a drummer and start a real band. They asked me if I knew of any drummers. "Not really" I said, "but if you can wait a month or so, I know that I can get there." We were off. Little did I know how this event would change my life. "The Iridescents" were born. For five years we worked many night spots in and around New York City, even Broadway's "Palladium Hall." We did our best to duplicate the Beatles and other famous groups of that era.

We practiced for hours and hours, rehearsing songs over and over again as we shared the noisy practice sessions between our homes. I preferred practicing at Sal's place; Sal had a younger sister with the most beautiful eyes I had ever seen. Whenever we practiced at Sal's, she and I were always exchanging glances, which wasn't easy. She was too young to date, but after one year, two years, three years, we just kept looking and getting to know one another. Finally, the timing was more appropriate, and I was her date for the senior prom. I was twenty-one and she was seventeen. We were already in love, and the next three years were spent waiting to get married. At twenty-four and twenty, we married. I never would have met Rosalie if it had not been for our unique set of circumstances. Neither would I understand that it was the hand of God that brought us together that day we first glanced into one another's eyes.

Married, with kids on the way, yet still with marijuana in the picture, life went on. We thought all was under "control," with just occasional use, but the good times slowly, imperceptibly faded away. I found that I was spending less time laughing and more time analyzing myself. I would retreat into my own little world of worry and guilt. What used to be "fun times" was now constant introspection. The more I looked, the less I liked what I saw. I didn't like my life or my work. I became more dissatisfied, yet less motivated.

Life was becoming unbearable. Where was I going, and what was I doing with my life? Why was I here? I felt that I had no purpose. Why do I do the things that make me feel guilty all the time, and why can't I stop doing them? I would smoke marijuana to feel a little better, but in the end would feel worse. Introspection slowly turned to paranoia. Fear would overwhelm me. I hated myself and was disgusted with my life. I felt irresponsible and guilty about my behavior but found it impossible to change. What was going on? My thoughts were never before so out of control. I had never experienced guilt as I did now. I always had a tender conscience, but not like this. I needed to get some answers.

During this time, I had a new secret. Those strange feelings I had when I was a child disappeared over time, but now something frightening seemed to have replaced them.

Spirit Mediums, Gurus, and Psychic Dreams

What is that sound? Sounds like music. No, not music, but some kind of steady, pleasant hum. Where is it coming from? It's coming from inside my head; and, what's this: I can make it louder and more intense by relaxing. This is really strange. I can feel the sound, and it's spreading all over my body. It feels electrical—like a vibration—an electrical vibration that feels as though it is reaching into the molecules of my body. Fascinating— no— frightening. Fascinating *and* frightening. Should I let it continue? The more I let it go, the more frightened I become. I don't like this, but I am intrigued by it. How do I stop it? I can't move. I'm wide awake, but paralyzed. This is too scary; I must make it stop. I've got to move—a leg, an arm, anything. It takes all the willpower I have to make myself move my leg, and it stops. I regain the use of my body, my heart is pounding, and I'm frightened, out of breath, and so very tired. I just want to let myself go to sleep, but I realize if I do, I'll fall right back into that state again, so I force myself to get up and walk around until I'm fully awake.

This happened two, three, sometimes ten times a week. What was it? I knew they weren't dreams because I was completely awake. What was happening to me? This was my new secret.

Concurrently, I was consumed with thoughts about the purpose of life. I reasoned that there is nothing more important for a human being to consider than searching for an answer to the age-old questions. What is the purpose of life? Why are we here? Where did we come from? Where are we going when we die? The thought that death was the end of existence drove me to my wits' end. It made no sense, but I had no answers. Nothing could take priority above searching for these answers.

It was lunchtime, and I decided to go into town and roam through a book store. Slowly walking down the aisle, a certain title caught my attention: *Journeys out of the Body*, by Dr. Robert Monroe. *Wonder what that's all about*, I thought. I purchased the book and began reading. Hmmm—astral projection. What's that? Leaving your body behind and traveling through various planes of existence! Is he for real? All right, how does he do that?

He explained it this way: he lay down, closed his eyes and allowed himself to drift lower and lower until it began to happen. He felt music, a vibration in his body that felt electrical and went right down to the molecular level. He could control the intensity by the power of relaxation. He explained how it could be frightening but was also fascinating. Then all of a sudden he separated from his body and could travel in the astral planes.

I couldn't believe it! He was describing exactly what had been happening to me for years, everything except the leaving of my body. Fairly instantly, my life changed. Finally, I had learned something that seemed to answer questions, and that had eternal and infinite implications. What could possibly be more important for me to apply my life's energy toward than to the truth about this?

If it was true that I could leave my body and travel through unknown astral planes of existence, then there must be other answers out there concerning the purpose of life and our existence. If there were other spheres of reality, I reasoned, perhaps this was where we went when we died. Is this heaven? Who would have an answer to all these questions flowing through my mind? My logic dictated that I needed to contact people well-versed in these things, people who had had the same experiences I had had. If anyone would have answers to all my questions, they would. Who were they?

I began searching through the teachings of the occult and the various religions and philosophies that incorporate supernatural phenomena. I spent six to eight hours a day reading the different teachings of all the religions of the world. Without a doubt, I was totally obsessed. Even at work, this was all I could think about. Included in my reading and searching was the Holy Bible. I found it difficult to understand, but began to consider the possibility of an evil supernatural power. Is there a devil? Is it possible that this supernatural activity was from him? Could it be part of a deception? Oh, how I wanted the truth! More than anything in this world, I wanted the truth. It seemed that every direction I searched in was filled with contradictions. There was always something that didn't fit or make sense. I was living under the conviction of sin in my life and wanted to change but didn't have the power. I prayed continuously, three, four, five hours a day, pleading with God, whoever He was, to lead me to the truth. I wanted the truth more than life itself.

My search led me through "mind control," spirit mediums, and Hinduism. After taking the Silva Mind Control course and sharing these experiences, I was referred to a spirit medium. Marcy was her name, and she lived in a very well-to-do neighborhood in Greenwich, Connecticut.

I felt I didn't belong in such a high-class neighborhood as I rang her doorbell. I remember being extremely nervous, yet strangely excited as her assistant welcomed me and invited me in. I glanced around at all the expensive works of art, elaborately framed paintings and many free-standing sculptures throughout the house. I looked down a number of steps through the living room into another room whose door was open and saw her watching me. Her assistant escorted me into her office, where we shook hands.

She invited me to sit down and went on to tell me that when she saw me enter in the front hall she noticed a very bright light or aura surrounding me, a characteristic, she said, of a very old soul, one who had lived many prior lives. She went into a semi-trance and with her eyelids fluttering and partially closed, began telling me about my previous lives as a healer and spiritual teacher. She saw me healing people on a beach and many other flattering notions. Then she began telling me facts about my life that she couldn't have possibly known. There was no doubt in my mind that she had some kind of genuine supernatural power.

She went on to say that I was awakening to this power in my current life at the present time and this was the reason for the many strange happenings. I was meant to be her disciple for a time, she said, as she trained me to do the work that she was involved with. There is a great awakening of spirituality in the world, and many people are being called to prepare the world for what is about to happen. I was to be one of them. The next step was for me to join their little group and come to the next meeting, a séance.

The Séance

My head was pounding. I had a most terrible headache and was sitting in a circle of Marcy's friends when the woman next to me said, "Who's got the headache?" "I do," I said. "Oh, I can feel it here on the right side of your head." She was right; that's exactly where it was. "Throbbing?" she asked. "Yup," I answered. The next thing I knew, everyone was meditating, and Marcy fell into a trance. She said there was the spirit of a little child there that had a message for me. The message was that "I was on the right track and that there was no turning back." I never felt more uncomfortable in my life than at that moment and knew I needed to get out of there. I left as soon as the meeting was over and upon arriving home, felt compelled to go directly to the Bible. I took the Bible off the shelf, placed it in my lap, opened it, looked down and began reading Deuteronomy 18, verse 10.

> There shall not be found among you anyone that maketh his son or his daughter to pass through the fire, or that useth divination, or an observer of times, or an enchanter, or a witch, or a charmer, or a consulter with familiar spirits, or a wizard, or a necromancer. For all that do these things are an abomination unto the Lord: and because of these abominations the Lord thy God doth drive them out from before thee. (Deuteronomy 18:10–12 KJV)

I couldn't believe what I was reading. Necromancy—what's that? What?! Communicating with the dead! That's what I was just doing. "Can't be," I rationalized, "they just didn't understand things back in the days this was written."

I became frightened and frustrated. I finally thought I had found something that had purpose, and now the Bible was condemning it. It seemed the Bible was getting in the way of what I wanted to do and what I wanted to believe, contradicting other teachings at every turn. I liked what these other writings said; it appealed to my interest in the supernatural. There was real power that I could have. These other writings placed me above most of the population of the world, taught me that I was farther along in spiritual maturity. I was one of the "old souls," I was told. I didn't want to stop believing that, and the Bible was ruining these proud thoughts, even if they did frighten me to a certain extent.

But I couldn't just ignore it; I couldn't stop reading it and considering what it taught. I feared that what I was fooling around with might be evil. I became so mentally confused that I believed my fellow workers were part of a satanic conspiracy against me, that they were part of a plot to involve me in their cult of psychics and witches.

The next few days were a blur. I began to believe that I was going to lose eternal life because I had gone to a spirit medium. For some reason, I thought I would die if I fell asleep; not just die, but slip into eternal nonexistence. This was a turning point, and without a doubt the most intense fear I have ever experienced.

I was fortunate. My loving wife and sister reasoned through the next few days with me, and I began to understand. But I vowed to stop my search—no more, no further reckoning, deciphering, parsing.

That declaration lasted a few short weeks. There was no stopping what I had started. This was the focus of my life, and I could not stop searching until I found answers to the mystery of life. I *did* decide, however, to take a different path, leaving spirit mediums and séances behind.

Time for the Guru

For as long as I can remember, India was the most fascinating place on earth to me. Simply upon hearing the word, I would envision a mystical fantasy of flying magic carpets, snow-capped mountains and meditating maharajas. The lost city of Shangri-La held a strong appeal; it was no fairy tale, but a place. I needed to believe there was a place somewhere in this world like Shangri-La, where we could all live in harmony and peace.

This appeal, this need, paved the way for the next leg of my journey. In New Rochelle, New York, there was an ashram for the renowned Hindu guru Sri Chinmoy. He was, and continued to be, until his death in 2007, the spiritual leader of the United Nations.

He also had many disciples with whom he systematically met at various locations around New York. I stopped by one of his ashrams and eagerly sought out someone to talk with concerning the things that had been happening in my life. I was given a picture of Chinmoy, taken while he was in a meditative state called *samadhi*. Hindus believe *samadhi* is when one's consciousness totally merges with the universal mind of God. I was instructed to concentrate on the picture during a time of quiet meditation and was to, in return, give to them a picture of my family, on which the guru would then meditate. We would both know by what we experienced whether we were to be his disciples.

That night I meditated on his picture. As soon as my eyes fell upon the picture, I had an occurrence I later learned to be of great consequence. I became totally paralyzed and stopped breathing. What appeared to be flames, varying in color from red to yellow to white, flashed out of the picture while his face disappeared and reappeared. It was a frightening and exhilarating supernatural experience. The following day, I delivered the picture of my family to the ashram and described what had happened to me the night before. I was told that the experience was very meaningful, that we were to become his disciples, that he was our savior. We were subsequently accepted into his highest order of disciples; among them were the famous musicians Santana and John McLaughlin, and we all met twice a week for fellowship and spiritual teaching.

The next year was one of learning meditative techniques through the study of occult literature as well as Hinduism's sacred writings. Throughout all the literature, there emerged a common teaching, a teaching that would eventually enable me to detect the very dangers this book was written to expose. I discovered through study and the actual practice of meditative techniques that all the religions and occult theories that enabled their followers to contact the world of the supernatural used certain meditative practices that eventually led to an altered level of consciousness.

I discovered that it was essential to learn these techniques to get to that certain mental level where I was able to contact the supernatural worlds. To leave my body in astral projection or to have any of numerous supernatural experiences, this unique corridor of the mind must be reached through certain meditative practices. These practices *always involved a focusing of the mind* on one thing to the exclusion of anything else. It could be reached by focusing on sounds such as music; or through chanting and repetition or recitation of words; through the sensation of touch; or the use of visual exercises. I learned that the most effective and most rapid method of attaining an altered level of consciousness was through the creation of mental images. By creating a mental image and sustaining that image, an altered state could rapidly be achieved.

I discovered that there was a fascinating and mysterious occurrence that took place for all who learned how to enter an altered level of consciousness—silence. It is a place where the thoughts that usually flit across the conscious mind up to 60 times every second slow down and eventually come to a stop. It is at that point that the devotee becomes an observer rather than a thinker and slips into that mysterious place of "repose" or "stillness" where awareness of reality is altered and the silence is attained, a supernatural and life-changing experience.

I would like to take the liberty at this point to explain to the reader that it is when a person enters this silence that they are entering a place where the powers of evil angels can create whatever illusion they desire. If a person is practicing Hinduism, they may experience during this demonically controlled moment their favorite Hindu guru, levitating over the river Ganges. The spirit medium will believe they are in contact with some spirit of a dead person, when they are really communicating with a fallen angel, a demon impersonating the one who passed away. A psychic enters that corridor of the mind when reading the mind of a subject. He will be given a thought by a demon, who gives the same thought to the one whose mind supposedly is being read. When the psychic reveals the thought, it appears as if they have read the mind of the subject, when in reality the thought was injected into both their minds by a fallen angel.

Finally, the modern-day Christian, upon entering the silence, will believe they have come into the presence of God, when in reality they are under the control of the same demons as the psychics, spirit mediums, and ancient mystics of the church, those of any religion or group that rely on supernatural experiences as evidence of their contact with God.

What must be remembered is that we do not control the timing of God's communication with us, He does. When we believe God is at our beck and call, by entering an altered state through the use of meditative or prayer techniques, we are deceiving ourselves and are committing the sin of presumption. And even more dangerous is the fact that this puts us in communication with demons and we would be actually practicing spiritualism—a deception we have been told about in the Spirit of Prophecy—which could place us under Satan's absolute control as we near the end of time.

Through meditation and the use of these practices, supernatural phenomena are made to occur in such a way that they fit the desired deception of the fallen angels in control. This is the power that Satan has over people who use these techniques, even if they are used unknowingly and are deceived, believing there is nothing wrong with their use. It is the purpose of this book to show how these methods have been used for thousands of years and are the secrets behind every mystical experience, whether by early mystics of the Christian church or a thousand years earlier, by Hindu masters. It is always the same—the entering into the silence necessary for the supernatural experience. Now, let's get back to what was occurring in our lives.

Astral projection, psychic dreams, and telepathy were occurring in our family. Even my three-year-old son was affected, describing events taking place elsewhere at the very time of their occurrence. We could not deny the power that was manifesting itself in our lives, but there was an everincreasing uneasiness concerning its source.

I continued to search both the Hindu Scriptures and the Holy Bible. The well-known and often referenced book *Autobiography of a Yogi*, authored by Paramahansa Yogananda in 1946, has been especially influential in bringing Eastern religions to the Western Christian mindset in a most appealing, acceptable, and believable manner. Yogananda supported the view that the Bible be used as a source of truth and repeatedly referred to Jesus as the Son of God. We were told by our guru, Chinmoy, that the Bible contained the truth and that Christ was truly God in the flesh, just as Chinmoy was God in the flesh. The difference, however, according to Chinmoy, is that he had transcended even beyond Christ's position.

As I searched the Bible and compared its teachings with those of the Eastern religions, I found many differences and contradictions, which led to great confusion and stress. In reality, most of my conflict was due to the fact that I could not change those aspects of my behavior that I knew were "unholy." My conscience was continually convicting me, but I could find no relief. I truly wanted to be a holy person, to reflect the goodness of God, whoever He was. I was assured time after time not to worry about such things—being the guru's disciple was what mattered—but this just reinforced the frustration and confusion. As I continued to study the teachings of the Eastern religions, as well as the Holy Bible, it became more and more evident that the contradictions were serious. The guru espoused one teaching, and the Bible, which he "accepted as truth," espoused another.

I reached a true fork in the road when, in my study of the Bible, I came across Acts 4:12. This verse made the claim that Jesus was the only name given among men whereby we can be saved; this created a huge problem for me. Chinmoy taught all of his disciples that *he* was their savior, that *he* took our sins upon himself, enabling us to advance in our spiritual life. He also taught that the Bible contained the truth. Thus, the Holy Bible, the book that Chinmoy said contained the truth, condemned him as a false teacher.

I had to find a solution to this apparent contradiction, so I sought his opinion about the difficulty. His answer was, "You can't believe everything in the Bible." It was becoming apparent to me that I would never be able to come to terms with these questions unless an absolute standard of truth existed. Did such a standard exist? How could I possibly know? In Chinmoy's opinion, he was his own standard because he considered himself an incarnation of God, even greater than Christ. The Bible claimed that *it* was the truth, as do the holy books of many other religions. Was truth subjective? If so, anything goes. It couldn't be. Oh, what confusion. Who to believe? What Scriptures should I study? Where was I to find the truth? Where was I to find victory and relief for my lack of holiness?

In desperation, I cast my life into the hands of God, whoever He was, and confessed to Him that I quit. It's over. I would search no more because I could not determine what is true. I knew one thing to be true: that there is a God, and I surrendered my life to Him, pleading to be led to the truth, wherever it was to be found. I would search no more, realizing that God knew my condition and He could lead me. Now it was up to Him. Give me truth, or let me die.

New Job, New Life

Six months earlier, I had sent resumes to a few chemical companies. Within days of this surrender to God, I received a call from Union Carbide Corporation in Tarrytown, New York. I interviewed and was offered a position that I could not refuse. It would mean relocating to the Tarrytown area, it being too far a commute from Long Island. While searching for our new home, I came across what seemed to be a perfect little cottage on a five-acre estate; it sounded too good to be true. Funny—I lived in the New York area all my life and never heard of the town where this home was located, in Crompond, New York.

Inquiring by phone, we found that it was still available and scheduled a time to meet with the owner and see the home. It was beautiful! The owner, who lived in a mansion on the back of the five acres, showed us through the house and grounds. While walking and talking, I noticed a neighboring home and asked who lived there. He said he did not know his name but that he was a minister. My heart began to pound, sensing that God just might be answering my prayer. Eventually, I came to know that His hand was guiding this entire process, and that He was leading me to the answers I sought. Being led next door to a minister was extremely significant to me at this time. I wanted help.

Most of my struggle now was coming to terms with how the Bible and all other spiritual teachings contradicted one another. I was still being drawn to the alluring attractions of spiritualism and its power and was unable to make a final decision one way or the other. In my deepest heart of hearts, I felt that Jesus was the answer, but had trouble dealing with the Bible's denunciation of the very teachings with which I was so intrigued. But this experience, this seeming providence of being led by God next door to a minister, was so powerful that it demanded immediate action on my part. It got my attention.

"What church does he pastor," I asked.

"The Seventh-day Adventist church," he said.

"What church? Seventh-day who?"

"Seventh-day Adventist," he reiterated.

"Who are they?"

"I don't really know," he said.

"All I know is that they go to church on Saturday."

What? Oh no. Please God, couldn't it be a more normal, mainstream religion? I was probably feeling concern about how our family and friends would feel. They watched us go from spirit mediums and séances to gurus and saris; but I pleaded for God to lead me to the truth, and He has led me next door to a Seventh-day Adventist minister. I prayed that prayer just three weeks earlier, and there we were. I had to meet the pastor and find out what the Seventh-day Adventist Church was all about.

One morning, shortly after we moved in, I saw him taking out the garbage and went to introduce myself. After initial pleasantries, I could not hold back telling him how it was that we had become his neighbor. As he listened to the story, I watched his face light up. His politeness turned into a broad smile that grew until he was beaming. We both knew the miracle that had taken place, and we set about a plan. We'd meet twice a week, John and I—John Luppens, the new young pastor of the Peekskill Church in the Greater New York Conference.

At that time, John was instituting the birth of a major self-supporting work in Peekskill, New York, a work that would include a vegetarian restaurant and a health retreat (Living Springs), while simultaneously evangelizing the city, employing the inspired E. G. White instruction specific to New York. After writing his book, *New York a Symbol*, he was anxious to relocate to New York from California to implement the plan that he felt God had given the church.

John asked a member of his church, one who was very familiar with the paths we had taken, to take charge of our Bible studies. Sidney (Pepper)

Sweet was the best Bible instructor we could have hoped for. For a year, we subjected this faithful servant of God to all of our most difficult and troubling inquiries imaginable. Sidney always answered our questions with Scripture. Those were wonderful days for Rosalie and me. At last we had what we were searching for, peace and truth, victory and purpose. The Lord used that little church in Peekskill, along with the Country Life restaurant, to intimately nurture us for the next few years—so many forever friends to enjoy an eternity together. We were baptized in 1974, and in 1977 the Lord opened the door for us to enter the ministry. Then it was that we even more fully understood why two young people from different worlds met and fell in love.

The story had to be told for you to understand why our love for the church, the remnant church, His bride, runs so deep. This "true church" is the church through which Jesus delivered us from drugs, spirit mediums, demons, Hindu gurus, Satan's supernatural snare, hopelessness, despair, and from sure eternal death. This is the church that is "the object of His supreme regard." He gave His life for it and watches over her jealously; and because of my love for Him, I am compelled to no longer keep silent concerning a perilous and deadly deception that will captivate the minds of any who are "not willing to heed the warning God has given."

Stories of God's Loving Care

We continue now, with a record of tales; true tales. Through childhood and into my early twenties, there were many occasions when I felt I was being watched over in a special way. Over and over it seemed some unseen power was watching over me and keeping me going, even while I was not a Christian.

Floating Can Be Dangerous

David's family and mine would often swim and picnic together on Long Island's North Shore at a place called Sunken Meadow State Park. The park was situated on the shore of a three-mile-deep cove on Long Island Sound, a body of water separating Long Island from Connecticut. The park had a beautiful beach where we all set our blankets, chairs, and barbecue. The swimming was always fun and extremely safe because the water deepened very gradually. We could walk out hundreds of feet before it became deep enough to be forced to swim.

On one of these excursions, David and I decided to have a contest, our competitive natures alive and well, to see who could float on their backs the longest. After half an hour or so, we both began to get tired and decided to call it a tie, give our arms a much needed rest and stand up. To our surprise, we discovered that our feet could not touch bottom. While we were floating, the tide began to move out, and we were, ever so gently, taken out with it.

David was taller than me, and when he put his tip-toes on the bottom, the water was a few inches above his nose. Okay, no problem. For ten-year-olds, we were both quite accomplished swimmers, so let's just swim back to shore, we thought. We swam and laughed and swam and laughed, until we realized that we were not getting closer to the shore, but farther and farther away. Our laughter turned to shouting, and then our shouting turned to sobs and panic when we realized that we were so far out, no one could possibly hear us. We were growing extremely tired, having drifted for such a long distance for an hour or more, so far that we were no longer visible from the shore line.

What were we going to do? We couldn't keep our arms moving much longer, and we were both very frightened, when way off in the distance, I saw a boat. It was the only boat in the entire cove, a cove three miles deep and three miles wide. One boat. The problem was, it didn't appear to be moving. It was standing still, and much too far away to see us in the water. We couldn't believe it. Here was our only hope, and he was too far away to see us, just sitting there. But wait, was it getting bigger, or was I just imagining it? Yes, it *was* getting bigger and bigger. I knew then that it must be heading right for us. It continued to come directly toward us. If he hadn't seen us floating in front of him, he would have run right over us.

When he saw us, he cut the engines, and the boat stopped dead in the water, ten feet in front of us. Slowly, he swaggered up to the front of the boat with a cigarette hanging out of his mouth, put his foot up on the rail with his elbow on his knee, looked down at us with a little grin and said real casually, "Hey, you guys want a ride?" I don't think David or I could have stayed afloat for another five minutes. We were crying and babbling to each other how we couldn't keep our arms moving any longer. "Yeah, we would like that ride. Thank you, thank you, thank you." He reached down with his strong arm and pulled us onboard. After we told our story, he gave us a little lecture, took us back to the beach and then disappeared off into Long Island Sound. Our parents didn't even know that we had any kind of a problem. Who was watching over me?

That's the way it was back then in our community. Parents just didn't have to worry about their kids every moment of the day. In those days, we would go off on our bikes and explore all day long without having the thoughts that worry so many now. When I was about ten years old, my dad gave me five dollars, and Allen's dad gave him five dollars, and they told us to get on the bus, go to One Hundred and 79th Street, take the IND subway line into Manhattan, get off at 8th Avenue and 42nd Street and ride the subways all day, until we got to know them. We'll see you tonight. That's the way it was; home, safe once more. Who was watching over me?

The Old Man

David and I would spend many hours playing in our, for the most part, user friendly neighborhood, but there was an old grumpy man who we simply called "The Old Man." In thinking back, he may have been mentally challenged because, on occasion, he would rush upon us while we were playing. We were just doing the things that kids do, being noisy the way kids can be when they play, when he would approach us, yelling and cursing, demanding that we go away and not play there anymore. He seemed to have violent tendencies, but was also old and not very mobile. We kept a safe distance, knowing we could outrun him if he should decide to come after us, which he did on occasion. We knew we were allowed to play where we were and tried to keep our distance from his place.

On one occasion while playing, we were unaware of his approach; he grabbed me from behind, turned me around and began to choke me. Really choke me. He seemed like a wild animal. With his face contorted and eyes raging, he said, "I finally got you. Do you know how long I have been waiting for this day? I am gonna kill you," and showered a few expletives on me. I was only ten years old and didn't have the strength to break away. He was squeezing my neck so tightly that my wind pipe was shut closed. From a safe distance, my friend David was screaming at him to let me go, but to no avail.

I couldn't do a thing and was about to lose consciousness, when he suddenly let go. His hands remained around my neck, but his grip simply released me. It was not as if his intentions had changed, for everything about him stayed the same. That insane, maniacal look on his face is the last thing I remember before turning and fleeing for my life. I was free and out of danger; I couldn't believe it. David asked me why he let me go. I couldn't answer. Neither could the man answer when the judge asked him why. He was warned never to touch any of the kids again—and he never did. Who was watching over me?

The Shinnecock Canal Event

A few years later, while a teenager, I was returning with friends by speed boat from a visit to Robins Island, an island in Peconic Bay between the forks of outer Long Island. We spent the day exploring, swimming and fishing. It was exciting being with these new and older friends of my neighbor. I felt a bit like an outsider and a little shy, too shy to say anything about the way they were driving the boat while entering the Shinnecock Canal that connects Peconic Bay with the Atlantic Ocean. They were foolishly gunning the throttle then cutting it, gunning it and cutting it. We were entering a lock with posts across the canal that had to be maneuvered carefully, and this was no time to be showing off. For sure, the beer that had been consumed all day encouraged the poor judgment. I was nervous, but too intimidated to say anything.

On one of these throttle up, throttle down scenarios, just as the boat was entering the canal, the engine stalled. We were in serious trouble. This is why: when the tide begins to go out, the level of the water way back at the beginning of the bay, the farthest from the open ocean, recedes much more slowly than the level in the open ocean. This is because it takes time for the change in the ocean level a hundred miles away, where the bay opens to the ocean, to affect the water level at the closed end of the bay, where the canal is.

The open ocean is on the other side of the Shinnecock Canal. After high tide, as the tide begins to change, the locks are not needed for the first few hours. With the locks open, the ocean level begins to drop, and water in the bay begins to flow out of the bay, through the canal, into the ocean. It moves more and more rapidly, until it becomes too dangerous to maneuver a boat safely. It is at this point that the canal is closed and the locks are used. We just happened to be going through the canal just before they closed it, when the water was flowing most rapidly.

Without power, we were completely at the mercy of the fast-moving current, flowing downhill and quickly approaching bridge supports that were rising out of the water every twenty feet or so. Suddenly, the boat turned sideways, smashed into one of the bridge supports and flipped, leaving all of us fighting the current and trying to stay afloat. Not one of us was wearing a life preserver—we were swimming as best we could toward the side of the canal where groups of people were screaming for help, but unable to help. All six of us were bunched together, floating straight down the middle of the canal. It was at this point that, finally, our circumstances greatly improved. For some reason, although the current was flowing straight ahead, we all began drifting, as a group, to the right toward the side of the canal. The onlookers were running along the side of the canal, some taking pictures for the next day's newspaper, others just watching the exciting saga unfold. Soon, we were close enough for them to reach us with fishing poles, which we anxiously grabbed. As we held on for our lives, they pulled us over to the edge, where we were lifted to safety.

We all grasped how fortunate we were as we watched the boat float right down the middle of the canal as it widened out into the Inter-coastal Waterway. We had to travel miles to retrieve it. Why had we, all of us, drifted toward the side of the canal while the boat continued to go straight? Again, as so many times before, unusual occurrences helped me out of a dangerous and life-threatening situation. Who was watching over me?

Sleep Driving

It was a Sunday morning, and I was driving home to Long Island from Stamford, Connecticut, where I worked as a chemist for American Cyanamid Company. In addition to my primary work, I was also the drummer in our rock band, "The Iridescents." We played four nights a week at a wellknown club, "The Molly & Me," in Glen Cove, Long Island.

This particular weekend, I committed to spend time on an important project at American Cyanamid. I foolishly chose to drive up to Connecticut after working until 2:00 a.m. Sunday morning. I would arrive by 3:00 a.m., work until 8:00 a.m. and return home to Long Island without losing my Sunday off. So what if I had been playing and drinking all night; I would just take a few amphetamines, and everything would work out.

On the way home, however, while driving on I-95 through the Bronx, I fell asleep; I don't know for how long, but it was a substantial amount of time. When I awakened in a panic, knowing I had been asleep, I was much farther down the road than when I was last conscious. The amazing thing to me, aside from how stupid I had been, was that when I awakened, I was in the middle of negotiating a curve perfectly, exactly in the middle of the passing lane, passing other cars at 65 miles per hour. Although startled and trembling, once again, all was well and I was safe— when I shouldn't have been. Who was watching over me?

Friends for Life

I don't remember the circumstances of our meeting, but Frank and I became good friends during the short time he attended New Hyde Park Memorial High School. Even though he lived five miles away, which on Long Island means there are a million people in between, we became pretty much inseparable. For many years I pondered over why I loved Frank like I did. I considered him my best friend right away. It truly was unusual and was something I thought about often.

Frank left for his new school after a few months, but our friendship continued to grow all the way through our college years. We worked together at our part time jobs, vacationed together at his grandfather's farm in upstate New York, played together, got in trouble together, fought together, right up to the time we both were married with kids. Strange, that I would meet someone when I was twelve years old who lived so far away, yet became such an important and influential part of my life.

Almost twenty years later, just a year or two after becoming a Christian, I received a call at 2:00 a.m. It was Frank. "Rick, I'm gonna kill somebody." What are you talking about? "I'm gonna kill someone." I knew Frank had a serious temper and was capable, especially since he had been drinking more than normal for a few years. I made him promise not to leave his house until I got there, a 3-hour drive away. When I arrived, Frank was standing in the doorway, with a Marlin .30-caliber lever-action rifle. He told me what had happened, and I made him promise once again not to leave the house until I got back.

It was 6:00 a.m. when I got to town and knocked on the door of his "employee," who would have deserved whatever happened to him. He answered the door, not knowing who I was, but when I told him, he followed my instructions to pack his bags and get out of town, fast, and forever, if he wanted to live. I know it sounds melodramatic, but it is true and was necessary. I returned to Frank's and did what I could to help him and his wife get through the crisis. It wasn't much, but was all I had to give.

Eight years later, when I was pastor of the Spartanburg Seventh-day Adventist Church in South Carolina, I was planning a trip to Miami for a conference when I remembered that Frank now lived in Florida and made plans to visit on my way down.

During those years, I had the blessing of sharing my new faith with my mom, my sister Gail, and her son Keith. As soon as Gail was baptized, God led her to be the secretary of the new "van ministry," in the Greater New York Conference. Merlin Kretchmar, president of the conference, and his wife, Juanita, were committed to the success of the new project. When Keith completed his service to our country in the United States Coast Guard, during which time I had the blessing of baptizing him, he joined the work at the van ministry also. There, he met and married Roberta and, shortly thereafter, they felt led to move to Spartanburg, where I was pastor. My sister Gail had been single for many, many years, waiting for the Lord to bring the one He wanted into her life.

When I arrived at Frank's in Melbourne, Florida, I soon learned that his wife had left him and that three years earlier he had found God. He hadn't had a drink in three years and had been delivered from the curse of alcoholism by his "Higher Power," through the ministry of AA. He didn't know who the "Higher Power" was, but whoever it was, his life was changed. I couldn't wait to share the three angels' messages with Frank, explaining who it was that had given him the victory. I contacted a local Bible worker from the Florida Conference and, after a few months, Frank accepted Jesus as his Savior.

During the time Frank was studying with a Bible worker in Florida, I found myself having the thought "Frank and Gail" go through my mind over and over. Not wanting to play Cupid, I tried to dismiss the thought, but it was futile. Frank and Gail, Frank and Gail; over and over in my mind, until I could resist the urge no longer. I called Frank and asked what he was doing the following weekend, telling him that I was thinking of inviting him up to Spartanburg to visit. Frank said, "Well, I guess I'm coming. Here's why. A few minutes before you called, I was praying about this weekend, got up and went to the calendar, circled it with a pencil and wrote two names, Rick and Benny. I was standing there at the calendar thinking about calling both of you to see what I might do this weekend, and the phone rang. Here we are talking about this weekend, so I guess I'm supposed to come to your place." He did, and guess who I made sure was there for a good part of the time?

Frank barely remembered Gail from the few fleeting glimpses he was lucky enough to have when visiting. To him, she was an older female "goddess" that he never really spoke with. What a difference a few years make! Now, let's get to the conclusion of the whole story. Perhaps it was six months later when I went down to the Melbourne, Florida, church and baptized Frank, my best friend. Then that afternoon I officiated the marriage of Frank and my sister Gail. Today, Frank and Gail minister together, as Frank serves as the East Coast coordinator for Regeneration Ministries.

I no longer have to wonder at how unusual it was that I would love a friend like I did when I was only twelve years old, someone who lived a world away and only came to my school for a couple of months. Isn't the Lord wonderful! Now, let's get back to the main subject of this book.

Chapter 4
Who Are We Anyway? Part I

L ong ago, in the far reaches of eternity past, God the Father and His Son clasped hands and made a solemn oath, a covenant between them, promising that if man fell, the Son would be the ransom for the lost race. He would be surety to meet the demands of justice and give His life as a ransom. It has always been purposed in the mind of God to save the fallen sons and daughters of Adam by giving His Son to die—His only Son.

> Herein is love; not that we loved God, but that He loved us, and sent His Son to be the propitiation for our sins. (1 John 4:10 KJV)

> The salvation of the human race has ever been the object of the councils of heaven. The covenant of mercy was made before the foundation of the world. It has existed from all eternity, and is called the everlasting covenant. So surely as there never was a time when God was not, so surely there never was a moment when it was not the delight of the eternal mind to manifest His grace to humanity. (*The Faith I Live By,* 76)

The promise of the everlasting covenant made in eternity past, when the Father and Son clasped hands together, was not easily fulfilled. After the creation of the world and the fall of man, there was a time that the eternal decision was actually *reconfirmed* in the presence of the heavenly host:

> He then made known to the angelic choir that a way of escape had been made for lost man; that He had been pleading with His Father, and had obtained permission to give His own life as a ransom for the race, to bear their sins, and take the sentence of death upon Himself, thus opening a way whereby they might, through the merits of His blood, find pardon for past transgressions, and by obedience be brought back to the garden from which they were driven.

Then they could again have access to the glorious, immortal fruit of the tree of life to which they had now forfeited all right. …

"Think ye that the Father yielded up His dearly beloved Son without a struggle? No, no." It was even a struggle with the God of heaven, whether to let guilty man perish, or to give His darling Son to die for them. (*Early Writings,* 126, 127)

Who are we anyway? What kind of relationship does Jesus have with His church? Looking beyond the surface and going deeper into the meaning of the cross, the cost of our redemption, our eyes will be opened to the wonderful love Jesus has for His church. It may take some effort for us to grasp the connection between who we are and Jesus' love for His church, but let us explore.

Love awakens love, and love is the only motivation strong enough to propel us in the Christian walk all the way, finishing the race and reaching the goal set before us. The theme of the cross will be the study of the redeemed forever and ever. As eternity rolls on and we look more and more deeply into the glory of the cross, we will be enlightened by the infinite mind of God, beholding heretofore unknown truths; truths that will expand our knowledge and draw us even closer to our Great and Mighty God.

A cursory look at the Lord's crucifixion and resurrection, knowing from Scripture of Jesus' foreknowledge concerning His resurrection on the third day, could lead us to conclude that this foreknowledge prevented Him from having to pass through a great deal of trial. This assumption, however, would diminish one of the greatest of God's realities: the cost of our salvation and the experience of the great power of love that comes from a deeper understanding of His sacrifice; this would be sorely missed.

Within the more nominal Christian understanding, the drama and literature teach that Christ's sufferings on the cross were mostly from the terrible physical torture He endured. Even though Jesus had foreknowledge of His victory and resurrection, this did not release Him from the mental torture of eternal separation from God. This truth is often unseen or misunderstood and can result in thinking that His sufferings were limited to the physical realm, where one might rightly claim that much greater physical agony was endured by many in the torture chambers of the Dark Ages.

If the sufferings of Christ consisted in physical pain alone, then His death was no more painful than that of some of the martyrs.

But bodily pain was but a small part of the agony of God's dear Son. The sins of the world were upon Him, also the sense of His Father's wrath as He suffered the penalty of the law transgressed. It was these that crushed His divine soul. It was the hiding of His Father's face—a sense that His own dear Father had forsaken Him—which brought despair. (*Testimonies for the Church*, vol. 2, 214)

As God's children, we need to understand that the penalty for sin is the second death and that Jesus, our substitute, must have endured its horror for every person that has ever walked the earth. This He did at Calvary, reconciling the world to God.

To wit, that God was in Christ, reconciling the world unto himself, not imputing their trespasses unto them; and hath committed unto us the word of reconciliation. (2 Corinthians 5:19 KJV)

Notice the text says "reconciling the world." That's everyone. We know that the whole world will not be saved, so what does it mean that all are reconciled? Many have tried to interpret this passage and have come up with theories of the science of salvation that are far from accurate. Instead of attempting to interpret this verse, here is a possible application.

Though the wages of sin is death, this reconciliation purchased *time* for all fallen humanity and is the reason we are not struck down immediately upon sinning. Jesus, by His death, purchased time; time for us to live out our lives and choose either to accept His substitutionary death personally or not; time to decide whether we want to be a part of God's eternal family or not. For every person who ever walked the face of this earth, Jesus purchased probationary time with the blood He spilled at Calvary's cross. Every breath we take has been purchased by that blood, and for this reason, our lives are not our own, but have been bought "for a price" of infinite value. Jesus' death released the tension that existed between God and man, reconciling the two.

Possibly, it is in this way that the whole world was reconciled to God by the death of His Son. We have not all been saved, but we have all been *reconciled* to God and given the time to choose.

Let's continue to consider more deeply the cross of Christ as He gave Himself for us.

Some have limited views of the atonement. They think that Christ suffered only a small portion of the penalty of the law of God; they suppose that, while the wrath of God was felt by His dear Son, he had, through all His painful sufferings, the evidence of His Father's love and acceptance; that the portals of the tomb before Him were illuminated with bright hope, and that He had the abiding evidence of His future glory. Here is a great mistake. (*Testimonies for the Church*, 213)

The ultimate fate of the lost is the second death. The second death means just what it says: a second "death." After the second resurrection, every responsible person ever born who is not among the redeemed lives, dies again, and this is their final demise. That "dying" again, the second death, is a living experience; an occurrence that takes place after the second resurrection. The horror arises from the all-consuming realization that they are about to cease to exist. Their suffering includes agonizing, unrelenting thoughts of how their sins have brought them to this place.

Only at this point do they know the ultimate seriousness and evil of sin. They realize what they have done to lose eternal life and are consumed with intolerable feelings of unrelenting desolation, knowing they are lost forever and can do nothing to stop their destruction. There is no one who can come to their aid or stop the carrying out of the sentence. They know they are going to die alone and cease to exist—forever. The gnashing of teeth may more be the result of these thoughts than the physical pain of being consumed by fire, the final consummation of which will come as a relief from the mental torture and agony.

This unimaginable experience was the price paid for our salvation, yet not ours alone, but for the salvation of the whole world, even the most heinous offender. This experience was the second death; the death Christ had to suffer to settle the just demands of the broken Law of God.

Satan with his fierce temptations wrung the heart of Jesus. The Savior *could not see through the portals of the tomb. Hope did not present to Him His coming forth from the grave a conqueror, or tell Him of the Father's acceptance of the sacrifice. He feared that sin was so offensive to God that Their separation was to be eternal. Christ felt the anguish that the sinner will feel when mercy shall no longer plead for the guilty race.* It was the sense of sin, bringing the

Father's wrath upon Him as the sinner's substitute that made the cup He drank so bitter, and broke the heart of the Son of God. (*The Desire of Ages,* 753, emphasis added)

The Spirit of Prophecy reveals that during those dark afternoon hours, the Father was at His Son's side, but because of the covenant they made together in eternity past—the everlasting covenant to save mankind—He must hide His presence during Jesus' suffering. He must not reach out to Him, for the salvation of the human race is dependent on His control at that moment. He must exert infinite, Godly restraint, to control His infinite, Godly desire, to help His frightened, suffering and dying Son, His only Son, whom He loves and with whom He has shared eternity past. Jesus must have no awareness of the Father's presence, nor the eternal bond of love that had always been between them.

The divine love of the Father for you and me restrained the overwhelming impulse to reach out and hold Him in His arms and assure Him that He was with Him at that time, His greatest hour of need. He couldn't, He wouldn't, for if He did we all would have been lost. It was this sense of His aloneness that forced from Jesus' parched lips the harrowing cry, "My God, My God, why hast thou forsaken me" (Ps. 22:1 KJV), when all the while, His Father was right at His side.

Awake, O sword, against my shepherd, and against the man (that is) my fellow, saith the Lord of hosts: smite the shepherd, and the sheep shall be scattered: and I will turn mine hand upon the little ones. (Zechariah 13:7 KJV)

The withdrawal of the divine countenance from the Savior in this hour of supreme anguish pierced His heart with a sorrow that can never be fully understood by us. So great was this agony that His physical pain was hardly felt. (*The Desire of Ages,* 753)

Oh, what pain the infinite heart of the Father must have endured, watching His beloved, innocent Son fear that He had been abandoned and left alone. How the Father withheld His divine embrace will be the study of the redeemed for endless ages of eternity. Reveal His presence? No; but there *was* one satisfaction the Father could allow as Jesus suffered alone. He could hide His Son's suffering from the sneering, sadistic crowd, who was staring in delight at His pain and torment, the pain and torment He was suffering for them. Oh, how the Godhead suffered; the Father, Son, and Holy Spirit were purchasing our redemption.

Inspiration informs us that there was only one time in all eternity that there was a "sundering" of the Trinity. Only once was the everlasting bond among them severed. Only once was one of the eternal trio forced to experience the total abandonment and separation from the others; a separation that literally broke the heart of the Son of God. Herein is the cost of our salvation, but not all; the rest will be for us to ponder in eternity.

> The Captain of our salvation was perfected through suffering. His soul was made an offering for sin. It was necessary for the awful darkness to gather about His soul because of the withdrawal of the Father's love and favor; for He was standing in the sinner's place, and this darkness every sinner must experience. The righteous One must suffer the condemnation and wrath of God, not in vindictiveness; for the heart of God yearned with greatest sorrow when His Son, the guiltless, was suffering the penalty of sin. This *sundering* of the divine powers will never again occur throughout the eternal ages. (*Seventh-day Adventist Bible Commentary*, 924)

The amazing love of God is demonstrated in the fact that while He "could not see through the portals of the tomb," and "hope did not present His coming forth a conqueror," and "He feared ... their separation was to be eternal," He did not save Himself, even when He feared He was lost forever. He knew He could call out, "Enough; let the sinful race perish," and every angel in heaven would come to His rescue. Yet, He did not exercise His right to come down from the cross to save Himself. Remember, this is God, our Creator. There never was a time He did not exist. Why would He do such a thing? Think this over for a few moments; then let's continue.

If Jesus came down from the cross and saved Himself, the human race would be lost. Even Moses, Enoch, Elijah, and possibly others already in heaven would have to perish with them. He knew that not one human would be saved, not one. Besides, He had already taken upon Himself humanity forever. What an interesting situation to ponder.

As He hung on the cross, Satan continued to tempt Him, hurling at Him discouraging thoughts, such as: there are so few who will take advantage of Your sacrifice, it's not worth all the suffering, no one cares; You are wasting Your life away for people who don't love you. They are an unthankful race of evil people. Let them perish, give up, come down from the cross and save Yourself.

> In the darkest hour, when Christ was enduring the greatest suffering that Satan could bring to torture His humanity, His Father hid from Him His face of love, comfort, and pity. In this trial His heart broke. He cried, "My God, My God, why hast Thou forsaken Me? [Matthew 27:46 KJV]. (*Manuscript Releases,* vol. 12, 407)

Jesus died of a broken heart.

What wonderful love. He did not consider life something to desire without you and me. The emotional pain the Son of God endured from the sense of His Father's frown, from the filthiness and shame of the sins of the world having been laid on His shoulders, from the anguish of a soul in the absence of mercy and being unable to sense His Father's presence—all these broke the heart of the Son of God.

This knowledge of His cross leads us to the most profound understanding of divine love. Simply, He chose death over life without us. He didn't want to be God if we couldn't be with Him. God chose not to exist forever if *you* couldn't be with Him forever. Only you! This is Christ's best demonstration—the grandest truth for us to grasp in our fallen condition—of His love for us, of His love for the church.

Yes, Jesus died of a broken heart, but the trial of the cross was the greatest victory the universe has ever witnessed, or ever will. Jesus' death was the victory of faith. For when His heart finally broke, the awareness of His Father's presence returned. Through the darkest hours of the cross, Jesus had to rely on His previous knowledge of the Father. It is this that sustained Him as He endured the sense of His disapproval and separation. It *did* break His heart, but at the same time He won the victory of faith, a marvelous mystery that will unfold during eternity.

> Amid the awful darkness, apparently forsaken of God, Christ had drained the last dregs in the cup of human woe. In those dreadful hours, He had relied upon the evidence of His Father's acceptance heretofore given Him. He was acquainted with the character of His Father; He understood His justice, His mercy, and His great love. By faith He rested in Him whom it had ever been His joy to obey. And as in submission He committed Himself to God, the sense of

the loss of His Father's favor was withdrawn. By faith, Christ was victor. (*The Desire of Ages,* 756)

As eternity unfolds, the contemplation of Christ's cross will yield ever and ever deeper insights into the character of God and the mystery of our existence. The infinite love of God, revealed in His selfless sacrifice to save our sinful race, will forever bind the hearts of all those who will inhabit eternity with Him. As the ages pass by, it will be the privilege of the redeemed to study the mysteries of the unfallen universe.

All the treasures of the universe will be open to the study of God's redeemed. Unfettered by mortality, they wing their tireless flight to world's afar—worlds that thrilled with sorrow at the spectacle of human woe and rang with songs of gladness at the tidings of a ransomed soul. With unutterable delight, the children of earth enter into the joy and the wisdom of unfallen beings. They share the treasures of knowledge and understanding gained through the ages upon ages in contemplation of God's handiwork. With undimmed vision they gaze upon the glory of creation—suns and stars and systems, all in their appointed order circling the throne of Deity. Upon all things, from the least to the greatest, the Creator's name is written, and in all are the riches of His power displayed. (*The Adventist Home,* 548)

The mystery of God is revealed in the salvation of the redeemed; how He takes those who fell to depths unimaginable, lower than any creatures in His Creation, and lifts them on high to be His special messengers of light, enjoying the closest relationship to Him throughout the endless ages of eternity, reveals the unsearchable mystery of our wonderful Savior's heart of love. What eternal splendor and joy we have to contemplate; "What a wonderful Savior is He."

The human race was to have a different relationship to God than all other creatures in His vast creation. "The life of Christ is to be revealed in humanity. Man was the crowning act of the creation of God, made in the image of God, and *designed to be a counterpart of God;* but Satan has labored to obliterate the image of God in man, and to imprint upon him his own image. Man is very dear to God, because he was formed in his own image" (*The Review and Herald,* June 18, 1895, emphasis added).

Just what it means to be a "counterpart of God," we will have to wait for life in the heavenly Canaan to comprehend fully, but the Spirit of Prophecy gives us some insight. "God designed that man, the crowning work of His creation, should express His thought and reveal His glory" (8T 264). Man's original design was for him to be the vehicle God would use to outsource revelations of His divine character throughout the myriads of inhabited worlds in His universal kingdom, to share His infinite wisdom and character throughout eternal ages.

> No other creature that God has made is capable of such improvement, such refinement, such nobility as man. ... Man cannot conceive what he may be and what he may become. Through the grace of Christ, he is capable of constant mental progress. (*Maranatha*, 229)

Satan was enraged. The thought that there was going to be a new world created with a race of beings who were of a "new and distinct order" (*The Review and Herald*, February 11, 1902) and had the ability to grow beyond all other beings in mental progress—beings who were meant to share the ever-increasing revelations of God's character to the universe—caused this jealous and selfish creature to become obsessed with their destruction. "It was the tempter's purpose to thwart the divine plan in man's creation, and fill the earth with woe and desolation. And he would point to all this evil as the result of God's work in creating man" (*Steps to Christ*, 17). Satan was infuriated by his exclusion from the planning process in man's creation.

Who are we, anyway? We are those who have seen the glory of God in His infinite sacrifice for us personally. We are those who recognize that God's love is mysterious, lifting those who have fallen to the sinful depths of His creation to the highest in His creation. We are those who have fallen at the foot of the cross, not trusting in self, knowing there is nothing redeemable in our carnal natures, and have been crucified with Him. We are those who have fallen, but will rise in Christ to heights unreachable before our fall.

> The life which Christ offers us is more perfect, more full, and more complete than was the life which Adam forfeited by transgression. (*Signs of the Times*, June 17, 1897)

Who are we, anyway? We are the ones who have glimpsed our wonderful Savior and responded to His call to pick up our cross and follow Him. We are the ones, because of our commitment to keep His commandments, who have been given the Spirit of Prophecy to guide us through to the end of this world. *We are His denominated people* who have come out of Babylon. We are the ones He beheld as He looked forward from His cross to the time of the end, who provided Him incentive to go all the way and not come down while dying on His cross. *We are His remnant church—that is who we are!*

Chapter 5
Who Are We Anyway? Part II

God has always had a people He considered His own; a people "set apart," who understand the requirements of the science of salvation He provided. A people whose hearts are filled with His Spirit and grasp the importance of sanctification, manifesting in themselves the loving character of God—and strive toward that expression, discerning evil and how lives are lost from its compromise. This is not a legalistic or proud lot, as they are often accused of being, but are a people jealous for the church that the Lord calls them to watch over, willing even to give their lives for God's honor and the safety of His people. These are people who can see how the dilutions of the principles of salvation invariably result in the loss of eternal life. Their upholding and jealous protection of the foundational truths upon which God's church is established is why they resist change for change's sake—the kind of change that inevitably results in losing connection with God and the loss of precious souls. Historically, such servants of God have been portrayed by those under Satan's influence as stubborn, proud, and often ignorant.

From the patriarchs and prophets through the chosen nation of Israel and down through the ages of the church, God has always had a designated people. These have always been those who possessed and lived by "the law and the testimony," or if they were inaccessible, lived up to all the light they had. They were those who were always in special relationship with the God of heaven. He chose, nurtured, and protected them for as long as they remained obedient. When they strayed, they were rebuked in His love and longsuffering, until they humbly repented and returned to His favor; He was and is "faithful and just to forgive them their sins and to cleanse them from all unrighteousness." When the nation of Israel had gone so far as to completely sever their relationship with Him, having forever rejected the Spirit of God by crucifying the Lord of glory, the Christian church became the chosen people of God.

But ye are a chosen generation, a royal priesthood, an holy nation, a peculiar people; that ye should show forth the praises of him who hath called you out of darkness into his marvelous light; which in time past were not a people, but are now the people of God: which had not obtained mercy, but now have obtained mercy. (1 Peter 2:9, 10 KJV)

Jesus Himself supported this truth when the Samaritan woman was contending with Him over where one could truly worship God. Jesus said:

Woman, believe me, the hour cometh, when ye shall neither in this mountain, nor yet at Jerusalem, worship the Father. Ye worship ye know not what: we know what we worship: for salvation is of the Jews. (John 4:21, 22 KJV)

I'm sure there were many who did not like that opinion. The statement Jesus made, "Salvation is of the Jews," is too separatist, too legalistic. They may have felt that Jesus was displaying pride and arrogance speaking in such a way; talking like that only creates barriers between the Jews and those of other religious persuasions. Of course, nothing could be further from the truth. He was not proud, arrogant, or legalistic; He was clarifying for those who were misinformed. In Jesus' day there were those who challenged the idea that salvation was of the Jews, or that God was such as He is, having a "chosen people." The Samaritans were an example, being Jews that in the past mingled their religion with others who infiltrated the land of Israel, bringing with them alternative beliefs. In Jesus' day, although they worshipped much like the Jews in Jerusalem, God was not with them, and Jesus had to make that truth understood by the woman at Jacob's well, or He would have been leading her astray. There were always some, even Jews, who did not like the "we are the only ones" idea.

What about today? Does Scripture uphold the idea that there will be a "chosen people" or "remnant church" during the time of the end? The "remnant" theme runs throughout the entire Bible. There has always been a "remnant," from Noah and his family to those returning to Jerusalem after the dispersion in Daniel's day; from the "remnant" in Israel, who accepted Jesus as their Messiah; and finally, a "remnant" from the church in the wilderness during the Dark Ages. This final "remnant" is identified scripturally in the book of Revelation, chapter 12:

The dragon was wroth with the woman, and went to make war with *the remnant of her seed, which keep the commandments of God, and have the testimony of Jesus Christ.* (Revelation 12:17 KJV, emphasis added)

The remnant is identified in the Spirit of Prophecy, as well:

The people of God are to guard carefully against the seductive influence of the deceiver. They are to hold firmly to the truths which called them out from the world, *and led them to stand as God's denominated people.* (*Counsels to Writers and Editors*, 109, emphasis added)

Seventh-day Adventists have a special work to do as messengers to labor for the souls and bodies of men.

Christ has said of His people, "Ye are the light of the world." We are the Lord's *denominated people,* to proclaim the truths of heavenly origin. The most solemn, sacred work ever given to mortals is the proclamation of the first, second, and third angels' messages to our world. (*Manuscript Releases*, vol. 7, 105, emphasis added)

God has called His church in this day, as He called ancient Israel, to stand as a light in the earth. By the mighty cleaver of truth, the messages of the first, second, and third angels, *He has separated them from the churches and from the world to bring them into a sacred nearness to Himself. He has made them the depositaries of His law and has committed to them the great truths of prophecy for this time.* Like the holy oracles committed to ancient Israel, these are a sacred trust to be communicated to the world. The three angels of Revelation 14 represent the people who accept the light of God's messages and go forth as His agents to sound the warning throughout the length and breadth of the earth. (*Testimonies for the Church*, vol. 5, 456, emphasis added)

The book of Revelation unfolds the history of the "great controversy" in wonderful detail. One purpose of the many prophecies in this book is to allow believers to identify their position in the history of time. Since the work God desires to be accomplished by His earthly army depends upon their place and time in history, it is essential for them to know where in the scheme of history they exist.

In the year 1840 there was an astonishing prediction made by Josiah Litch, one of the Advent believers. He was studying the history revealed in the blowing of the trumpets in Revelation chapter 9 and determined that the blowing of the sixth trumpet would meet its fulfillment by the fall of the Ottoman Empire, sometime in the month of August. A few days before the 11th, he determined that the exact date was August 11, 1840. To calculate the timing of this event, he used the year/day principle to reckon the length of time in the time prophecy of Revelation chapter 9, concerning the blowing of the sixth trumpet. This method of calculating time in Biblical prophecies was acceptable to most Protestant theologians of his day, especially those of the Advent awakening during the 1830s.

After prayerfully considering the importance of this new light and impressed by God that this was Bible truth, he made public his discovery. His prediction found its way to the major newspapers of the day, all across America. When the event occurred exactly as predicted, great energy was infused into the Advent awakening. Thousands realized the accuracy of the methods the Adventists were using to explain and unfold the meaning of the great prophecies in the books of Daniel and Revelation. Ellen White comments on this event, not as an interpretation of the prophecy concerning the sixth trumpet, but as verification that these historical events did take place as predicted, strengthening the movement:

> At the very time specified, Turkey, through her ambassadors, accepted the protection of the allied powers of Europe, and thus placed herself under the control of Christian nations. The event exactly fulfilled the prediction. When it became known, multitudes were convinced of the correctness of the principles of prophetic interpretation adopted by Miller and his associates, and a wonderful impetus was given to the advent movement. Men of learning and position united with Miller, both in preaching and in publishing his views, and from 1840 to 1844 the work rapidly extended. (*The Great Controversy*, 335)

This revival spread around the world, reaching every missionary outpost in existence at the time. Hundreds of thousands were rejoicing in the light of the soon coming of the Lord. The witness of God's Spirit verified His presence amidst the believers in this Great Awakening, an awakening with the power of the Spirit the world had not witnessed since apostolic times.

Suffice it to say that this "Great Awakening" was a revival of profound importance. We read from *The Great Controversy*:

> All classes flocked to the Adventist meetings. Rich and poor, high and low, were, from various causes, anxious to hear for themselves the doctrine of the Second Advent. The Lord held the spirit of opposition in check while His servants explained the reasons of their faith. Sometimes the instrument was feeble; but the Spirit of God gave power to His truth. The presence of holy angels was felt in these assemblies, and many were daily added to the believers. As the evidences of Christ's soon coming were repeated, vast crowds listened in breathless silence to the solemn words. Heaven and earth seemed to approach each other. The power of God was felt upon old and young and middle-aged. Men sought their homes with praises upon their lips, and the glad sound rang out upon the still night air. None who attended those meetings can ever forget those scenes of deepest interest. (*The Great Controversy*, 369)

The time for the Lord to appear came and went and Jesus did *not* appear. The sadness and disappointment the Adventists experienced cannot be expressed in words. Let us look at just one aspect of this period of history that begs examination.

Some who are uncomfortable about the beginnings of our movement feel that The Great Disappointment was the result of poor methods of Bible study; that if the Adventists had studied harder, prayed more, or were more careful in their analysis of Scripture, they would not have made such an embarrassing mistake. The Great Disappointment is often a part of our history that some want to forget or conveniently avoid, feeling that it truly was the result of uneducated farmers attempting to understand Scripture that was simply over their heads. These opinions are not correct and, in reality, reveal a shameful lack of understanding of the mighty working of God during the Advent awakening.

No matter how much they studied, or how long they prayed and sought for a proper understanding of the Scriptures that led them to believe Jesus would return in 1843/1844, they never would have arrived at any other explanation. Never! God, for His divine purpose, withheld their minds from a proper interpretation of the Bible verses they were studying, causing them to misapply them to the second coming of Christ. It was His will that they would make this mistake, not a result of wrongdoing. The Holy Spirit led them each step of the way in this great revival, preventing the truth from being seen. This was done for a reason and is so very important for Adventists to understand, especially at this time.

> The time of expectation passed, and Christ did not appear for the deliverance of His people. Those who with sincere faith and love had looked for their Savior, experienced a bitter disappointment. Yet the purposes of God were being accomplished; He was testing the hearts of those who professed to be waiting for His appearing. There were among them many who had been actuated by no higher motive than fear. Their profession of faith had not affected their hearts or their lives. When the expected event failed to take place, these persons declared that they were not disappointed; they had never believed that Christ would come. They were among the first to ridicule the sorrow of the true believers.

> But Jesus and all the heavenly host looked with love and sympathy upon the tried and faithful yet disappointed ones. Could the veil separating the visible world have been swept back, angels would have been seen drawing near to these steadfast souls and shielding them from the shafts of Satan. (*The Great Controversy,* 374)

Just as the disciples believed Jesus was about to take the throne of David as they led out in Christ's triumphal entry into Jerusalem, but were mistaken, so the Advent believers thought Jesus was going to come in the clouds of heaven, when it was another event that was to take place. Both of these events fulfilled Bible prophecy and would never have met their fulfillment if the believers knew the truth. Their actions, although misconceived, precisely met the Bible's predictions according to God's predetermined plan. Christ's triumphal entry was predicted by the prophet Zechariah in chapter 9, verse 9, while the Advent awakening and Great Disappointment were the fulfillment of Revelation chapter 10.

This is something that Adventists need to understand; yes, there was an error made, but it was God's will that the error was made. As the Spirit of God led them in their studies, He prevented the truth from being seen. Whoever accuses the Advent believers of wrongdoing, either from poor study methods or just being a fanatical group of uneducated farmers, *is mistakenly blaming the Holy Spirit of wrongdoing.* The Advent awakening was solemnly led forward, step by step, by the Almighty God and there is great danger in making incorrect accusations of how the Spirit of God led this movement, especially for those who have the Spirit of Prophecy in their midst, explaining these facts in detail.

> In like manner, Miller and his associates fulfilled prophecy and gave a message which Inspiration had foretold should be given to the world, but which they could not have given had they fully understood the prophecies pointing out their disappointment, and presenting another message to be preached to all nations before the Lord should come. The first and second angels' messages were given at the right time and accomplished the work which God designed to accomplish by them. (*The Great Controversy*, 405)

Even though the Great Awakening was based on a misunderstanding of Scripture, it accomplished exactly what God wanted it to accomplish. It brought the attention of the world, and especially the Protestant churches, to the great prophecies of the books of Daniel and Revelation and enlightened the world with the first and second angels' messages. In these two messages, the Protestant churches, God's people of that day, where receiving their last message of warning and mercy. This was their opportunity to respond to the new light flashing around the world through the Advent awakening as those prophecies previously sealed up and closed, until the time of the end, were now unsealed, opened, and understood by many, as the Protestant Reformation rolled on. The great question history awaited was: would the Protestant churches believe and commit to the truth of this new revival inspired by the Holy Spirit? Would they accept the new light God was shining throughout the world?

Sadly, as we look back into the history of those days, the records speak loudly and are extremely accurate, revealing how they did not accept the unique, life-changing message for that day, but rejected it and sadly disfellowshipped those who brought it to them. Denominationally, the Protestant churches turned their collective backs on the Spirit of God, leaving themselves in darkness, no longer being the people of God, but giving themselves over to the deceptions of satanic powers.

After the Great Disappointment, Revelation chapters 10 and 11 were understood as never before. Those few who remained confident that it truly was God who led them, saw how the book of Revelation accurately recorded almost 2,000 years ago all they had gone through. They must now "prophesy again," being the elect that accepted the first and second angels' messages, which the other churches rejected.

Now, as the Lord's new "chosen people," they must prophesy again to the whole world a message containing the full truth, proclaiming "the hour of His judgment and the Commandments of God," focusing on the Sabbath, the memorial of Creation. There must be another call to come out of Babylon, now that Babylon was filling up with "spirits of devils." This was a more complete message, directing God's children to the temple in heaven, where Jesus is making application of His atoning sacrifice as He ministers on our behalf. The world will witness a final revelation of God's true character of self-sacrificing love.

Along with the warning not to receive the "mark of the beast," the Lord's chosen, clothed in Christ's righteousness, having faces shining with the glory of God, will give the final "three angels' messages" to a perishing world. Then Jesus will return.

My purpose here is not to interpret prophecy, but to show how the light received as God's Spirit opened the interpretations of the prophecies in Daniel and Revelation to the Advent believers was the very light they needed to know, without doubt, that they were now God's denominated people, His remnant church.

Near the end of Revelation 9, at the blowing of the sixth trumpet, Turkey fell, just as predicted, establishing without doubt that the methods and counting of time used by the Adventists were correct. This being so, it was between the sixth trumpet of Revelation 9, verse 13, which was fulfilled on August 11, 1840, and the seventh trumpet of Revelation 11:15, announcing the final scenes of earth's history, that the Advent movement was portrayed in Revelation, chapter 10, where the entire Great Awakening and Great Disappointment were foretold in every detail. My friends, I hope and pray you see, as many do, how the Seventh-day Adventist Church is a church predicted in Bible prophecy, arising exactly as predicted in Revelation, chapter 10.

Who are we, anyway? Scripture leaves no doubt who we are. We are God's "remnant church," His denominated people. We are they who "keep the commandments of God and have the testimony of Jesus." We are God's "chosen people." God Himself made it undeniably clear who we are; we are Seventh-day Adventists, a people He Himself named, chosen to give the last message of mercy to a dying world, and that, brothers and sisters, is why Satan hates us.

How he hates us and *his plan to destroy us* is the rest of the story.

Chapter 6
Shall We Mingle?

There is an essential foundation to lay here that should be held throughout this study. There are many circumstances in which we are to collaborate and dialogue with the sisterhood of Protestant churches: sharing ministry and information—creation science, temperance work, religious liberty—to name a few, with personal friendship and witnessing of the highest priority. The danger is when we seek to learn from them in matters of theology, personal spiritual growth, and also methods of evangelism and church growth. To do so is a slippery, then almost mind-numbing slope that may have the potential to land us right in the middle of an element of the omega, one that takes away our God-given discernment and sensitivity to the clear Word of God and His prophetic gift. This is the very reason we've been given such clear and pointed warning against seeking to gain this kind of information from the other Protestant churches.

The spirit of ecumenism pervades the Christian world and more than a few Adventists are of the opinion that it is unwise *not* to participate in the sharing of ideas and methods used in the exploding evangelical Protestant community. The huge success of these approaches evidenced by the tens and even hundreds of thousands attending their congregations and meetings fairly begs us to discover and apply them to our "Laodicea" churches. "Why not?" is the appeal of many; if it works for them, it may work for us. And so the machinery is put in motion, without the much-needed caution, to learn from them and to become skilled at the modern science of "church growth." Feelings of embarrassment and frustration associated with our image as legalists and separatists, coupled with the obvious differences between "theirs and ours," lead them to the desire for Adventism to be viewed as a normal Protestant denomination, a sister in the sisterhood of all the other Christian churches in the Protestant community.

On our General Conference web page, we have a realistic and appropriate statement addressing how we, as a church, should relate to the ecumenical movement. In this statement, wise counsel is given to the conditions of our involvement with the other churches. Here are a few remarks lifted directly from the web page:

> In the focalized light of its prophetic understanding … She begins by "calling out" God's children from "fallen" ecclesial bodies that will increasingly form organized religious opposition to the purposes of God. Together with the "calling out" there is a positive "calling in" to a united, worldwide—that is, ecumenical—movement characterized by "faith of Jesus" and keeping "the commandments of God" (Rev. 14:12). In the World Council of Churches the emphasis is first of all on "coming in" to a fellowship of churches and then hopefully and gradually "coming out" of corporate disunity. In the Advent Movement the accent is first on "coming out" of Babylonian disunity and confusion and then immediately "coming in" to a fellowship of unity, truth, and love within the globe-encircling Advent family.[5]

Ellen White wrote:

> Our ministers should seek to come near to the ministers of other denominations. Pray for and with these men, for whom Christ is interceding. A solemn responsibility is theirs. As Christ's messengers we should manifest a deep, earnest interest in these shepherds of the flock. (*Testimonies for the Church*, vol. 6, 78)

Here we are counseled to "pray for and with," but not to go to their seminars to learn new techniques of evangelism, prayer, and discipleship. We are not told to seek their knowledge and methods. On the contrary, we are counseled:

> There is to be no compromise with those who make void the law of God. It is not safe to rely upon them as counselors. (*Selected Messages*, Book 2, 371)

Then, again from the GC web page:

---

5 "Seventh-day Adventists and the Ecumenical Movement," General Conference of Seventh-day Adventists web site, http://adventist.org/beliefs/other-documents/other-doc3.htm.

Should Adventists cooperate ecumenically? Adventists should co-operate insofar as the authentic gospel is proclaimed and crying human needs are being met. The Seventh-day Adventist Church wants no entangling memberships and refuses any compromising relationships that might tend to water down her distinct witness. However, Adventists wish to be "conscientious cooperators." The ecumenical movement as an agency of cooperation has accept-able aspects; as an agency for organic unity of churches, it is much more suspect.

Experience has taught that the best relationship to the various councils of churches (national, regional, and world) is that of ob-server-consultant status. This helps the church to keep informed and to understand trends and developments. It helps to know Christian thinkers and leaders. Adventists are provided the oppor-tunity to *exert a* presence and make the church's viewpoint known. Membership is not advisable.[6]

Notice that the above statement says we are to attend their meetings in an "observer-consultant status" to keep "informed" and for the purpose of making our "viewpoint known." Making our viewpoint known is not seeking what they have to teach and applying it to our lives and the lives of our parishioners without concern for where it might have come from. As we have already suggested, this is occurring now, as many in our beloved church have learned to practice dangerous methods of ancient Christian disciplines; practices thought to improve our relationship with Jesus, but in reality are satanic methods of mind control.

Why are we so prone to this behavior that is so contrary to the counsel we have in the Spirit of Prophecy? What is the need of our people that is ap-parently not being met, and what is the special attraction of these practices that makes them so alluring to the SDA Christian? We need to examine these things and understand as best we can the motivations involved, for it is not beyond any of us to be thus deceived.

Acceptance by our peers is a need we all have and is a tremendous influence in our lives. There are times when this need can be used for good and is necessary to be a holy witness for the Lord, but there are times when

6   Ibid.

Satan will take advantage of this innate desire and use it for his evil work. When God requests His denominated people to stand firm on the pillars of truth upon which His kingdom is established, truths which the other churches rejected 150 years ago, the temptation can exist to compromise those truths to improve our image.

Those in our church who have allowed the need to be accepted to overrule their better judgment and counsel from our inspired writings are often discomfited by some of the "old fashioned" beliefs: that we are the remnant church, have the truth, are God's special "chosen people" and are the only ones who have the unique last-day message for the world. For them this kind of thinking is indicative of elitism, pride, separatism, and sometimes even ignorance. These beliefs are often thought to be backward, uncreative, and closed-minded and are thought to be the cause of much considered wrong with the church today.

So for years we have been involved with the other churches, ignoring our own counsel referenced above from our web page, dialoguing with Christians of other faiths in an attempt to emerge from the Dark Ages of Adventism into the postmodern world. In seminars, workshops, and on our college campuses, workers meetings, conference office workshops and retreats, Seventh-day Adventists are learning the methods and techniques of the other Protestant churches, attempting to "fix" our church and bring it up to par, joining with the sisterhood of Protestant churches.

Could these efforts have far-reaching and destructive effects on our ability to sound the three angels' messages to the world? We may think that our knowledge and clear understanding of Scripture protects us from being deceived by the erroneous beliefs and doctrines of those we mingle with and invite to "teach" us, but here the Lord tells us we are making a disastrous mistake.

There is to be *no compromise* with those who make void the law of God. It is not safe to rely upon them as counselors. Our testimony is not to be less decided now than formerly; our real position is not to be cloaked in order to please the world's great men. They may desire us to unite with them and accept their plans, and may make propositions in regard to our course of action which may give the enemy an advantage over us … You are not to look to the world in order to learn what you shall write and publish or what you shall speak. Let all your words and works testify, "We have not followed cunningly devised fables" (2 Peter 1:16 KJV). "We have also a more sure word of prophecy; whereunto ye do well that ye take heed, as unto a light that shineth in a dark place" (2 Peter 1:19 KJV). (*Selected Messages,* Book 2, 371, emphasis added)

Through Ellen White, the Spirit of God is strongly reminding us that "we have also a more sure word of prophecy," to take heed and not look to the other churches, whence we have been delivered, but rely on the light God has shined upon *us* for instruction and the planning of His work.

The danger in thinking that the Protestant evangelicals have something to offer and that we should learn from them to design our plans is that to do so, we must *disregard* and thus *reject* the light we have warning us not to do such things. We are entertaining the spirit of antagonism toward the Spirit of Prophecy and rejecting its counsel in receiving instruction from them. History reveals that Satan's warfare against Israel and the church is most successful when he can pervert their understanding of God's character and His requirements for them to maintain a saving relationship. He knows that the best way to bring this condition about is to cause the rejection of the inspired messages brought by the prophets to His people.

One aspect of Israel's history is a sad commentary on how they continually rejected the Spirit of God.

O Jerusalem, Jerusalem, thou that killest the prophets, and stonest them which are sent unto thee, how often would I have gathered thy children together, even as a hen gathereth her chickens under her wings, and ye would not! (Matthew 23:37 KJV)

One of Satan's most effective devices in leading God's people astray is by suggesting that God does not require such strict obedience to His requirements as some may think. Observe the following quotation:

This is what will distinguish between those who honor God and those who dishonor him. Here is where we are to prove our loyalty. The history of God's dealings with his people in all ages shows that he *demands exact obedience.* (*Counsels for the Church,* 268, emphasis added)

Obedience to what? is the question. His divinely inspired instructions! In addition to the Holy Bible, the Lord in His mercy and great love, sent

His bride His final love letter, filled with instructions on how to get to the wedding banquet. The Spirit of Prophecy is this love letter.

The requirements to stay in a saving relationship with Him are the same today as they have ever been. The way we approach Him, how we are to behave, the music we listen to, the books we read for pleasure or for education, how we pray, how we contemplate and meditate on His Word, how we are to worship, and how we relate to the Spirit of Prophecy is the same today as it ever has been. *God does not change.* God spoke to His people in Old Testament times through the prophets; there were hundreds, if not thousands, of prophets over the years whom God called to be His mouthpiece and safely instruct Israel as they shared the message of salvation with the world. And when His people obeyed, they continued to have God's counsel available, at every moment and in every circumstance. There was never a reason for not understanding God's leading other than outright rebellion or people believing that their own wisdom exceeded that of the prophets. Self-sufficiency and repeatedly doubting the requirements of God led His people to ignore and even murder His messengers until, "last of all," they even ignored and murdered His Son. Satan consistently won the day, deceiving God's people, the Israelites, over and over by convincing them that they did not have to so strictly follow the divine counsel. This deception, along with their desire to be like the heathen nations around them and participate in their more exciting style of worship, to eat their more stimulating foods, to take their women to be their wives, along with their desire not to be considered "peculiar," led to their final separation from God and the eternal loss of their status as God's "chosen people."

Israel's history is a lesson we ignore at our own peril. We can suffer today from the same delusions as did those who brought about the downfall of Israel, as Satan employs his age-old temptations that work so well in any given generation. Like Israel of old, many in the church today believe we are misled when we think of ourselves as God's chosen people; and still some believe we are, but think we should never talk as if we are, or act in any way that reveals we believe it.

For many, the desire for acceptance into the sisterhood of Christian churches mandates the concealment of the unique truths that is the framework for who we are. There is the desire to clean up our vocabulary of those words or phrases that reveal our uniqueness, or point to the special truths that define us, such as "remnant," or "the truth." It is often felt that the use of these words or phrases reveals our pride and arrogance and only adds to the negative perception other Christian groups have of the Seventh-day

Adventist Church. Some also feel that the use of these terms that reveal the uniqueness of our church hinders the efforts to advance the persona of our church. This is a slippery slope and a grave deception.

> We are under obligation to declare faithfully the whole counsel of God. We are *not* to make less prominent the special truths that have separated us from the world, and made us what we are ...

> At this time, when we are so near the end, shall we become so like the world in practice that men may look in vain to find God's denominated people? Shall any man sell our peculiar characteristics as God's chosen people for any advantage the world has to give? Shall the favor of those who transgress the law of God be looked upon as of great value? Shall those whom the Lord has named His people suppose that there is any power higher than the great I AM? Shall we endeavor to blot out the distinguishing points of faith that have made us Seventh-day Adventists? (*Evangelism*, 121, emphasis added)

For those thus deceived to continue in their work, striving for acceptance into the sisterhood of Protestant churches, counsel such as this must be ignored.

Chapter 7
History Repeated

Section A

During the month of February 1904, the same month she had to deal with Kellogg's "alpha" apostasy, Ellen White wrote a letter to Brother Craw, a friend and steadfast supporter of the work. She was requesting a loan or gift to be used to publish recent writings on Old and New Testament history that she felt the church needed as quickly as possible. She wrote to Brother Craw of the urgent need for funds to continue spreading the message around the world, and how she and others were helping in any way possible. She mentioned Elder Conradi's work in Europe and his contribution of $500 used in publishing some of her work. Repayment would come from sales. Then, there were believers in Africa from Elder Haskell's labors who donated $2,000 to the work she began in Australia. During this time, committed believers were investing every penny they could find to spread the three angels' messages.

She asked Brother Craw, "Will you place a copy of this letter in the hands of those whom you think might be sufficiently interested in the work of God to make me their agent, and entrust me with their means, either as a loan or a gift? Let us do all we can to help advance the work."

She expressed the burden of her heart in these words: "My soul is in distress as I see souls perishing out of Christ. I long to see them, coming in to the truth. I see many places where means is greatly needed, that a beginning may be made" (*Manuscript Releases*, vol. 13, 393). She went on to say that the medical missionary work is the pioneer of the gospel and also the method through which the Lord planned to reach the wealthy, as well as the means of breaking down any prejudice against evangelism. After making this statement defining the importance of our medical work, she made this most interesting statement:

We have no time to lose. Troublous times are before us. The world is stirred with the spirit of war. Soon the scenes of trouble spoken of in the prophecies will take place. The prophecy in the eleventh of Daniel has nearly reached its complete fulfillment. Much of the history that has taken place in fulfillment of this prophecy *will be repeated*. In the thirtieth verse a power is spoken of that "shall be grieved, and return, and have indignation against the holy covenant: so shall he do; he shall even return, and have intelligence with them that forsake the holy covenant." (*Manuscript Releases*, vol. 13, 393, emphasis added)

Then she quoted the following verses from Daniel 11: 31–36 (KJV, emphasis added).

- 31. "And arms shall stand on his part, and they shall *pollute the sanctuary of strength,* and shall *take away the daily sacrifice*, and they shall *place the abomination* that maketh desolate."

- 32. "And such as do wickedly against the covenant shall *he corrupt by flatteries:* but the people that do know their God shall be strong, and do exploits."

- 33. "And they that understand among the people shall instruct many: yet they shall fall by the sword, and by flame, by captivity, and by spoil, many days."

- 34. "Now when they shall fall, they shall be holpen with a little help: but many shall cleave to them with flatteries."

- 35. "And some of them of understanding shall fall, to try them, and to purge, and to make them white, even to the time of the end: because it is yet for a time appointed."

- 36. "And the king shall do according to his will; and he shall exalt himself, and magnify himself above every god, and shall speak marvelous things against the God of gods, and shall prosper till the indignation be accomplished: for that that is determined shall be done."

After quoting these Bible verses she said:

Scenes similar to those described in these words *will take place.* We see evidence that Satan is fast obtaining the control of human minds who have not the fear of God before them. Let all read and understand the prophecies of this book, for we are now entering upon the time of trouble spoken of: "And at that time shall Michael stand up, the great prince which standeth for the children of thy people: and there shall be a time of trouble, such as never was since there was a nation even to that same time: "and at that time thy people shall be delivered, every one that shall be found written in the book. And many of them that sleep in the dust of the earth shall awake, some to everlasting life, and some to shame and everlasting contempt. And they that be wise shall shine as the brightness of the firmament; and they that turn many to righteousness as the stars for ever and ever. But thou, O Daniel, shut up the words and seal the book, even to the time of the end: many shall run to and fro , and knowledge shall be increased." (Daniel 12:1–4 KJV)

The Spirit of the Lord is being withdrawn from the world. It is no time now for men to exalt themselves. It is no time for the people of God to be erecting costly buildings, or to be using the Lord's entrusted talent of means in glorifying themselves. Whatever we do we should do economically. The buildings we erect should be plain, without useless display. Let us beware of selfish greed." (*Manuscript Releases*, vol. 13, 394)

Ellen White made few comments about the prophecy in Daniel, chapter 11, the last and most detailed of all the prophecies in the book of Daniel. Her comments in the letter she wrote to Brother Craw, noted above, imply a repeat of history, which would most definitely include Satan's attacks against the remnant church.

Concerned that time was short and trouble was coming in the world, she referenced the prophecy in Daniel 11, saying it had almost reached its complete fulfillment, and indeed it had. When she made that statement, the *only* part of the prophecy in Daniel 11 yet to be fulfilled was the segment from verses 40 to 45, beginning with the words, "And at the time of the end." Could there be a connection between the end-time fulfillment of these verses and the intriguing statement concerning Daniel 11:30, that, "much of the *history* that has taken place in the fulfillment of this prophecy *will be repeated*"?

Her words do not suggest a dual or multiple fulfillment, nor is this the intent of the author. She is saying that "*much of the history*" that took place in its *past* fulfillment "will be repeated." Another way to say it is that the *historical results of verse 30's past fulfillment will occur once again.* The reader must not miss this point. Ellen White was implying that history will be repeated, not the prophecy or the exact manner in which it was fulfilled.

The King of the North (papal Rome) is destined to regain the position it previously held during the Dark Ages, having authority and control over the world. "His deadly wound was healed, and all the world wondered after the beast" (Revelation 13:3). Then, having regained great power and authority, he will be in a position to execute a final assault on God's people, the subject of that segment of Daniel 11's prophecy in verses 40–45, yet unfulfilled in Ellen White's day.

Remember, the papacy must "resurrect" from the deadly wound received in 1798, so what Ellen White most likely had in mind when saying, "will be repeated," was a reoccurrence of the results of the prophecy—the papal dominion of the Dark Ages, and this history will be repeated. To be clear, this is not a dual fulfillment or a repeat of the original prophecy, but is a repeat of the history's original fulfillment. This is the meaning of Ellen White's statement.

To recap:

> The prophecy in the eleventh of Daniel, has nearly reached its complete fulfillment. Much of the history that has taken place in fulfillment of this prophecy *will be repeated.* In the thirtieth verse a power is spoken of that "shall be grieved, and return, and have indignation against the holy covenant: so shall he do; he shall even return, and have intelligence with them that forsake the holy covenant. (*Manuscript Releases*, vol. 13, 394, emphasis added)

We can also conclude from this statement that Ellen White was implying that Daniel 11:30 is definitely one of the verses among those she quoted, whose history "will be repeated."

Verse 30 states that the King of the North is grieved, predicted he will have indignation against the Holy Covenant, and would have "intelligence" with those who had forsaken the Holy Covenant. The *historical* fulfillment of this prophecy was the papal domination of the civilized world during the Dark Ages and arresting the progress of the Protestant Reformation in Europe, forcing their exodus to the New World. We will not study the details of this development, but it is important to know that similar results can be expected in our day, when history "will be repeated," and the world will once again come under the control of the Roman Catholic power.

Section B

Personal note: You will find many quotations from the Spirit of Prophecy in this chapter. The purpose of this book is to expose the sophistries and deceptions being used to prevent the remnant church from carrying out its mission of proclaiming the three angels' messages to the world. Satan's strategy for the last battle in this conflict is to make of none effect the inspired writings God has given the church. We are revealing the danger in plans and practices present in our church today, originating from sources other than the inspired ones God instructs us to use for this purpose. We have shown previously that to fulfill our mission, the church must heed the counsel and warnings contained in the Spirit of Prophecy. In this chapter we show how inspiration identifies the papacy as the enemy of God's church in the final conflict and instructs us how to be victorious. We quote extensively because we want to know God's plan for His church, not man's.

We are entering the final conflict of a war that has raged for more than 6,000 years, and the Lord has called us to be His representatives. We are the soldiers in His army, and our most powerful weapon is to reflect the brightness of His glory; the light that exposes the darkness of Satan's deceptions. Every true follower of Jesus will shine with this light, but to gain the ultimate victory we are responsible for more than merely reflecting His glory. It is crucial to learn all we can about the enemy. It is true that Jesus is our Omniscient Commander-in-Chief, but His omniscience would not have us be ignorant of the enemies ways, unable to discern his plans and strategy. As faithful disciples, we will accept the Lord's direction, as if it was our own will. We are called to learn the enemy's ways, but only by the methods revealed through inspiration.

There is precious instruction for the church in Ellen White's "preface" to *The Great Controversy*, 1888 edition. She says:

> As the Spirit of God has opened to my mind the great truths of His word, and the scenes of the past and the future, I have been bidden to make known to others that which has thus been revealed,—to trace the history of the controversy in past ages, and especially so to present it as to *shed a light on the fast-approaching struggle of the future. In pursuance of this purpose*, I have endeavored to select and group together events in the history of the church …

In these records we may see a foreshadowing of the conflict before us. ... We may see unveiled *the devices of the wicked one, and the dangers which they must shun* who would be found "without fault" before the Lord at His coming.

It is not so much the object of this book to present new truths concerning the struggles of former times, as to bring out facts and principles which *have a bearing on coming events. ... through them a light is cast upon the future, illumining the pathway of those who, like the reformers of past ages, will be called, even at the peril of all earthly good, to witness "for the word of God, and for the testimony of Jesus Christ.*

In the great final conflict, Satan will employ the same policy, manifest the same spirit, and work for the same end as in all preceding ages. That which has been, will be, except that the coming struggle will be marked *with a terrible intensity such as the world has never witnessed.* Satan's deceptions *will be more subtle,* his assaults *more determined.* If it were possible, he would lead astray the elect. Mark 13:22, R.V. (*The Great Controversy*, 1888 edition, vii–xi, emphasis added)

Ellen White's purpose in reviewing the history of God's people is not for history's sake, but that we, who are about to enter the final conflict, can understand the plans the enemy has to destroy us. We are told, "In these records we may see a foreshadowing of the conflict before us," and that, *"Satan will employ the same policy, manifest the same spirit, and work for the same end as in all preceding ages."*
She goes on to say:

If we desire to understand the determined cruelty of Satan, manifested for hundreds of years, not among those who never heard of God, but in the very heart and throughout the extent of Christendom, we have only to look at the history of Romanism. Through this mammoth system of deception the prince of evil achieves his purpose of bringing dishonor to God and wretchedness to man. (*The Great Controversy*, 570)

Among God's people it is often declared that Roman Catholicism has changed and that the Adventist Church should no longer maintain the stance it took more than one hundred years ago. This begs the question; should we change what we have taught in the past about the papacy? Is it true that she has changed?

In order for the answer to these questions to be meaningful, we will need to agree with two basic Adventist teachings held since the inception of our church; teachings about which, our beliefs will likely determine our salvation. Two chapters in this book, "Who are We Anyway?" parts I and II, were written first to convince the reader that it is essential for us to believe the Seventh-day Adventist Church is the remnant church of Bible prophecy. Second, the true biblical gift of prophecy, providing all the counsel and warnings needed by God's people, was manifested in the life and writings of Ellen G. White. The conviction that these two teachings are true is the only way for us to be saved from the constant stream of satanic delusions we will encounter until probation closes.

Before we use the Spirit of Prophecy to answer the questions raised, it must be understood that if even one statement concerning important issues of salvation is doubted, or considered out of touch with reality, nothing written by the hand of Ellen White can be trusted—nothing! Every sentence written would be open to scrutiny and personal opinion. To think we have the ability to judge what the Holy Spirit has inspired His messenger to write is the pinnacle of arrogance and egotism and leads blindly down the path to rebellion.

> God speaks through his appointed agencies, and let no man, or confederacy of men, insult the Spirit of God by refusing to hear the message of God's word from the lips of his chosen messengers. By refusing to hear the message of God, men close themselves in a chamber of darkness. They shut their own souls away from vast blessings, and rob Christ of the glory that should come to him, by showing disrespect to his appointed agencies. (*The Review and Herald*, September 12, 1893)

Please consider the following:

AD GENTES
ON THE MISSION ACTIVITY
OF THE CHURCH

This is a document from Vatican II, instructing churches around the world on mission activity. The instruction is filled with information on the importance of spiritual formation to the success of their outreach program: "Since the *contemplative life belongs to the fullness of the church's presence,* let it be put into practice everywhere."

The "contemplative life" consists of those mystical teachings learned in the discipline called "spiritual formation," brought to us through the visions of Ignatius Loyola, founder of the Jesuits. The document first claims that these teachings belong to the Roman Catholic Church, and should be put into practice everywhere. For what purpose would they want this practice to be spread everywhere? The document answers by saying these words about this practice:

> 40. Religious institutes of the contemplative and of the active life have so far played, and still do *play, the main role in the evangelization of the world.*

The Vatican II instruction is saying that the Roman Catholic practice known as spiritual formation, plays "the main role" in evangelizing the whole world. I pray you will see how this practice called spiritual formation is truly a child of the papacy. The dangers of the mystical practices which lie at the heart of this discipline will be explored in the chapters to come.

We have seen some of the papacy's plans for the future and need to carefully consider the counsel and information in *The Great Controversy,* but first, without relying on inspiration, just history, let us examine a quote from Pope Paul VI:

DOGMATIC CONSTITUTION ON DIVINE REVELATION,
DEI VERBUM,
SOLEMNLY PROMULGATED BY HIS HOLINESS
POPE PAUL VI ON NOVEMBER 18, 1965:

> 21. *The Church has always venerated the divine Scriptures* just as she venerates the body of the Lord, since, especially in the sacred liturgy, she *unceasingly receives and offers to the faithful the bread of life from the table both of God's word and of Christ's body. She has always maintained them, and continues to do so,* together with sacred tradition, as the supreme rule of faith, since, as inspired by God and committed once and for all to writing, they impart the word of God Himself without change, and make the voice of the Holy Spirit resound in the words of the prophets and Apostles.

We ask, has Roman Catholicism changed her ways? This document claims she has always provided people with *"the bread of life."* Is the church speaking the truth through this official document about Scripture, penned in 1965 by Pope Paul VI? Or is the documented and proven history of the Dark Ages true? We know for a fact that if people, even a small child, were caught carrying just one page of Scripture by officials of the church they would lose their lives, commonly by a most unthinkable and tortuous method. According to *Fox's Book of Martyrs*, fifty million lost their lives. Fifty million!

Let us continue now with the inspired statements from the Spirit of Prophecy. They will help us to see how this practice may fit into their future plans:

> The Romish Church now presents a fair front to the world ... but she is unchanged. ... Popery is just what prophecy declared that she would be, *the apostasy of the latter times.* (*The Great Controversy*, 1888 edition, 570, 571, emphasis added)

> A prayerful study of the Bible would show Protestants the real character of the papacy, and would cause them to abhor and to shun it; *but many are so wise in their own conceit that they feel no need of humbly seeking God that they may be led into the truth.* (*The Great Controversy*, 1888 edition, 572, emphasis added)

> If the reader would understand the agencies to be employed in the soon-coming contest, he has but to *trace the record of the means which Rome employed for the same object in ages past.* (*The Great Controversy*, 1888 edition, 573, emphasis added)

> There has been a change; but the change is not in the papacy. Catholicism indeed resembles much of the Protestantism that now exists, *because Protestantism has so greatly degenerated since the days of the reformers.* (*The Great Controversy*, 1888 edition, 571, emphasis added)

This remarkable prediction by the Lord's servant should awaken any sincere Adventist to the urgency of our mission:

But Romanism as a system is no more in harmony with the gospel of Christ now than at any former period in her history. . . . She is employing every device to extend her influence and increase her power in preparation for a fierce and determined conflict *to regain control of the world, to re-establish persecution, and to undo all that Protestantism has done. Catholicism is gaining ground upon every side.* (*The Great Controversy*, 1888 edition, 572, emphasis added)

Has the papacy changed? Should we cease our warnings to the world concerning what Scripture and the Spirit of Prophecy predict is coming upon the world? Not if we choose to believe Scripture and that the Lord inspired Ellen White to write *The Great Controversy*. Friends, as we demonstrated a few paragraphs back, if we choose to believe that what Ellen White wrote in *The Great Controversy* is no longer applicable, then the only logical thing to do would be to throw out everything she wrote, for how could one decide what applies, and what does not? With that settled, let us continue to learn, for this next statement gives every one of us direction for the future:

As we near the close of time, there will be greater and still greater external parade of heathen power ... *All need wisdom carefully to search out the mystery of iniquity that figures so largely in the winding up of this earth's history.* ... In the very time in which we live, the Lord *has called ... them a message to bear. He has called them* to expose the wickedness of the man of sin who has made the Sunday law a distinctive power. (*Testimonies to Ministers and Gospel Workers*, 117, emphasis added)

We must carefully "search out the mystery of iniquity" and have been called to "expose the wickedness of the man of sin." It is not difficult to know what God has called us to and what we should be doing with our lives. It is not difficult to recognize deception when we are confronted by it. It is not difficult for our schools to decide which courses are acceptable to teach and which should be avoided, and it is not difficult to discern which of the many supernatural voices heard by Christians today is the true voice of God.

All we need is to distrust self, faithfully relying on the guidance of the Holy Spirit, whom the Lord sent to guide us into all truth. This is the same Spirit who inspired Bible writers thousands of years ago, and who today has given the remnant church the writings of Ellen G. White. We learn from these inspired writings that God will guide us, using at least four different methods. One is through impressions the Holy Spirit makes upon our hearts. The second is by words that have been written by the inspired writers of the Bible. Third, we have in our day through the counsels of the Spirit of Prophecy, the genuine expression of the gift of prophecy. The fourth and most important is by Providence.

In these four ways, the Lord protects and leads His people to the surrender of self, to rely upon the teachings contained in inspired writings, and finally, to cooperate with heavenly beings dedicated to helping us carry out God's will. Situations will arise that will actually be the unfolding of God's plan. When these four elements of the true Christian life are present in our lives, we can have the assurance of God's leading and guidance. If one's spiritual life is lacking one of these prerequisites, and supernatural manifestations occur, God's people will know that deception is taking place.

In chapter 2, "Spiritual Formation," we compared the spiritual experiences of Ignatius Loyola and Martin Luther. We saw how Martin Luther trusted in Scripture, the Word of God, while his contemporary, Loyola, was determined to have God speak to him by his desired method—supernatural revelation. Loyola wanted to see God everywhere and in everything, a pantheistic concept of God. He refused to respond to his guilty conscience, and chose not to seek what the Bible taught concerning sin and repentance. Thoughts about these things disturbed him, so he avoided God's word containing instruction on those subjects, following his own inclinations instead. Nevertheless, Loyola's practices did result in supernatural revelations, which today are called "the spiritual exercises" of Ignatius Loyola, and are the teachings used by the Roman Catholic Church to develop the discipline known as spiritual formation.

Luther on the other hand, surrendered self and refused to follow his own inclinations, seeking instruction from God's Word. The Lord spoke to Luther as he studied, revealing His supernatural power by giving Luther victory over sin and by providentially leading him in his life. The prerequisites mentioned above were present in Luther's experience and he became the greatest of the reformers, dedicating his life to leading people out of the corrupt Roman system. Meanwhile, Loyola rose to the highest recognition in that same Roman system, founding the Jesuit order, which inspiration claims is one of the most cruel organizations that has ever existed.

When the lives of these two men are compared, we can see the result of seeking God on one's own terms, as Loyola did, imagining Him to be the way you want Him to be, and how it can result in a spiritual experience, even a supernatural experience, but devoid of the presence of God. We find that the mystical experiences of Loyola originate from the same deceptive supernatural source upon which the theology of Roman Catholicism is structured. The worship experience is centered around the performance of the sacraments, intended to induce a mystical experience where God's grace is received. The foremost of the sacraments is the Eucharist, the center of every mass or worship service, where it is believed the priest has the special power to actually transform the bread and wine into the body and blood of the Lord. It is this teaching, called transubstantiation, which is the major roadblock to the merging of the Protestant and Catholic churches.

The traditional worship in the Roman Catholic Church teaches the participant that God's grace is received by simply performing the sacrament, making the entire process one of salvation by works, not faith. The Roman Catholic system is an elaborate process, extremely attractive to those who would rather not be troubled with a guilty conscience, or with the idea that victory over sin is necessary. It is believed that God's grace does not contain the transforming power of God, just forgiveness, and can be received without exercising faith or having a personal relationship with God. All that is needed to stand right with God is to perform the sacraments and go to confession to have sins forgiven and their results eradicated. The mysticism involved in the true performance of the sacraments, is why the Scriptures have given the system the names "Man of Sin" and "Mystery of Iniquity."

Roman Catholic theology is steeped in mysticisms—a power over which God has allowed Satan complete control. Accordingly, anyone who practices mysticism comes under the control of satanic agencies. This truth is absolutely essential for God's people to understand and explains why there is such danger in the practice of spiritual formation.

We need to consider what is occurring in the world today and how the papacy is involved. If inspiration is to be believed, then considering a repetition of strategies the papacy used in the past is necessary to understand how she will attempt to overthrow God's people today.

The Jesuit order thrives today and is governed by the same policies set forth by Ignatius Loyola. The order conceals its real purpose beneath a covering of religiosity, using an outward display of care for the poor and needy to deceive society. The Spirit of Prophecy tells us this truth and is why our trust in it is our only hope; otherwise, we would be deceived as those will be without the inspired writings.

The only way for those in God's church to teach and preach that we should no longer fear Roman Catholicism is for them to no longer trust in the Spirit of Prophecy. Satan has control of their minds and the inspiration God gave the remnant church has been made "of none effect." They have rejected the only means of their defense and the fruit of this rejection demonstrates the importance of trusting in inspiration.

When the Jesuits are in a position where they lack power, they patiently bide their time, and are silent, but when conditions in the world change, and they believe their plans will succeed, they will act. They are dedicated and sworn to do anything to carry out the pope's plans, even to give their lives. It is difficult to believe these things in the world we live in today, having been surrounded and brought up with political correctness and anti-prejudicial legislation, but as Christians, we must allow inspiration to speak louder than the voice of the media and educational institutions. Our nature is no different than those who took part in the Inquisition, and in observing the increase in atrocities taking place in the world today, there is adequate evidence that what we have gleaned from the Spirit of Prophecy can be trusted.

The following segment was copied directly, from an editorial in the February 2012 edition of *Inside the Vatican*, a Roman Catholic publication. It is written by the editor, Dr. Robert Moynihan, and contains quotations from a message given by Pope Benedict XVI that was read in Roman Catholic Churches on Youth Day, May 12, 2012.

Silence can be what we need most of all in our noisy world, Pope Benedict said recently. In fact, silence may be the best way to evangelize, to communicate the grandeur and glory of Christ, whose divine nature transcends the power of all words to express.

The Pope expressed his thoughts on silence in a remarkable letter issued on January 24, entitled "Silence and Word: Path of Evangelization." The letter was released at the Vatican press office by Archbishop Claudio Maria Celli, head of the Pontifical Council for Social Communications, for World Communications Day 2012.

"When messages and information are plentiful, silence becomes essential if we are to distinguish what is important from what is insignificant or secondary," the Pope wrote in the message, which was read in Catholic churches around the world on May 20, 2012. Silence, he said, is "often more eloquent than a hasty answer" because it "permits seekers to reach into the depths of their being and open themselves to the path toward knowledge that God has inscribed in human hearts."

The Pope says silence has been a key part of Christian life from the earliest times. He points to the "eloquence of God's love, lived to the point of the supreme gift," which is seen "in the *silence of the cross," when, after Christ's death "there is a great silence over the earth." Silent contemplation also "immerses us in the source of that Love, who directs us toward our neighbors so that we may feel their suffering and offer them the light of Christ, his message of life and his saving gift of the fullness of love," he wrote.

Roman Catholicism's thrust to win the world over is called the "New Evangelization." We can see in the statement above, that the present pope has placed his confidence to accomplish their goals, in the mysticism of "silence," or "Ignatiun Spirituality."

Some claim to have avoided the danger by not practicing contemplative prayer, and that they have taken only the good teachings from what they learned. What must be understood is that it is not only the practice of the mystical component of spiritual formation that makes it so dangerous. It is where souls place themselves in relation to God's calling and the *Three Angels' Messages*, when they choose to go outside the church to learn a discipline created and taught to them by the very power God called them to expose—the antichrist.

I pray you see the absurdity and the danger in believing that it is acceptable to learn spiritual formation and bring it into our schools and churches. The facts are that we have been given all the counsel and warnings needed to identify the dangers in these practices, and that they are tools of the enemy to win people back to Roman Catholicism through placing their minds in a state where they can be controlled by satanic forces without being aware of it.

Learning the discipline of spiritual formation will not improve one's spiritual life as many believe. Advocates of this Roman Catholic discipline will eventually discover that they have fallen under the hypnotic delusions of the enemy, obsessed with preventing them from giving the *Three Angels' Messages* to the world.

Chapter 8
Who Will Recognize the Omega?

For almost 2,000 years, God's people lived without prophetic guidance. The Holy Spirit led individuals to break from the oppression of papal Rome, guided the reformers as they stood against this power for hundreds of years, and many groups of Protestants formed various denominations from the 15th to the 19th century. During this period, the faithful of all these churches were God's chosen people as the Spirit continued to unfold truths that had been lost by years of papal oppression. The Protestant denominations fell out of God's favor when they rejected the first and second angels' messages in the early 1840s.

Like the great reformers before them, the Adventists' hope of reviving their own dead churches was crushed. They had hoped that the beautiful line of prophetic truth and the wonderful Savior they all had found as He guided them in their preparation for His soon coming would thrill their hearts as it did theirs, but it was not to be. Instead of rejoicing with them, those churches rejected the truth brought to them and excommunicated the messengers, members of their own church families. Then by rejecting the light illuminating Christ's ministry in the Most Holy Place, the only place Jesus could now be found, they turned their backs on their Savior, having no other way of finding salvation. There was no hope for those denominations after that rejection. What a sad, sad history for the Protestant churches.

Those who rejected the first message could not be benefited by the second; neither were they benefited by the midnight cry, which was to prepare them to enter with Jesus by faith into the most holy place of the heavenly sanctuary. And by rejecting the two former messages, they have so darkened their understanding that they can see no light in the third angel's message, which shows the way into the most holy place. I saw that as the Jews crucified Jesus, so the nominal churches had crucified these messages, and therefore they have no knowledge of the way into the most holy, and they cannot be benefited by the intercession of Jesus there. … they offer up their useless prayers to the apartment which Jesus has left; and Satan, pleased with the deception, assumes a religious character, and leads the minds of these professed Christians to himself, working with his power, his signs and lying wonders, to fasten them in his snare … Satan deceives some with Spiritualism. He also comes as an angel of light and spreads his influence over the land by means of false reformations. The churches are elated, and consider that God is working marvelously for them, when it is the work of another spirit. The excitement will die away and leave the world and the church in a worse condition than before. (*Early Writings*, 260)

In analyzing this statement, the Spirit of Prophecy definitely predicts that there will *never* be a future time when the Protestant denominations will accept the three angels' messages, neither will they ever come back into favor with God; to the contrary, their condition will only worsen as Satan brings in false revival. They rejected the message God gave them to usher in the coming of the Lord, hardened their hearts against the working of the Holy Spirit, and *denominationally* sealed their doom. They were no longer "God's chosen" people; the Seventh-day Adventists became such.

It is important at this point to analyze what occurred back at that time. The body of Christians in the many Protestant denominations, by their rejection of the first and second angels' messages, lost their favor as God's denominated people, as did Israel by her rejection of the Messiah. By no means is the door shut for Christians in all those churches to be saved; it wasn't then and it isn't now.

We are told that most of the people that will make up God's commandment-keeping church are still members of those churches, awaiting the repeat of the call to "come out of her my people" (Revelation 18:4 KJV). This is our mission, to repeat the first and second angels' messages, adding to it the third angel's message, which is an appeal and witness—a proclamation and demonstration of Christ's righteousness in the lives of His people. The world will see and hear the way of salvation. They will witness with their own eyes the beauty and holiness of God in His servants as they proclaim the last message of mercy to a world about to perish. They will also see and understand the fate of those who reject this offer as the truth is revealed about the beast and its image and what it means to receive their "mark." The entire world will make their choice; the gospel will be heard and seen by every living person as God's commandment-keeping people love them to the end. This is why we exist; the church is to love them into eternal life.

God's true church consists of visible and invisible members. *His visible church on earth is the denominated Seventh-day Adventist Church.* The invisible members that are also a part of His true church are those following God by walking honestly and faithfully in the light they have. They are *spread all over the world,* waiting to hear the three angels' messages, which will be given with power under the light of the Fourth Angel when the visible church is ready to receive them at God's appointed time. In the end, when Jesus comes in the clouds of heaven to receive His bride, She will be visible for the entire world to see. The invisible members will have all responded to the "loud cry," symbolized by what we call the Fourth Angel in Revelation 18:1–4. It is at this time, the call of the Fourth Angel, that Babylon's fall becomes complete.

> After these things I saw another angel come down from heaven, having great power; and the earth was lightened with his glory. And he cried mightily with a strong voice, saying, Babylon the great is fallen, is fallen, and is become the habitation of devils, and the hold of every foul spirit, and a cage of every unclean and hateful bird. For all nations have drunk of the wine of the wrath of her fornication, and the kings of the earth have committed fornication with her, and the merchants of the earth are waxed rich through the abundance of her delicacies. And I heard another voice from heaven, saying, Come out of her, my people, that ye be not partakers of her sins, and that ye receive not of her plagues. (Revelation 18:1–4 KJV)

Those who respond to the call come out of the fallen churches and join with the Lord's denominated, commandment-keeping people.

It is interesting to note that back in the 1840s, as soon as God's law was honored and became the standard of righteousness in His church, the Lord restored to it the Spirit of Prophecy, the prophetic gift.

Ellen White wrote:

> As the third angel's message arose in the world, which is to reveal the law of God to the church *in its fullness and power,* the prophetic gift was immediately restored. (*Loma Linda Messages,* 33, emphasis added)

In the light of all we have studied from the inspired writings and what will follow, revealing that the Protestant world has rejected God's last-day message and that the Seventh-day Adventist Church is the "remnant," we will summarize three of this book's most important conclusions. Our willingness to accept these paraphrased counsels, implied in the Spirit of Prophecy, is our only safeguard from the subtle delusions of the omega.

My dear brothers and sisters, I know that for many these statements will be difficult to accept. For many years we have ignored the inspired counsel warning us that God is displeased with us when we turn back to the fallen churches, thinking they have light for us to improve our spiritual lives or help us with new methods of doing ministry. I pray that you will seek God's Spirit for guidance and reject your own or anyone else's opinions. It is Scripture and the Spirit of Prophecy that is inspired—that is what we must trust for truth.

1. Writing under the power of the Almighty God, Ellen White wrote that God's Spirit was withdrawn from the Protestant churches when they rejected the first and second angels' messages in 1843/44; and that what is believed to be the working of the Holy Spirit in their midst at any level—aside from that of sincere individual seekers—is not the Holy Spirit, but the deceptive power of Satan and his host doing the supposed work of God. This is not a popular view of her counsel in our church today, but ignoring or refusing to believe this counsel is ignoring or refusing to believe the Holy Spirit and can result in losing the ability to discern the truth—and more (to be explained). Again, this is not to say that there are not true, Spirit-led Christians, spread among the various churches in the world today who have a saving relationship with God and are members of His invisible church; there are, but the Spirit of Prophecy clearly states that the denominated Protestant churches are under the influence of satanic power and falsely believe that God is working for them, when He is not.

I saw that God has honest children among the nominal Adventists and *the fallen churches*, and before the plagues shall be poured out, ministers and people will be called out from these churches and will gladly receive the truth. Satan knows this; and before the loud cry of the third angel is given, he raises an excitement in these religious bodies, that those who have rejected the truth may *think that God is with them*. He hopes to deceive the honest and lead them to *think that God is still working for the churches*. But the light will shine, and all who are honest will leave the fallen churches, and take their stand with the remnant. (*Early Writings*, 261, emphasis added)

In analyzing this statement, Ellen White is saying that the fallen churches will be deceived right up until the time of the "loud cry," and that it will only become worse as Satan ushers in a false revival just prior to it. True believers will be called out before the plagues are poured out. Again, this demonstrates that there is *never a time* when the Protestant churches come back into favor with God. *They are deceived and under satanic influence now*, the daughters of Babylon, and will be to the close of probation. *This point must be understood and accepted to be able to discern the "omega."* Again:

I saw that as the Jews crucified Jesus, so the nominal churches had crucified these messages, and therefore *they have no knowledge of the way into the most holy, and they cannot be benefited by the intercession of Jesus there.* ... they offer up their useless prayers to the apartment which Jesus has left; and Satan, pleased with the deception, assumes a religious character, and leads the minds of these professed Christians to himself, working with his power, his signs and lying wonders, to fasten them in his snare. ... Satan deceives some with Spiritualism. He also comes as an angel of light and spreads his influence over the land by means of false reformations. The churches are elated, and *consider that God is working marvelously for them, when it is the work of another spirit.* The excitement will die away and leave the world and the church in a worse condition than before. (*Early Writings*, 260, emphasis added)

The "nominal Adventists" were those in the Advent movement who never accepted the Sabbath truth and the Spirit of Prophecy following the Great Disappointment. They formed their own Sunday-keeping churches. All other Protestant denominations would be those described above as the "nominal" and "fallen" churches. Every one of them had opportunity to receive the message of truth that was presented to them, but rejected those messages.

In light of this truth, here are conclusions two and three, which God's people need to understand and accept if they are to comprehend the deceptive working of the omega:

2. To attend meetings held by other denominations without God providentially directing us to attend, or to invite speakers from other Christian denominations to specifically enhance our spiritual insight, or receive instruction, training, and education in spiritual things will eventually result in losing the ability to discern truth from error, and more (to be explained).

3. To read books, watch videos, or listen to recordings of authors or instructors of other Christian denominations for the purpose of receiving instruction, training, education, or spiritual insight of any kind, without God providentially leading us to do so, will eventually result in losing the ability to discern truth from error, and more (to be explained).

Logic dictates that it makes no difference whether we go to other Protestant churches to learn something new or invite them to our churches or colleges for the same reason. There is no difference between going to listen and listening to a CD; between going to listen and reading their books or watching their presentations on DVD. *If we do any of these things for the purpose of gaining spiritual insight or for spiritual growth, or just go to be there without the Lord's providential direction to go, it means we are rejecting the counsel God gave us in the Spirit of Prophecy.*

When we choose to ignore warnings God has given, we are placing ourselves outside of His protective care where we come under the influence of demonic power. What is most alarming is that we are not aware of our situation; a very dangerous place to be.

I direct your attention once again to Ellen White's inspired advice:

I was shown the necessity of those who believe that we are having the last message of mercy, *being separate* from those who are daily imbibing new errors. I saw that neither young *nor old should attend their meetings;* for it is wrong to thus encourage them while they teach error that is a deadly poison to the soul and teach for doctrines the commandments of men. The influence of such gatherings is not good. If God has delivered us from such darkness and error, *we should stand fast* in the liberty wherewith He has set us free and rejoice in the truth. *God is displeased* with us when we go to listen to error, without being obliged to go." (*Early Writings*, 124, emphasis added)

I would point out that when Ellen White states "obliged to go," she could never have meant there would be a time to go to improve our methods of labor, receive any new light that God has given them, or to receive any beneficial instruction on spiritual topics, for we have been warned that God will never let any new light shine on them, but will always give it to His denominated remnant church.

It may be that the Lord would send a strong and mature believer to gain insight into how the enemy is at work, or to represent our church as a witness for God in some way, but it would never mean to learn anything worthwhile or to receive new light or understanding of any kind. God will always shine any new light needed upon His beloved and chosen people.

Why is it so dangerous to receive instruction from any teacher of the fallen churches? Can't we acquire some good information? Don't they have any new ideas that we can use, or teachings we can take advantage of? Can't we learn something we never thought of before? What if we hear only of that which we agree? These are all logical questions to ask, but we need to understand that there is another principle at work—a principle we have been ignoring for many years.

The principle is this: ignoring the Lord's directive to *not* go outside the church for any new light *gives Satan immediate access to our minds where he begins his hypnotic process.* By choosing to go, we will have chosen to allow it, and God will not stop it—nay, cannot stop it—because He would be violating our freedom of choice. When we go, having been counseled *not* to go, Satan and his evil angels will gain control of our minds, using a type of hypnosis we *cannot* detect; it nevertheless *is hypnosis.*

Just as long as men consent to listen to these sophistries, a subtle influence will weave the fine threads of these seductive theories into their minds, and *men who should turn away from the first sound of such teaching will learn to love it.* As loyal subjects *we must refuse even to listen to these sophistries.* Their influence is something like a deadly viper, poisoning the minds of all who listen. *It is a branch of hypnotism, deadening the sensibilities of the soul.* (*Manuscript Releases,* vol. 10, 163, emphasis added)

It is "a branch of hypnotism." Are you beginning to see what might have startled Ellen White? A branch of hypnotism, unrecognized as hypnotism, is far more dangerous than any kind of deception that is recognizable.

> He approached Eve, not in the form of an angel, but as a serpent, subtle, cunning, and deceitful. With a voice that appeared to proceed from the serpent, he spoke to her, and his conversation was like the words which today wise and wicked angels speak through various agencies. *As Eve listened, the warnings that God had given faded from her mind.* (*Signs of the Times*, May 29, 1901, emphasis added)

As we listen to what we have been warned against, these warnings of God will fade from our minds. Again we have the counsel:

> Just as long as men *consent to listen* to these sophistries, a subtle influence will weave the fine threads of these seductive theories into their minds, and men who should turn away from the first sound of such teaching will learn to love it. As loyal subjects we must *refuse* even to listen to these sophistries. Their influence is something like a deadly viper, poisoning the minds of all who listen. *It is a branch of hypnotism, deadening the sensibilities of the soul.* (*Manuscript Releases*, vol. 10, 163, emphasis added)

At the very moment we assent to receive teaching—listen, read, watch videos, invite speakers, go to seminars, in any genre—from teachers of the fallen churches, we will *immediately* begin to fall under the *hypnotic power* of Satan.

> If our eyes could be opened to discern the fallen angels at their work with those who feel at ease and consider themselves safe, we should not feel so secure. Evil angels are upon our track *every moment.* (*Spiritual Gifts*, vol. 4b, 92)

When the divinely inspired counsels, quoted above, are comprehended, believed, and accepted, then and only then will we be able to discern the omega deception. If we disagree and seek the knowledge of the fallen churches we become hypnotized, unknowingly, as Kellogg and his associates. That is a frightening proposition, but is the only logical conclusion considering the inspired counsel of Ellen White.

To enter into dialogue with these deceived churches for the purpose of being instructed by them is disobeying the counsel we have in the Spirit of Prophecy willfully or because of being ignorant of it.

If God has any new light to communicate, *He will let His chosen and beloved understand it, without their going* to have their minds enlightened by hearing those who are in darkness and error.

I was shown the necessity of those who believe that we are having the last message of mercy, *being separate* from those who are daily imbibing new errors. I saw that neither young nor old should attend *their meetings*; for it is wrong to thus encourage them while they teach error that is a deadly poison to the soul and teach for doctrines the commandments of men. (*Early Writings,* 124, emphasis added)

Once again:

If God has any new light to communicate, He will let His chosen and beloved understand it, without their going to have their minds enlightened by hearing those who are in darkness and error. (*Early Writings,* 124)

If we refuse this counsel, or don't know it, we are in a condition where deception can easily take place. God has promised to lead us in the way we should go, and because we are His special people, we need not go to the fallen churches, thinking we will gain insight into anything that will benefit the church or our own spiritual experience. On the contrary, we have been warned that the opposite will occur, and we will lose our way. Roman Catholicism and fallen Protestantism, are rapidly joining hands through the power of spiritualism.

The Roman Catholic teaching of spiritual formation, with spiritualism its driving force, is not considered a threat by the Protestant churches because they have chosen as their master, he who is also in control of Roman Catholicism. It was shown previously in this chapter that because of their rejection of the first and second angels' messages, the Protestant denominations have fallen under Satan's control, and have lost the ability to discern the deception. In spite of this sad development of the mid nineteenth century, there are many in those fallen churches that belong to God's invisible church, and they are living faithful Christian lives. When the time comes, these faithful believers will respond to the loud cry of the second angel of Revelation 14, who will enlighten the entire world with his glory, saying "come out of her my people," and they will, uniting with the Lord's Sabbath keeping, remnant church.

As history repeats itself, the papacy will once again attempt to regain control over the world and prevent God's remnant church from fulfilling its mission. The Jesuit led counter-reformation, when nothing was considered too corrupt or immoral to overthrow, sought to bring to a halt the Protestant Reformation. This is a warning to God's people that in the final conflict we can expect a papal assault upon our church. This assault, led by fallen angelic beings far superior to us in intelligence, will not only use supernatural forces and civil authorities as weapons, but it will also use the deceit of having no moral restrictions. It is this truth that makes our adherence to the special end-time counsel and warnings in Scripture and the Spirit of Prophecy an absolute necessity.

We have been instructed to learn all we can of this cunning and deceitful power, for the reasons just given. Looking back through time, it is stunning to see the methods the enemy used to mislead God's people. Like a chameleon that adjusts its outer appearance to go unnoticed, so does the church of Rome conceal its real intentions through outward sanctimony and virtue, but once it acquires the authority it constantly seeks, the persecutions of the past will occur once again.

God's people must not be deceived by this power, or the voices within our own church that would have us believe she has changed, and that we need not fear her as they did in centuries past. The church of Rome intends to regain control of the whole world, ruling as she did during the Dark Ages. She is the unseen force in the world behind all the activity to centralize political and national authority.

When she ruled during the Dark Ages, many European nations had to be dominated and kept under control. Today, still seeking to dominate the world, and having learned from past experience, she sees that it is now possible to reach her goal through an easier and more convenient process. Working stealthily behind the scenes, she is attempting to bring the world under a centralized authority. When she succeeds, she will be its one moral authority and will have achieved her ultimate goal. This is what is driving the history we see unfolding in the world today.

Know this: I am not suggesting any kind of conspiracy in the Seventh-day Adventist Church with the Roman Catholic Church. I have no personal knowledge, for example, of any Jesuit infiltration; neither do I believe this to be the case. God is in His holy temple, overseeing the work and safety of His church, but even He will not stop Satan from influencing the minds of those in His church who refuse to follow the counsel in the Spirit of Prophecy, for they have that "freedom of choice" with which God created them, a freedom Jesus would never take away. So, is it possible that papal falsehoods are being taught by Roman Catholic teachers to Seventh-day Adventist people? Yes. Absolutely, yes! Pantheistic teachings entered the church more than one hundred years ago because some refused to "heed the warnings God has given," and we have been warned that it would happen again.

I say once again, the Lord saved my life by leading me to this church and I would never, ever knowingly say or do anything that would result in harm to the church or the family of saints for whom Jesus died; neither would I want to detract from its mission. On the other hand, I am compelled to say what I believe needs to be said, to save and preserve the foundational pillars of our faith; pillars that have stood the test for 150 years.

The Seventh-day Adventist Church is God's remnant church, arising precisely as foretold in chapters nine through eleven of Revelation. Jesus is the Head of the church and will see it through whatever crisis it must confront. Leaving it is not an option for anyone who wants to be among the redeemed. We are the church militant and exist at a time when the wheat and tares grow up together. There will come a time when the church will be glorified, pure, and without sin, but that time is not now. To leave the church because it has tares who cause problems, or because there are those not following the counsel we have, or any other of a thousand reasons that bad decisions are made by those in the church, is faulty thinking.

Remember this: Jesus is God and is in His holy temple. As He had to enlighten Ezekiel, He also wants us to understand that He is in absolute control of everything that takes place in His church, at every moment in time, always. Nothing sneaks into the church behind His back—nothing! No false teaching, no leader who makes wrong decisions because of poor judgment, no false theology that deceives many of His people; not one thing occurs in His church that He does not permit and is not cognizant of. Every occurrence has a purpose and is under His omniscient control. Every occurrence!

Like Ezekiel, who the Lord in His merciful concern gave the vision of the wheels within wheels, we also need to learn the lesson it taught. God is God, and He wants us to know Him. He longs for us to see Him as He is, for only then will our worship be pleasing and acceptable. He desires us to grasp the eternal glory of His being, manifested and out-sourced to the universe by the cross of Jesus. He wants us to understand, as He wanted Ezekiel to understand, that nothing, not one thing in this universe, takes place without His awareness and that is not under His control. What is happening in the church and the whole of creation is progressing according to His plan, which is far beyond our ability to comprehend. We can be confident though that no mistakes are occurring. This is the meaning of the complicated yet perfect movements of the wheels within wheels.

So never doubt that Jesus is in control of His church, never leave His church, and never think you have the responsibility to separate the wheat from the tares. That's the work of angels. In Scripture and in the Spirit of Prophecy there cannot be found the suggestion that the "wheat" leaves the church to start another, purified church. It is always the "tares" that are separated out from the "wheat," and that process is accomplished by angels, not men. This leaves the church purified, ready to meet her Savior. It would do us good to remember this fact, for there will not be the raising up of another purified church. Never!

We can't see into the hearts of people, so let God use the angels to accomplish that important work. God is not limited by our stunted conception of His infinite characteristics, or of His intimate and absolute involvement in human affairs. Our duty is to preach the three angels' messages, to teach the three angels' messages, and to live the three angels' messages; the heart of which is the message of Christ our righteousness and His current ministry in the Most Holy Place of the heavenly temple, preparing to come back to this earth and take us home.

There will be a shaking and many will flee, but as the faithful in Babylon hear and respond to the three angels' messages sounding throughout the entire world, they will take their stand with those who "keep the commandments of God and have the testimony of Jesus."

Inspired counsel has warned us that there would be a satanic assault more intense than that which almost caused the church to fall 100 years ago. Ellen White trembled for the safety of God's people and the potential effects this assault might have if left unmet and was extremely concerned for the safety of the church. The characteristics of this "omega" must be something terribly threatening and dangerous. What could possibly have made her react the way she did? We shall see.

The history of the fulfillment of Daniel 11's prophecy, which Ellen White said "will be repeated," was, as we have already mentioned, fulfilled by the papal domination of Europe and the "counter-reformation" attack against Protestantism, God's people of the day. That history, which is to be repeated, was the placing of the abomination of desolation and the taking away of the daily by replacing Christ's ministry in the heavenly sanctuary with the Roman Catholic mass. The repeat of this history suggests there will be an attempt to compromise the message pointing the world to Christ's ministry in the heavenly sanctuary, a major part of the message God's people are proclaiming to the world. This agrees with the warnings in the Spirit of Prophecy, which say that his strategy is to sweep away this fundamental pillar of God's church.

In *The Great Controversy*, page 26, we can gain some insight into what the "abomination that maketh desolate" may refer to. In the context of this phrase she says, "When the idolatrous standards of the Romans should be set up in the holy ground ..." The "abominations" of Rome, both pagan and papal, are myriad, and history records that many have "desolated" the people of God for the last two thousand years, so it is not necessary for us to apply this term to any guess we might make.

What we know for sure is that some idolatrous standards of the Roman church may threaten the holy ground of the Seventh-day Adventist Church at the end of time, if this aspect of the prophecy is one that Ellen White meant would be repeated. We know one application is the primary "abomination" of the union of church and state, as it was during the 1,260 years of the Dark Ages, and will eventually result in a death decree, but there are obviously other "abominations" also attacking the holy ground.

What are the forces at work that could sweep away the most important "pillar of the faith," Christ's ministry in the Most Holy Place, substituting in its place some deceptive counterfeit? She makes reference to this occurring, so how will we know when it occurs?

In the alpha, the deceptive teachings of Dr. Kellogg were dangerously undermining the truth of Christ's ministry in the heavenly sanctuary by presenting God as energy instead of a personal Being who ministers on our behalf in the temple in heaven. Ellen White explained the technique used by Dr. Kellogg to overwhelm the minds of those under his authority:

The long night interviews which Dr. Kellogg holds are one of his most effective means of gaining his point. His *constant stream of talk confuses the minds* of those he is seeking to influence. *He misstates and misquotes words,* and places those who argue with him in so false a light that their powers of discernment are benumbed. *He takes their words and gives them an impress which makes them seem to mean exactly the opposite of what they said.* (*Battle Creek Letters*, June 23, 1904, emphasis added)

Sounds like "smooth talk," doesn't it? It was Kellogg's use of "smooth talk" that convinced the medical workers of Ellen White's day to accept his pantheistic teachings. He would use gossip, misinformation, and false accusations to win over the sympathies of those he needed to stand with him to support the changes he wanted to bring to the church.

Another tactic used was to pretend to support the Spirit of Prophecy, taking Ellen White's counsel out of context, creating the illusion that she agreed with his plans. This truly was a crisis having to do with control of the church by those desiring change. It was argued that change was necessary, especially if we wanted to keep our young people in the church. This argument was used to convince parents to send their children to Battle Creek, who would then be the targets of Kellogg's new ideas, trained accordingly, and then used to implement them. The plan was to win over the youth, then their future success was guaranteed. The Lord revealed these hidden agendas to Ellen White, and she counseled parents over and over not to send their youth to Battle Creek.

> I was bidden to warn our people on no account to send their children to Battle Creek to receive an education, because these delusive, scientific theories would be presented in the most seducing forms. The matter has been working in his mind in such a way that he thinks he is to be the channel to infuse other minds with great light regarding certain scientific problems. Words and sentiments from my books will be taken and presented as being in harmony with his theories. But the Lord has forbidden us to enter into any discussion with him. (*Testimonies to the Church Regarding Our Youth Going to Battle Creek Obtain an Education*, 42)

Sound familiar? The *Testimonies* were seldom referenced in any of the decision-making, most assuredly because they always spoke against their plans.

These methods of mind manipulation originated with Satan, and were used by him in the courts of heaven after his fall. These were the spiritualistic sophistries Ellen White warned the church about in the alpha, and they were used by Dr. Kellogg to confuse the minds of those who listened. Because of the hold these false theories had on the leadership in Battle

Creek, she warned the church against sending their children to school in Battle Creek.

It may be extremely important for us to consider her counsel to the church at that time and the reasons she warned the church not to send their children to Battle Creek. Perhaps we should compare the dangers of that time with what is taking place in our schools today. In her day, she warned against studying pantheistic theories and false teachings, like the personality of God, where His presence was located, and sciences that used hypnotism or mind control. These were the subjects of the false theories contained in the alpha of Kellogg's day, and those which caused her strong counsel.

Roman Catholic disciplines, containing the very same theories and practices in Kellogg's day that caused Ellen White's strong counsel to both the leaders of the church and to parents not to send their children to schools in Battle Creek, have been studied by some of our administrators and teachers in non-Adventist institutes and colleges, who brought these teachings to our colleges and are being taught to our young men and women.

Those leaders and teachers, who advocate spiritual formation, learned these disciplines by attending institutes established by the very churches we have considered Babylon for more than 150 years. My friends, how can we possibly give the three angels' messages to the world, which warns them of the dangers of spiritualistic, Roman Catholic teachings when we are teaching the very same disciplines, and have learned them by attending their institutions.

Is it any wonder that there are those in God's church who believe and teach that Roman Catholicism has changed, and we need not worry as we once did? Is it any wonder that those who teach such things are almost all advocates of spiritual formation, and is it also possible that they believe the Spirit of Prophecy is no longer relevant and Roman Catholicism is no longer a threat because they know what they have done violates the warnings and counsel it contains?

The sad reality and very real possibility is these people who believe, teach, and preach these errors, do so because they are in rebellion, a condition attained by the decision to do what pleased them, instead of what Inspiration warned them against doing.

Even though many will be thus deceived, history tells us that there will also be those who understand what is happening. They will, in turn, take action against the deceptions these people have accepted by refusing to heed the warnings God has given them.

God has honest believers who will take action, standing against the corrupting influences, against those who have "forsaken the Holy covenant" and have accepted the deceptive and corrupt "instructions."

> God speaks through his appointed agencies, and let no man, or confederacy of men, insult the Spirit of God by refusing to hear the message of God's word from the lips of his chosen messengers. By refusing to hear the message of God, men close themselves in a chamber of darkness. They shut their own souls away from vast blessings, and rob Christ of the glory that should come to him, by showing disrespect to his appointed agencies. (*The Review and Herald*, September 12, 1893)

Ellen White is obviously making reference to those who reject the counsels in the Spirit of Prophecy. They close themselves in a "chamber of darkness" and place themselves beyond the reach of the only means given by God for them to be protected from deception. These have rejected God's messenger, preparing themselves to be deceived by the omega.

Chapter 9
Is the Church Under Attack?

Spiritual formation, a teaching originating with the king of the north, papal Rome, is becoming somewhat established in our church. Its acceptance is the result of some Seventh-day Adventists succumbing to the "intelligence" with papal Rome or their representatives. There have been certain things in our church that have changed, and it behooves us to discover if these changes correspond to what we have been warned would occur if the church would reflect characteristics of the omega apostasy.

Inspiration claims that there would be a desire to restructure, to publish books and magazines of a new order, to change the way things have been done in the past, to lightly regard the Sabbath and de-emphasize the doctrinal pillars of the church. We are told the changes would be disguised in the garb of "revival," doing a wonderful work that focuses on the youth, holding exciting meetings in our big cities. This movement would have great momentum, appearing to perform a wonderful work for God, but to a certain degree it would disregard the Spirit of Prophecy and, in general, lower the standards of the church.

Many faithful Adventists believe that this is occurring presently. Something new is happening in our church. Things are different and continue to change at a rapid pace. It is not the same church it was even twenty-five years ago, and there is a degree of change that has become alarming to many.

There are countless new organizations, visually high-tech, entrancing web sites advertising new secular themes. There are exciting programs for our youth, perhaps not wrong in themselves, but programs incorporating previously rejected agendas such as famous evangelical speakers from other denominations; speakers the Spirit of Prophecy warns us not to listen to. These speakers are often accompanied by Christian rock groups and questionable video presentations.

We invite men and women to train and teach our youth who are members of denominations who disfellowshipped the founders of our church for Sabbath-keeping; churches who actively war against the Ten Commandments and warn people to beware of Seventh-day Adventists.

Most of the organizers of these exciting meetings for our young people have been trained in and practice spiritual formation; a fact not generally known, but a fact nonetheless. It is not our desire to mention names or point fingers, but as an example of the fact just mentioned, I want to point this out: a Seventh-day Adventist administrator and co-founder of the popular SDA youth movement called "GODencounters," wrote the following:

> Prayer room coordinator [Name Given] believes that introducing people to corporate contemplative practices such as lectio divina and centering prayer, and also to experimental prayer rooms like the ones set up to allow visitors to pray through the different stations of the Cross and the Old Testament sanctuary, helps to stretch them out of their comfort zones.[7]

It seems that training in spiritual formation has become a prerequisite for those involved in the preparation of material used throughout our church for the spiritual education of our youth. How does this occur?

How is it that most of those who participate in the making of videos for the youth, in both the production and on screen, have been trained in spiritual formation; obviously, not by accident.

The practice is moving explosively through the Protestant world and has now entrenched in the Seventh-day Adventist Church. It is not a new discipline and in most instances incorporates a renewal of Roman Catholic teachings based on the spiritual exercises of Ignatius Loyola. Central to its teachings is the discerning of spirits and the mystical experience of centering and contemplative prayer. Roman Catholic doctrine teaches that supernatural manifestations experienced when the disciple enters the mystical state called the silence, where the presence of God is experienced, are absolutely required for there to be any genuine Christian growth, for that is where God's grace is received, according to their theology.

---

7   Erika Larson-Hueneke, "In the Presence of GOD and Each Other," in A. Allan Martin, Shayna Bailey, Lynell LaMountain, eds., *God Encounters: Pursuing a 24-7 Experience of Jesus* (Nampa, ID: Pacific Press Publishing Association, 2009), 11.

In the chapters to come we will show how the incorporation of this ancient form of mystical prayer, which has spread into the Protestant churches over the last 50 years, is a planned strategy of the Roman Catholic Church and is why it is one of the primary disciplines learned in almost all spiritual formation seminars held at the many and varied learning facilities all around our country. We insert the word "mystical" when referring to this type of prayer because it is the truth and more accurately portrays what this type of prayer really is, "ancient mysticism."

This "contemplative/mystical" prayer refers to a method of prayer that leads to a level of consciousness where thoughts have ceased and the individual enters this special silence, where many believe they experience the presence of God. Attaining this "contemplative" state is facilitated by what is called centering prayer; one of various methods or techniques of focusing or centering the mind, leading eventually to an altered state.

Once mastered, this centering method submerges the disciples to a level of consciousness that is on par with the trance of hypnosis. It is where they experience "utter repose" and are blessed with a new understanding of themselves and their relationship to the rest of the universe. This altered state of mind is called by many names: the silence, the quiet place, and the stillness are a few used by spiritual formation enthusiasts.

It is here, in this "mystical silence," where all mental activity ceases, a place in the mind where there are no images or awareness of the flow of thoughts, and where one has the most profound and life-changing experiences, including a sense of God's presence as they have never experienced before. It is here where the devotees come to understand their unity and "oneness" with all created things and all other people. They become acutely aware of their new mission in life, having much greater insight into how God leads them in everything they do. It is also in this "mystical silence" that some hear what they believe is Jesus as He speaks with them personally.

Before we read some of the actual testimonies of those who have experienced the silence, we need to learn how the methods used today came to be. The following is the testimony of Father Thomas Keating, a Roman Catholic priest who experimented with representatives of various Eastern religions at an abbey in the Northeastern United States around 50 years ago. Today's methods and techniques of centering prayer and contemplative prayer come, to a great degree, from those experiments.

Contemplative Outreach
Fr. Thomas Keating

Fr. Thomas Keating is a founding member and the spiritual guide of Contemplative Outreach, LTD.

He has served on Contemplative Outreach's Board of Trustees since the organization's beginning and is currently serving as the Chairman of the Board. Fr. Keating is one of the principal architects and teachers of the Christian contemplative prayer movement and, in many ways, Contemplative Outreach is a manifestation of his longtime desire to contribute to the recovery of the contemplative dimension of Christianity.

Fr. Keating's interest in contemplative prayer began during his freshman year at Yale University in 1940 when he became aware of the Church's history and of the writings of Christian mystics. Prompted by these studies and time spent in prayer and meditation, he experienced a profound realization that, on a spiritual level, the Scriptures call people to a personal relationship with God. Fr. Keating took this call to heart. He transferred to Fordham University in New York and, while waiting to be drafted for service in World War II, he received a deferment to enter seminary. Shortly after graduating from an accelerated program at Fordham, Fr. Keating entered an austere monastic community of the Trappist Order in Valley Falls, Rhode Island in January of 1944, at the age of 20. He was ordained a priest in June of 1949.

In March of 1950 the monastery in Valley Falls burned down and, as a result, the community moved to Spencer, Massachusetts. Shortly after the move, Fr. Keating became ill with a lung condition and was put into isolation in the city hospital of Worcester, Massachusetts for nine weeks. After returning to the monastery, he stayed in the infirmary for two years. Fr. Keating was sent to Snowmass, Colorado in April of 1958 to help start a new monastic community called St. Benedict's. He remained in Snowmass until 1961, when he was elected abbot of St. Joseph's in Spencer, prompting his move back to Massachusetts. He served as abbot of St. Joseph's for twenty years until he retired in 1981 and returned to Snowmass, where he still resides today.

During Fr. Keating's term as abbot at St. Joseph's and in response to the reforms of Vatican II, he invited teachers from the East to the monastery. As a result of this exposure to Eastern spiritual traditions, Fr. Keating and several of the monks at St. Joseph's were led to develop the modern form of Christian contemplative prayer called Centering Prayer. Fr. Keating was a central figure in the initiation of the Centering Prayer movement. He offered Centering Prayer workshops and retreats to clergy and laypeople and authored articles and books on the method and fruits of Centering Prayer. In 1983, he presented a two-week intensive Centering Prayer retreat at the Lama Foundation in San Cristabol, New Mexico, which proved to be a watershed event. Many of the people prominent in the Centering Prayer movement today attended this retreat. Contemplative Outreach was created in 1984 to support the growing spiritual network of Centering Prayer practitioners. Fr. Keating became the community's president in 1985, a position he held until 1999.

Fr. Keating is an internationally renowned theologian and an accomplished author. He has traveled the world to speak with laypeople and communities about contemplative Christian practices and the psychology of the spiritual journey, which is the subject of his Spiritual Journey video and DVD series. Since the reforms of Vatican II, Fr. Keating has been a core participant in and supporter of interreligious dialogue. He helped found the Snowmass Interreligious Conference, which had its first meeting in the fall of 1983 and continues to meet each spring. Fr. Keating also is a past president of the Temple of Understanding and of the Monastic Interreligious Dialogue.[8]

Let us define the terms spiritual formation and "contemplative" spirituality, or contemplative prayer. These definitions are also from the same Protestant organization, Lighthouse Ministries.

---

8   Fr. Thomas Keating, "Contemplative Outreach,"
    http://www.contemplativeoutreach.org/fr-thomas-keating
    (accessed April 26, 2012).

Spiritual formation: A movement that has provided a platform and a channel through which contemplative prayer is entering the church. Find spiritual formation being used, and in nearly every case you will find contemplative spirituality. In fact, contemplative spirituality is the heartbeat of the spiritual formation movement.

Contemplative Spirituality: a belief system that uses ancient mystical practices to induce altered states of consciousness (the silence) and is often wrapped in Christian terminology; the premise of contemplative spirituality is pantheistic (God is all) and panentheistic (God is in all).

It can be seen that modern contemplative prayer has its roots in the practices of the religions of the East, whose methods and techniques are undoubtedly ancient mysticism. It needs to be mentioned also that the Christian mystics, dating back almost two thousand years, understood and practiced these same mind-altering techniques, which were, in fact, the secret and means of their supernatural experiences (more on that later).

Now, here are some testimonies of those that have prayed for and experienced the silence. The few quotes below without references or page numbers were all taken off the Lighthouse Trails Research web site.

Augustine:

"With the flash of one trembling glance, my mind arrived at, that which is, but I could not fix my gaze thereon."

Thomas Keating:

"Our spiritual journey, especially contemplative prayer, together with its practices for daily life, are processes of becoming aware of just how profound that unity is with God, ourselves, other people, other living beings, the earth, and all creation."

Marie of the Incarnation:

"Seeing God in everything and everything in God, with completely extraordinary clearness and delicacy."

In Chuck Swindoll's well-known book, *So You Want to be Like Christ: Eight Essential Disciplines to Get You There*, Swindoll defines the difference between solitude and silence. "Solitude" he defines as simply finding a place where you can be alone, without any disruptions from the outside world. "Silence" he describes in a very different way. He says it is a "stillness" of the mind.

> I do not believe anyone can ever become a deep person (intimate with God) without stillness and silence. [9]

Swindoll claims, "I do not believe anyone *can ever become a deep person without the 'stillness,' and 'silence.'*" Notice the similarity between Swindoll's statement of how he doubts anyone could become a "deep person," without spiritual formation's mystical silence and the following statement by a Seventh-day Adventist pastor:

> Without spiritual formation, a person would be "spiritually uncivilized." It is the process by which they can go from being a spiritual infant to spiritual maturity ... developing the potential that God's put within you. [10]

The quote by Swindoll comes shortly after quoting Henri Nouwen, the father of modern spiritual formation. Here is a quote revealing Nouwen's thinking in this excerpt from Ray Yungen's "A Time of Departing" second edition:

> Prayer is soul work because our souls are those sacred centers where *all is one* ... It is in the heart of God that we can come to the full realization of the *unity of all that is*. [11]

---

9 Charles Swindoll, *So You Want to be Like Christ: Eight Essential Disciplines to Get You There* (Nashville, TN: W Publishing Group, a Division of Thomas Nelson Inc., 2005), 190.

10 Wendi Rogers, "Church, Congregations Increase Focus on 'Spiritual Formation,'" *Adventist News Network,* February 3, 2004.

11 Ray Yungen, *A Time of Departing* (Silverton, OR: Lighthouse Trails Publishing Company, 2002), 61–64.

Nouwen's mentor, the Trappist monk Thomas Merton, describes "contemplative/mystical prayer" this way:

> When one enters the deeper layers of contemplative prayer one sooner or later experiences the *void, the emptiness, the nothingness ... the profound mystical silence ... an absence of thought.* [12]

Notice how the Roman Catholic Trappist monk, Merton, used the phrase *"profound mystical silence."* He obviously understood exactly what was happening.

Nouwen, the Roman Catholic priest, wrote *The Way of the Heart*, one of spiritual formation's most essential books of instruction. He also happens to be the mentor of Richard Foster, a name those familiar with spiritual formation recognize as one of the foremost leaders of today's "emerging church" the name of the spiritual formation movement sweeping the Protestant world. This is the same Richard Foster interviewed in an issue of the *Review* a few years ago, an issue in which his personal Renovare Spiritual Formation Bible was advertised and recommended by one of our organizations affiliated with a conference here in America. Here is a quotation of Richard Foster, revealing his perspective.

> Progress in intimacy with God *means progress toward silence.* It is this *recreating silence* to which we are called in *Contemplative Prayer.* [13]

Notice how the opinion exists with Foster, Nouwen, and the unnamed Adventist pastor that spiritual advancement will only take place when one masters the ability to enter into the mystical silence of contemplative prayer.

Now, it is time for the facts concerning this satanic practice.

What you are about to read in the next few paragraphs I pray will be taken in the right spirit, for your eternal destiny may depend on it.

Henry J. M. Nouwen, one of the fathers of modern spiritual formation, and others during the last few centuries have simply revived an ancient

---

12 William Johnston, *Letters to Contemplatives* (Maryknoll, NY: Orbis Books, 1996), 13.

13 *Be Still: and Know That I Am God*, DVD, directed by Amy Reinhold, David Kirkpatrick, Judge Reinhold (2006; Los Angeles, CA: 20th Century Fox).

mystical method of altering one's consciousness, through the knowledge and control of certain mental processes. They gave these processes the names centering prayer and contemplative prayer, tucking them nicely within the Roman Catholic discipline called spiritual formation, deceiving Christians into believing this is a blessing, promoting the spiritual growth of the Christian and eventually leading to a new experience with God; the experience of coming into His presence.

What makes this deception so treacherous is that Satan has designed and initiated the entire process, and that the mystical place called the silence is the same as the trance of psychics or spirit mediums, occultists, and magicians; it is the same as the *samadhi* of the Hindu yogi, the trance of the hypnotist, or mental realms of the two great literary mystics of the eighteenth century, Emerson and Thoreau. *They are all the same thing!* It is a place in the mind where *normal thought processes cease,* hence, the quiet place, or silence. This altered state is necessary to have the supernatural experience sought after by all the mystics down through the ages. It is also necessary to hear "Jesus'" voice speak to us and to have the mystical experiences of those practicing spiritual formation today.

I know these things because I have been there. I was there during the time I practiced meditation under the tutorship of a "spirit medium." I was there during the time I practiced meditation, learning to use supernatural and psychic powers in the mind-control courses I took. I was there when I thought I left my body practicing astral projection. I was there when I was possessed by a spirit preparing to do automatic writing. I was there at a séance when communicating with a spirit. I was there when paralyzed and ceased to breathe, meditating and engulfed in flames emanating from a picture of my guru, the great Hindu master Sri Chinmoy, spiritual leader of the United Nations in the 1970s.

I know about the silence, the quiet place, the stillness, and, once again, so you will understand, so does any other person who ever lived and meditated as a mystic, occultist, magician, witch, soothsayer, ancient Greek priestess of temple gods and goddesses, or witch doctor, or voodoo priest, or New Ager, and on and on and on.

Please listen carefully!

It is an absolute error for any Seventh-day Adventist pastor, educator, church elder, member, conference president or administrator, to attempt to explain, justify, excuse or claim in any way that this experience is different and is not a satanically-inspired supernatural and hypnotic form of mysticism. *It is not different,* and we, who have been there and have been saved by the grace of God, know *it is not different,* no matter what anyone might say as they try to justify the practice of spiritual formation's "contemplative/mystical prayer." *It is ancient* satanic *mysticism, and that is that!*

God, in His infinite wisdom and by His unerring providence, led some of us to be in the positions we are in today because we know *it is not different.* God, whose ways are beyond our understanding, brought us into His remnant church, not only to save us, but prior to our deliverance allowed us to desperately search through the confusing, deceptive, and supernatural world of the occult, waiting until the right moment to miraculously facilitate our escape. Why? So He would have some of us in His church with the experience necessary to know about these things; to know it is not different.

These are people He can trust to "never leave a soul unwarned" and call this deception the satanic evil that it is; people who cannot keep silent when they see innocent souls encouraged to attend classes where mysticism is taught by teachers in God's remnant church; teachers who have been trained at Catholic or Protestant institutes, such as the Shalem Institute near Washington, D.C., established as a part of a plan to win over the whole world in preparation for the final conflict of the ongoing Battle of Armageddon (evidence revealed in the chapters to come).

These are people in His church who know the dangers because they have been through it before. They are people who have experienced the "unholy spiritual love" warned of in the Spirit of Prophecy, but were willing to resist the temptation to return to it in their search for truth.

> I have seen the results of these fanciful views of God, in apostasy, spiritualism, and free-lovism. The free-love tendency of these teachings was so concealed that at first it was difficult to make plain its real character. Until the Lord presented it to me, I knew not what to call it, but I was instructed to call it unholy spiritual love. (*Evangelism,* 602)

There are those of us who have experienced the horror of the satanic deception of spiritualism who would never, ever attempt to pray this way, neither would we justify our practice of contemplative/mystical prayer because it is exciting, or take God's precious time to go to seminars and institutes established by the Babylonian churches that God so miraculously delivered us from, to learn spiritual formation. Neither would we find it exciting or desirous to be a teacher of this new Roman Catholic tool to evangelize the world (see *The Omega Rebellion,* 196, 197), deceiving our own brothers and sisters in God's church to possibly sell books or teach classes, for any reason, ever. Neither would the power tempt us, power never before imagined; power to move young people by the thousands, or perhaps to be a part of the "in crowd" that all practice these new and exciting methods, from which they see new and exciting strategies and plans emerge; plans to reach the massive crowds, and on, and on, and on. Finally, we would not desire to be a part of that elite group who hear Jesus speaking to them, who think they know beyond a shadow of a doubt that this is the power of God and can be used to reach the whole world and if we don't join in we'll remain stunted in our spiritual growth, as that Adventist pastor believes. No, we want none of it, because *we know about these things.*

After conversing with a teacher of spiritual formation at one of our universities for over an hour, revealing the dangers and the counsels contained in the Spirit of Prophecy and my own experience with the supernatural and how many of us were delivered from this very same experience, this doctor and college professor received not one word—not one. He was only able to communicate at an emotional level about his experience and how wonderful it was, telling me that I needed to experience it myself to understand. Then I would know it is the Spirit of God and that I am mistaken.

My friends, the most difficult thing to do for those who believe they have come into the "presence of God" by entering the silence, through "contemplative/mystical prayer," is to deny their feelings and accept the inspired warning in the Spirit of Prophecy. Satan takes control and offers the deceptive "free-lovism" experience, an overwhelming emotional feeling of love and unity with everyone and everything that exists (pantheistic in nature)—the same feelings experienced in altered states of consciousness.

There is no doubt Satan's mysticism has appeared once again, this time in the revival of the discipline called spiritual formation. It will only be as we stand upon the sea of glass that we will be sure of all things. But this we can be sure of—this deception has all of the omega-like characteristics and has most assuredly already gained a foothold among God's people.

> They will act as though it was their prerogative to use the Holy Spirit instead of letting the Holy Spirit use them, and mold and fashion them after the pattern of the divine. ...
>
> But ministers who bear the last message of mercy to fallen men must utter no random works; they must not open doors whereby Satan shall find access to human minds. It is not our work to

experiment, to study out something new and startling that will create excitement. Satan is watching his chance to take advantage of anything of this order that he may bring in his deceiving elements. (*Selected Messages*, 59, 60)

There is a common thread running through the testimonies of those who have experienced the silence: a profound sense of oneness with the universe, all humanity, peoples of all religions and cultures, including the life-changing awareness that God exists everywhere, in all things. The ecstatic experience of beholding the presence of God in them and in everything around them re-awakens their intensity to mission and is powerfully brought into their daily life and experience. They perceive God moving in them and in everything around them. This is a life-changing experience and re-motivates them to service. Here is a quotation from a Seventh-day Adventist leader:

Real spiritual formation is a process of growing more and more in tune to discernment of *God's voice* as well as more and more tuned to discernment of God's moving in my life, in the ordinary of life, as well as even in the difficult times of life. That's where real spiritual formation, or at least the value of spiritual formation, is seen.[14]

Notice how this pastor spoke of the "discernment of God's voice" as a part of his experience. This must be extremely powerful and is often the "main attraction" of contemplative prayer. Entering the mystical silence to meet with God and hear His voice has to be very appealing and fascinating. Imagine learning a spiritual discipline where you have the opportunity to "talk with God" *anytime you feel like it*. All that is required is the time and place to pray. I don't think I would want to do anything else, especially if I experienced the emotional ecstasy that often accompanies the perception of God in me and those around me, moving through me and them as we go through life together. What an experience! My heart would be overflowing with excitement and motivation as I would be endlessly seeking after the solitude of prayer. Here is another example:

---

14 "Church, Congregations Increase Focus on 'Spiritual Formation,'" *Adventist News Network*, February 3, 2004.

Second Point. The second, to look how God dwells in creatures, in the elements, giving them being, in the plants vegetating, in the animals feeling in them, in men giving them to understand: and so in me, giving me being, animating me, giving me sensation and making me to understand; likewise making a temple of me, being created to the likeness and image of His Divine Majesty; reflecting as much on myself in the way which is said in the first Point, or in another which I feel to be better. In the same manner will be done on each Point which follows. [15]

When God revealed to Ellen White how the supernatural powers associated with the "alpha" affected those involved, she was at a loss for words in describing the change in their behavior and personality. They seemed to be experiencing a type of ecstasy or loving feelings, beyond her capacity to address, or give a name. God gave her the words He wanted her to use: "free-lovism" and "unholy, spiritual love." See below:

The sophistries regarding God and nature that are flooding the world with skepticism are the inspiration of the fallen foe, who is himself a Bible student, who knows the truth that it is essential for the people to receive, and whose study it is to divert minds from the great truths given to prepare them for what is coming upon the world.

I have seen the results of these fanciful views of God, in apostasy, spiritualism, and *free-lovism*. The free-love tendency of these teachings was so concealed that at first it was difficult to make plain its real character. Until the Lord presented it to me, I knew not what to call it, *but I was instructed to call it unholy spiritual love.* (*Testimonies for the Church*, vol. 8, 292)

These "unholy spiritual love" experiences *were always associated with speculative theories regarding the nature of God and "where His presence is"* (*Selected Messages*, Book 1, 270). This fact is extremely important to understand, because we are strongly warned not to speculate on these two themes.

---

15 Ignatius of Loyola, "The Spiritual Exercises of St. Ignatius of Loyola," (The Christian Classics Ethereal Library), http://www.ccel.org/ccel/ignatius/exercises.pdf.

To study this science is to pluck the fruit from the tree of knowledge of good and evil. God forbids you or any other mortal to learn or to teach such a science ... Cut away from yourselves everything that savors of hypnotism, the science by which satanic agencies work. (*Selected Messages*, Book 2, 350)

Remember that Satan has come down with great power to take possession of minds and to hold them captive under his sway. (*Mind, Character, and Personality*, vol. 2, 716)

Through the channel of phrenology, psychology, and mesmerism, he comes more directly to the people of this generation, and works with that power *which is to characterize his efforts near the close of probation*. (*The Signs of the Times*, November 6, 1884)

Richard Foster is one of the gurus of the present spiritual formation movement in America. In a recent DVD he put it this way: "This silence is like a *portable sanctuary*, where all carry around with us the presence of God."

I hope you see the significance of this remark. It reveals the belief of all that practice spiritual formation's "contemplative and mystical prayer," including those in the Seventh-day Adventist Church. Satan's deception has led them to believe they have been in Jesus' presence and many have heard His voice. To them, it is as if they were carrying around with them a "portable sanctuary." If we carry with us a *"portable sanctuary"* and have Jesus speak to us any time we enter into the silence, *who needs the sanctuary in heaven,* or for that matter, who needs the Seventh-day Adventist Church to tell the world that Jesus is in the *Most Holy Place, of heaven's sanctuary?* What does it matter that Jesus entered the Most Holy Place? There would be no need for a Most Holy Place, for they always carry Jesus with them in their hearts' sanctuary, all their own, with Jesus available when needed. All they have to do is slip into the silence to conjure Him up and do their bidding.

Remember the "omega-like characteristic." People would be deceived concerning God's personality and *"where His presence is"* (*Selected Messages,* Book 1, 201). They would even find themselves in a position where *"Satan can talk with them."* Remember, it would rob them of their past experience and give them instead a false science, a science that would have no need of the sanctuary and the three angels' messages. Remember?

Now, here is what may be the most startling fact about the "omega," that surely could have caused Ellen White to "tremble." She saw and then wrote the warning for us to heed that the "omega" would result in the "control of men's minds." At first, this thought might not be so startling, but consider the following scenario. Ellen White saw something that caused her to tremble. What if she saw:

Thousands of Seventh-day Adventists all over the world, many of them in responsible positions, making plans and carrying on with the work of God, but the truth was they were all deceived and under Satan's control, carrying out his plans. What if she saw another spirit leading many of them, spirits under the control of Satan. What if she saw this group of God's people, hypnotized in a mass hypnosis, different than any type of hypnosis they were ever exposed to or familiar with; a hypnosis that was not like a trance or stupor, but a kind of hypnosis in which those hypnotized were carrying on with their normal life in the church, at work, recreation and travel, but they were actually under Satan's hypnotic spell because they rejected divine counsel and had erroneous spiritual convictions? If you saw that happening to today's church one hundred years ago, might that have caused you to "tremble"? Dearly beloved, read on very carefully.

This is exactly the condition Kellogg and all his associates were in when she claimed they were hypnotized. They did not know they were hypnotized, neither did they believe her when she told them they were. She said they were all under the hypnotic influence of the father of lies. These were the administrative and thought leaders of the Seventh-day Adventist Church, hypnotized and under Satan's control, without any awareness of the fact.

Please remember this is not to say that this is the way it is or the way it will be. Ellen White saw what *might* happen *if* the "omega" was not confronted and defeated. What she saw made her tremble for the church. I do believe this is a bona fide threat and that the prerequisites are in place right now. This is how mass hypnosis took place during the alpha in Kellogg's day:

> You should understand clearly that satanic agencies are clothing
> false theories in an attractive garb, even as Satan in the garden
> of Eden concealed his identity from our first parents by speak-
> ing through the serpent. You are instilling into human minds that
> which to you seems to be a very beautiful truth, but which in real-
> ity is error. *The hypnotic influence of Satan* is upon you, and upon

all others who turn from the plain word of God to pleasing fables." (*Spalding and Magan Collection*, 332, emphasis added)

Kellogg and his associates rejected years of warnings from Ellen White concerning the speculative theories they believed. The very essence of these theories had to do with the "*personality of God and the location of His presence.*" She warned them very pointedly that their beliefs were false theories and violated the teachings of Scripture. Their persistence in these beliefs, after 20 years of warnings from the pen of inspiration, confirmed their rejection of the Spirit of Prophecy, the only hope they had of seeing their error. Upon these subjects, the *personality of God and the location of His presence, they had no right to speculate.*

> Human talent and human conjecture have tried by searching to find out God. Many have trodden this pathway. The highest intellect may tax itself until it is wearied out in conjectures regarding God, but the effort will be fruitless, and the fact will remain that man by searching cannot find out God. This problem has not been given us to solve. All that man needs to know and can know of God has been revealed in the life and character of His Son, the Great Teacher. As we learn more and more of what man is, of what we ourselves are in God's sight, we shall fear and tremble before Him. (*The Upward Look*, 323)

So today, we too turn from the plain word of God and the counsel of the Spirit of Prophecy to pleasing fables, when we seek a knowledge of the discipline of spiritual formation—and thousands are. This spiritual discipline is being taught at seminars held by those denominations we have, for 150 years, identified as Babylon, after they rejected the first and second angels' messages. Attending those seminars is a clear rejection of the Bible and Spirit of Prophecy. It is no less a rejection when we invite teachers, educators, and pastors of those other denominations to instruct and guide our people. Kellogg and his associates would have done well to examine their verbal assent of the Spirit of Prophecy, while refusing to accept the inspired counsels it contained that forbade their endeavors; and we would, too.

We have learned principles from the Spirit of Prophecy that reveal that when we reject or ignore its counsel, or even simply enter into research or discussion of sciences such as spiritual formation, Satan has the right to cast his bewitching spell upon us. Why would this be? Because divine inspiration has warned us not to, and to do so is a rejection of the Spirit's direction. When we reject God's direction it gives Satan the right to control us, and God will not and cannot protect us. We have chosen the course we are on, and God will not violate our freedom to have made that choice.

> Satan so often controls in such a way that does not frighten us or reveal that he, in fact, is in control, but subtly infiltrates our minds and weaves in threads of error and apostasy.
>
> Satan is not ignorant of the result of trying to define God and Jesus Christ in a spiritualistic way that sets God and Christ as a nonentity. The moments occupied in this kind of science are, in the place of preparing the way of the Lord, making a way for Satan to come in and confuse the minds with mysticisms of his own devising. Although they are dressed up in angel robes they have made our God and our Christ a nonentity. Why? —because Satan sees the minds are all fitted for his working. Men have lost track of Christ and the Lord God, and have been obtaining an experience that is omega to one of the most *subtle delusions that will ever captivate the minds of men. We are forbidden* to ... set the imagination in a train of conjecture." (*Manuscript Releases*, vol. 11, 211, emphasis added)

Here is the "omega": *the control of human minds—mass hypnotism without awareness.* We are forbidden to set the mind in a "train of conjecture," in other words, *speculate concerning subjects in which we have not been given divine light.* Like a chameleon, the "omega" continually changes its outward appearance, until it will appear in its final, most destructive and subtle form. Spiritual formation owns the characteristics that match the Spirit of Prophecy's description and is the modern revival of a Roman Catholic teaching. The rapid spread of this dangerous discipleship program throughout our church is a possible application of Ellen White's warning that Daniel's prophecy in Chapter 11:30–36 would be repeated, claiming that *papal Rome, the "king of the north," would have "intelligence" with those in the church who have forsaken the holy covenant.*

Spiritual formation's pantheistic theory of God contains within it the belief and practice of what Ellen White termed "free-lovism," and "unholy spiritual love."

Satan is attempting to establish his deceptions in the hearts of those in God's church, just as the Spirit of Prophecy predicted. The "quiet place" or "mystical silence," the central and most important teaching of spiritual formation, often hidden within its other teachings, allows Satan to talk with those who practice this discipline, deceiving them into thinking they are hearing Jesus speak with them, thus removing His presence from the Most Holy Place and relocating Him into their presence at their command. In believing this, one has an erroneous concept of the *personhood*, or *personality*, of God. It relegates the Lord Jesus Christ to a "nonentity," demanding Him to be an essence, capable of existing everywhere simultaneously, existing in the hearts of all men personally. This removes Jesus from the sanctuary in heaven, changing His personhood into a panentheistic essence pervading the hearts of His people. These beliefs make the Lord an essence and not an actual being who dwells in heaven.

> When I first left the State of Maine, it was to go through Vermont and Massachusetts, to bear a testimony against these sentiments. "Living Temple" contains the alpha of these theories. I *knew that the omega would follow in a little while;* and I trembled for our people. I knew that I must warn our brethren and sisters *not to enter into controversy over the presence and personality of God.* (*Selected Messages*, Book 1, 203, emphasis added)

To reiterate, "Although they are dressed up in angel robes *they have made our God and our Christ a nonentity.* Why?—because Satan sees the minds are all fitted for his working. Men have lost track of Christ and the Lord God, *and have been obtaining an experience that is omega to one of the most subtle delusions that will ever captivate the minds of men. We are forbidden to ... set the imagination in a train of conjecture"* (*Manuscript Releases*, vol. 11, 211, emphasis added).

Note the "omega" experience in the above quotation. The Lord's servant is defining an aspect of the "omega," *considering the person of God to be in the hearts of men and in the objects of His creation, making Him an "essence."* This is why, she says, they have lost track of Christ and the Lord God. *These erroneous views are the revelations people have who experience the mystical silence of spiritual formation.*

They, like all who have embraced the mystical experience and believe they have been in God's presence, see Him as a pantheistic/panentheistic god, everywhere, in everything, or they see His fullness dwelling in the hearts of all people. These are erroneous views of God. The Spirit of

Prophecy makes it clear that God dwells in the hearts of the redeemed, while it is Satan who dwells in the hearts of the wicked.

> In *Living Temple* the assertion is made that God is in the flower, in the leaf, in the sinner. *But God does not live in the sinner.* The Word declares that He abides only in the hearts of those who love Him and do righteousness. *God does not abide in the heart of the sinner; it is the enemy who abides there."* (*Sermons and Talks*, vol. 1, 343, emphasis added)

Let us look at how God dwells in the hearts of the redeemed. Instead of having an actual presence, the god of spiritual formation is, in fact, a kind of essence located in the hearts of all men. It contradicts the certainty that the Father and Son have a presence in heaven, relocating their presence to the hearts of all human beings, renewed or not. Scripture and the Spirit of Prophecy reveal that the miraculous work of God upon the renewed human heart in the process of salvation is accomplished not by the personal presence of the Father or of His Son, *but by Jesus' presence through His Spirit, the Holy Spirit.*

Consider this: by His infinite sacrifice to save us, Jesus carries to this day, and forever, certain limitations of humanity. As He told His disciples, He had to leave them so that the Comforter could come and guide them in every aspect of their spiritual lives. He said, "The Spirit of truth" … will abide with you forever … *"for He dwelleth with you, and shall be in you"* (John 14:17 KJV, emphasis added).

This is how God works in the life. It is Christ in you and you in Christ *through His Spirit.* For now, this is a mystery that we will have to accept. It is speculation, which we have been warned against, to believe that the person of Jesus is in us; this is not what has been revealed. This entire area of thought must be left alone, as we have been warned.

"Much of the history that has taken place in past fulfillment of this prophecy will be repeated." We cannot positively know what aspects of this prophecy "will be repeated." It is our understanding of the alpha and omega that informs us of which aspects to consider.

For instance, we know the omega will attempt to sweep away the entire Christian economy, or Christ's ministry in the heavenly temple. We know that those deceived will believe Jesus is talking with them. We know it will contain elements of the "alpha," meaning we can look for pantheism, false doctrines concerning what God is like, how He communicates with us, His personhood and work as High Priest, or any other teachings we know were a part of the alpha.

In this verse, reference is made to "polluting the sanctuary of strength (heavenly sanctuary), the taking away of the daily (tamid) or the "continual," and the placing of the abomination that maketh desolate.

In the Old Testament the "daily" always referred to the ministry of the Holy Place. Consider this: if Ellen White's prediction that "much" of this prophecy would have another fulfillment in the future included the part concerning the taking away of the "daily" by the king of the north, papal Rome, it could not refer to the Holy Place, but must refer to the Most Holy Place, since that is where there is daily activity now, at the "time of the end." It was on October 22, 1844, when Jesus our High Priest went behind the veil to begin the application of His atoning sacrifice to all the saved and the investigative judgment began. Jesus' ministry in the heavenly temple's Holy Place had ended and the time had come for cleansing and for judgment. The proclamation of these new developments in the process of our salvation was a continuation of Reformation theology and was given by the early Adventists to every denomination in the messages of the first and second angels of Revelation, chapter 14.

In the context of the time of the end of which inspiration is speaking, it is consistent to believe that it is Christ's ministry in the Most Holy under attack and counterfeited by the omega. This would be the sweeping away of the entire Christian economy Ellen White was speaking of. She made it very clear that the ministry of Jesus in the heavenly sanctuary would be in the bull's eye of Satan's attacks before the end of time. Jesus' ministry in the Most Holy is the center of our salvation's activity and would most definitely be the target of Satan's counterfeits and deceptions; the Spirit of Prophecy tells us so.

With these things in mind, consider what Ellen White is suggesting. It is not a stretch to assume that the "daily" or "continual" is referring to Christ's ongoing ministry in the Most Holy Place at the time of the end. That would be in context if the "daily" was one of the events in the prophecy to be fulfilled, which seems plausible since Christ's ministry lies at the heart of the atoning work. We have inspiration claiming His ministry is the object of Satan's hatred and wrath.

Consider this: As we just discovered above, she said "much of the history that has taken place in fulfillment of this prophecy will be repeated." As history is repeated, we can expect an attack on the doctrine of Christ's ministry in the sanctuary in heaven. The truth preached during the Reformation was attacked and we have warnings in the Spirit of Prophecy that once again, false teachings will come into the church attempting to sweep away this vital pillar of Adventism.

We need to consider the possibility that this attack, by Daniel's king of the north, could be the mysticism of Roman Catholicism's spiritual formation, which is rapidly overtaking all Christianity. Spiritual formation's deceptions generate the false awareness of the personal presence of Jesus in the heart of the believer. The entrance into spiritual formation's "silence," necessary to experience what is believed to be Jesus presence, is truly the same self-induced trance of the spirit medium, a deception that renders Christ's ministry in the Most Holy of heaven's sanctuary useless and unnecessary.

Here is the Roman Catholic teaching on contemplative prayer, taken from the New Roman Catholic Catechism:

III. CONTEMPLATIVE PRAYER

2711   *Entering into contemplative prayer is like entering into the Eucharistic liturgy:* we "gather up" the heart, recollect our whole being under the prompting of the Holy Spirit, abide in the dwelling place of the Lord which we are, awaken our faith in order to enter into the presence of him who awaits us. We let our masks fall and turn our hearts back to the Lord who loves us, so as to hand ourselves over to him as an offering to be purified and transformed.

2715   *Contemplation is a gaze of faith, fixed on Jesus.* "I look at him and he looks at me": this is what a certain peasant of Ares in the time of his holy curé used to say while praying before the tabernacle. This focus on Jesus is a renunciation of self. His gaze purifies our heart; the light of the countenance of Jesus illumines the eyes of our heart and teaches us to see everything in the light of his truth and his compassion for all men. *Contemplation also turns its gaze on the mysteries of the life of Christ. Thus it learns the "interior knowledge of our Lord,"* the more to love him and follow him.

2717   *Contemplative prayer is silence, the "symbol of the world to come"* or "silent love." Words in this kind of prayer are not speeches; they are like kindling that feeds the fire of love. In this silence, unbearable to the "outer" man, the Father speaks to us his incarnate Word, who suffered, died, and rose; in this silence the Spirit of adoption enables us to share in the prayer of Jesus."

Could aspects of spiritual formation have characteristics of an abominable doctrine that sweeps away the entire Christian economy, reflecting elements of the end-time "omega"?

Contemplative/mystical prayers, pantheistic theology, places Jesus' presence in *people,* and as we noted, allows Satan to create the illusion that God is speaking to them, when it is he, Satan, speaking to them, just as the Spirit of Prophecy predicted.

It is when one enters into the "mystical silence," a corridor in the mind connecting the human mind with supernatural spheres occupied by fallen supernatural beings, that Satan performs his communication. Spiritual formation's contemplative/mystical prayer relies on this communication and connection for the acquisition of all the emotional spiritual gifts of "freelovism," and all that it brings with it. Could it be considered that those who practice spiritual formation have their own personal sanctuary, which they carry with them in their hearts; a sanctuary replacing the genuine, the one "the Lord pitched, and not man?" Unquestionably, if so, these concepts would undermine the "pillars of our faith" and "sweep away the whole Christian economy."

To place the person of Jesus inside all human hearts is without doubt panentheistic, Roman Catholic mysticism. Pantheism teaches that God is actually in everything that exists, everywhere. Panentheism is the belief that the fullness of God's person exists in everything, everywhere. Remember the theology concerning the personality (personhood) and presence of God, necessary for the discipline of spiritual formation to do its deceptive work came right out of the Roman Catholic Church. Saint Ignatius Loyola, founder of the Jesuit order, besides his own supernatural experiences, used the mystical teachings of Aquinas and Augustine, both considered among the greatest of all Roman Catholic theologians.

As history is repeated, we know the king of the north will attempt to gain control of the world and deceive God's people. Since spiritual formation and the mysticism that empowers it are thoroughly Roman Catholic in origin, they definitely seem to agree with the prophetic predictions about the deceptions Satan will use at the end of time against God's church. As we study the warnings and cautions given by Inspiration, there is no doubt about the dangers of these practices. They surely fit the description revealed in the Spirit of Prophecy of what we can expect from the end-time omega. Time will tell.

As God's remnant church, we must come to grips with the reality of what is happening! There is a new movement within the church, with books of a new order containing mystical teachings and leaders who seem unstoppable in their enthusiasm for these "new" ideas and teachings, learned by attending training centers for spiritual formation. These centers were established by denominations that we, through inspiration, have been warned about and have believed for 150 years are the daughters of their mother, Babylon the Great, the mother of harlots. It is happening now!

Remember, many of the teachings included within the model called spiritual formation are good Christian concepts. It is the learning and practice of contemplative/mystical prayer, which leads to altered states of consciousness and the supernatural experience of the silence, or quiet place, that is the idolatrous teaching we are exposing as a teaching of Romanism. There are many in God's remnant church who have written about their experience of the silence and have recommended literature authored by admitted mystics. This is part of the deception.

The earliest mystics of the Roman Catholic Church, whose writings we have, verify the use of contemplative prayer's silence as the tool used to experience supernatural phenomena. There are other "idolatrous standards" included in spiritual formation's teachings, such as the use of spiritual directors and confession, but we are focusing on the supernatural element of the mystical experience.

Before our next chapter, please prayerfully consider this quotation from a General Conference bulletin, informing the church at large of its plans to implement the teaching of spiritual formation around the world.

The Adventist world church created the International Board of Ministerial and Theological Education (IBMTE) in September 2001, designed to provide overall guidance and standards to the professional training of pastors, evangelists, theologians, teachers, chaplains and other denominational employees involved in ministerial and religious formation, or spiritual formation, in each of the church's 13 regions around the world. (ATN News)

Considering all we have learned thus far, are you "trembling" yet? Let us search our hearts together.

Chapter 10
A Fearful Warning

We have all heard the words meditation and contemplation, defined as thought, consideration, and reflection. These are words that people of almost every religious persuasion use regularly to describe what are considered normal spiritual exercises. Spiritual formation enthusiasts, however, distort the accepted meaning of contemplation and meditation in their use of contemplative prayer. When teaching this prayer they are in fact assisting students in their subjugation to evil supernatural powers, as they become spellbound by the fascination of entering the silence, a place in their minds they perceive has brought to them the presence of God. In reality, what it has brought to them is a delusion; a satanically fabricated hallucination constructed to fit their brand of Christianity.

In spiritual formation seminars, students are taught to use contemplative prayer as the tool to gain entry into this silence, whose realms can only be reached by the total *absence* of thought, consideration, and reflection, the exact opposite of what contemplation and meditation really mean. *This is the distorted and deceptive use of these words by those involved with spiritual formation.*

In the meditative practices of the occult, Hinduism, New Age or ancient mystical Christianity, devotees have learned from the very start that the mind's ability to focus, concentrate, and visualize are the very abilities that, if controlled in a certain way, will slow down the train of thoughts that naturally fly across the conscious part of the mind. It has always been essential knowledge among the initiated that this slowing down of the thoughts is the mechanism that enables contact with the "supernatural realms."

These are the practices taught at the thousands of spiritual formation seminars held across the country, even though abstractly, as students learn contemplative/mystical prayer. What is meant by abstractly is through the teaching of repetitive prayer, repetitive Scripture reading, willful emptying of the mind during prayer and meditation, and the use of visualization. All these practices seem harmless to the uninformed Christian, but if it were made known that these are the very same techniques used in occult circles to alter consciousness most would flee the practice.

In the year 2008, one Roman Catholic retreat alone, The Jesuit Retreat House in Ohio, had more than 7,000 students who received training in spiritual formation's contemplative/mystical prayer. That's 7,000 at one retreat center, in one year. Presently, in the USA there are more than 4,000 Roman Catholic and Protestant retreats and conference centers that hold spiritual formation seminars. Do the math to realize what is happening on the American Christian scene! My friends, this is the "emerging church," which has as its most popular leaders Richard Foster, George Barna, and Leonard Sweet, speakers who we often invite to speak at our seminars and our universities.

The occultist practitioners of the mystical sciences understand that there is a definite corridor or passageway between the conscious and the subconscious, and that the entrance into this passageway is the secret to obtaining supernatural power and experiencing the other realms of reality. The practice of certain kinds of these techniques, as taught in spiritual formation seminars, helps gain entry into that "corridor" of the mind. It is in this corridor that the spirit medium communicates with the alleged spirits of the dead; it is here where the yogi theoretically leaves his body in the state of astral projection, or the psychic experiences a vision of the future. It is into this corridor that the hypnotist, through diverse methods, moves his subject to delve into the subconscious.

The Hindu calls this place *samadhi*; the New Ager calls it tuning in; the occultist or spirit medium, a trance. Today, Christians are going to this same corridor of the mind and have given it a new name: "the silence" or "quiet place." Little do they realize they are going to a place where Satan has been escorting deceived souls for thousands of years, a place where he maneuvered them to accept as true his myriad deceptions.

These teachings are not new, neither are they unfamiliar to those with the spiritual agenda of winning over the whole world. We will look again at the quotations listed below by Pope John Paul II in chapter 12, "Evangelizing the World," but consider now also what he believes and teaches through what he has written.

APOSTOLIC LETTER
VICESIMUS QUINTUS ANNUS
A valid method ...

27. We should not be surprised that our relationship with Christ makes use of a *method*. ... our human nature and *its vital rhythms*. Hence, while Christian spirituality is familiar with the most sublime forms of *mystical silence* in which images, words and gestures are all, so to speak, superseded *by an intense and ineffable* union with God.

31. Listening and meditation are nourished by silence. ... A discovery of the importance of silence is one of the secrets of practicing contemplation and meditation.

28. I mentioned in my Apostolic Letter Novo Millennio Ineunte that the West is now experiencing a renewed demand for meditation, which at times leads to a keen interest in aspects of other religions. Some Christians, limited in their knowledge of the Christian contemplative tradition, are attracted by those forms of prayer. In effect, the Rosary is simply a method of contemplation. As a method, it serves as a means to an end. ... Such is the intent of the addition of the new series of mysteria lucis to the overall cycle of mysteries and of the few suggestions which I am proposing in this Letter regarding its manner of recitation."

We will more fully examine the quotations above in Chapter 12. They are included here so the connection can be seen between spiritual formation's contemplative prayer methods of meditation and the mysticism and contemplative traditions of the Roman Catholic Church at the very highest level, that of Pope John Paul II. What this connection is, what it means, and how it is being used to influence the world is the subject of the coming chapters.

Consider the following passage from the book *Milarepa: Tibet's Great Yogi*:

In realizing the non-existence of the personal Ego, *the mind must be kept in quiescence*. On being enabled, *by various methods, to put the mind in that state* as a result of a variety of causes, *all (thoughts, ideas, and cognition) cease*, and the mind passeth from consciousness (of objects) into *a state of perfect tranquility*, so that days, months, and years may pass without the person himself perceiving it; thus the passing of time hath to be marked for him by others. This state is called Shi-ney (Tranquil Rest) ... *Thus, by thought-process and visualization, one treadeth the path.*[16] (emphasis added)

This is where the occultist is deceived by familiar spirits into believing he has power to read minds, the New Ager imagines he is merging his consciousness with the universal mind of this god, and the yogi sees his favorite guru floating over the Ganges.

Today, while practicing spiritual formation's contemplative and mystical prayer and entering into the silence, the Christian believes he is communicating directly with God, sensing His presence in all things. He listens as God talks with him, feels His nearness as God walks with him from moment to moment, and has a most profound and emotional experience of "free-lovism," feeling immersed in the wonderful, all-encompassing love of God.

Again, unknown to them, is that the process used to enter into the silence, that same ancient process used to teach deceived souls since Adam and Eve fell in the Garden of Eden, is the science we've been warned against studying and becoming skilled at in the Spirit of Prophecy. The various techniques used to reach the silence taught in spiritual formation seminars, such as the use of repetitive Scripture and prayers, chanting, listening, focusing, mantras all variations of satanic, and hypnotic procedures were used for thousands of years to accomplish one goal: the slowing down of the *natural* thought process. A shocking truth, they are learning to open the door of their mind to *altered states of consciousness*. This is an *occult science fundamental* and is the reason for Ellen White's warnings to not even discuss this science. For our purposes, we have and will address the facts sufficient to demonstrate the danger, which is great and is already being practiced by some in our church, but *not* for the benefit of learning something new to "help us in our spiritual walk."

Modern mystics describe the silence in the book *Three Magic Words*.

The brain is stilled. The man, at last let's go; he glides below it into the *quiet feeling*, the quiet sense of his own identity with the self

---

16 W. Y. Evans-Wentz, *Tibet's Great Yogi: Milarepa* (NY: Oxford University Press, Inc., 1971), 141.

of other things—of the universe. He glides past the feeling into the very identity itself where a glorious all consciousness leaves no room for separate self thoughts or emotions.

I turn from the world about me to the world of consciousness that lies within. I shut out all memories of the past, create no images of the future. I concentrate on my being, on my awareness. I slide deep into the very recesses of my soul to a place of utter repose. I know, I know that this is Immortal Self, this is God, this is me. I am, I always was, I always will be.[17] (emphasis added)

This place of "utter repose" is the silence, or quiet place of spiritual formation's "contemplative/mystical prayer."

U.S. Anderson, the author of *Three Magic Words*, and the other mystics he quotes, have all fallen under a delusion from intruding into Satan's territory, supernatural-altered states of consciousness. Through these hypnotic experiences, they have come to believe in a pantheistic god; a god who is actually made up of, and is, his creation. The logical conclusion of this belief is to think you are the same as everything else that exists—god. So, now we have the surprise teaching of Anderson's book, the *Three Magic Words*, "I am god."

These poor deluded souls, believed they discovered God when they entered the quiet feeling, learning the method of getting there from Hindu masters. This is the silence of their mystical experience, where they imagined merging with God's consciousness. They believed Him to be an essence, pervading all things and consisting of all things, concluding that since He is His creation, they too must be God; hence, the three magic words, "I am God."

Today, spiritual formation's mystical silence leads to similar experiences: God in everything, God as everything, everywhere, and in every heart—moving, feeling, seeing, and living with them in all they do, also experiencing a dramatic sense and feeling of love for everyone, everywhere. Spiritual formation's contemplative/mystical prayer results in pantheistic and panentheistic experiences, with advocates united in practicing methods and techniques we have been warned about, leading to belief in concepts that falsely define the personality of God and where His presence is

---

17 Uell S. Anderson, *Three Magic Words* (Chatsworth, CA: Melvin Powers Wilshire Book Company, 1954) 315–319.

located. These two concepts we are warned never to speculate on in the Spirit of Prophecy.

> It introduces that which is nought but speculation in regard to the personality of God and where His presence is. No one on this earth has a right to speculate on this question. The more fanciful theories are discussed, the less men will know of God and of the truth that sanctifies the soul. (*Selected Messages,* Book 1, 201)

It is a fact that many in our beloved church have received training in spiritual formation, where they have learned to practice "contemplative/mystical prayer" and have had the wonderful and exciting experiences it assures those who pass through its portals into the esoteric realms of the supernatural. They will be excited, renewed, with a new sense of mission. They will be highly motivated to carry on the work of God, yet will be under the control of a "different god" and, disturbingly, will not believe it. Evidence strongly confirms that "contemplative/mystical prayer's" silence is an altered-state of consciousness, similar to the trance of hypnotism and leads to a satanic mystical experience.

My dear church family, I have been to this place. I know the tremendous power that bewitches those who have had a mystical experience, in which they believe God has spoken with them. I know and have experienced the incredible, ecstatic feeling of love and "unity" with all things. My escape was the result of the fact that I yearned for truth and to be set free from the bondage of sin, more than the wonderful "free love" emotions this supernatural experience provided. There is but one way of escape for any Seventh-day Adventist practicing the "contemplative/mystical prayer" of spiritual formation: the acceptance of the veracity of the Spirit of Prophecy as divinely inspired truth, which warns us of the dangers of investigating, practicing, and even discussing these theories for the purpose of spiritual advancement. Furthermore, a determination to spread this practice, a masterpiece of deception tears down, rather than builds, God's remnant church.

Spiritual formation's contemplative/mystical prayer is a different form of the same deception employed by Satan in my own past, more than thirty years ago. It was the most difficult battle of my life to deny my feelings and accept the truth of the Bible and Spirit of Prophecy, as it will be for those practicing this mystical science in the church today. Those who have learned to practice the mystical prayer of spiritual formation, a form of prayer first used in Christianity by the early Roman Catholic mystics and then repackaged by Jesuit priests in the 16th century, are described in the Spirit of Prophecy in this way:

> To study this science is to pluck the fruit from the tree of knowledge of good and evil. God forbids you or any other mortal to preach or to teach such a science ... Cut away from yourselves everything that savors of hypnotism, the science by which satanic agencies work." (*Mind, Character, and Personality*, vol. 2, 716)

> Through the channel of phrenology, psychology, and mesmerism, he comes more directly to the people of this generation, and *works with that power which is to characterize his efforts near the close of probation.*" (*The Signs of the Times*, November 6, 1884, emphasis added)

Notice how Satan will intensify his efforts to deceive as we near probation's end. We can be sure that he will do all in his power to cloak this deception, attempting to prevent God's people from discerning even the possibility that spiritual formation's contemplative/mystical prayer may be the supernatural channel through which he will attempt to tear down the remnant church. He has already disguised his efforts in the wrappings of Christian discipleship, spreading this false teaching, with roots in Roman Catholicism, to many of the Protestant churches and at the same time has tempted us by their seeming successes to seek their knowledge and methods of work. Using every device at his disposal, just as he did to Israel of old, he maneuvers God's people to turn away from seeking the instruction given by inspiration, the prophets of old and the Spirit of Prophecy today.

This short review of what has been happening is precisely how we have been warned that the "omega" would become a threat to God's church. He will develop among the people of God a satanic hatred of the Testimonies. Amazing!

> The very last deception of Satan will be to make of none effect the testimony of the Spirit of God. Where there is no vision, the people perish (Proverbs 29:18). Satan will work ingeniously, in different ways and through different agencies, to unsettle the confidence of God's remnant people in the true testimony. ...

There will be a hatred kindled against the testimonies which is satanic. The workings of Satan will be to unsettle the faith of the churches in them for this reason: Satan cannot have so clear a track to bring in his deceptions and bind up souls in his delusions if the warnings and reproofs and counsels of the Spirit of God are heeded. (*Selected Messages*, Book 1, 48)

The Spirit of Prophecy helps us understand why there are those who are so open to this deception.

It is a masterpiece of Satan's deceptions to keep the minds of men searching and conjecturing in regard to that which God has not made known and which He does not intend that we shall understand. It was thus that Lucifer lost his place in heaven. He became dissatisfied because all the secrets of God's purposes were not confided to him, and he entirely disregarded that which was revealed concerning his own work in the lofty position assigned him. By arousing the same discontent in the angels under his command, he caused their fall. Now he seeks to imbue the minds of men with the same spirit and to lead them also to disregard the direct commands of God. (*The Great Controversy*, 523)

Considering the fact that characteristics of the omega are supernatural, such as believing that one is hearing Jesus' voice when it is the voice of Satan, and the luring aspects of entering into the "silence," it is reasonable to assume this deception will contain theories and/or practices that God never intended for them to understand.

We read:

Thus many err from the faith and are seduced by the devil. ... human philosophy has attempted to search out and explain mysteries which will never be revealed through the eternal ages. If men would but search and understand what God has made known of Himself and His purposes, they would obtain such a view of the glory, majesty, and power of Jehovah that they would realize their own littleness and would be content with that which has been revealed. (*The Great Controversy*, 522)

These observations are consistent with the practices and teachings contained in the discipline we call spiritual formation and its contemplative/mystical prayer, and it seems those predisposed to involve themselves with these teachings invariably are those who will not consider what the Spirit of Prophecy has to say.

My friends, a satanic hatred of the Testimonies does not necessarily mean that those thus described will reveal their true feelings, or would ever make themselves known, for such would lose their good standing in the church. This satanic hatred could manifest in such a way to raise no eyebrows, simply a willful ignoring of the counsels contained in the Spirit of Prophecy. No open controversy, but just a willful ignoring of the warnings they contain.

We are God's chosen people, and He has given us the prophetic gift—a most precious, living gift. The words written are for our instruction and counsel and are *meant* to lead us through the confusion and deceptions of the last days. We are no match for the devices of the enemy and greatly need to humble ourselves before God, accept His counsel and rest in the arms of our loving Savior, with the original simplicity of life that Adam and Eve had before their fall. The constant pulling apart and doubting of the Spirit of Prophecy is a sure warning sign that a closer, more judicious relationship with Jesus is needed.

There are some who think they are able to measure the character and to estimate the importance of the work the Lord has given me to do. *Their own mind and judgment is the standard by which they would weigh the testimonies.*

My Instructor said to me, *Tell these men that God has not committed to them the work of measuring, classifying, and defining the character of the testimonies. Those who attempt this are sure to err in their conclusions. The Lord would have men adhere to their appointed work. If they will keep the way of the Lord, they will be able to discern clearly that the work which He has appointed me to do is not a work of human devising.*

Those who carefully read the testimonies as they have appeared from the early days, need not be perplexed as to their origin. *The many books, written by the help of the Spirit of God, bear a living witness to the character of the testimonies."* (*Selected Messages*, Book 1, 49, emphasis added)

In examining the following pages, you will need to decide for yourself if characteristics of the described omega may already be impacting God's church, doing its deceptive work.

Chapter 11
Rebellion

The Spirit of Prophecy strongly warns against speculating about the "personality" of God and the "location" of His presence, implying that those with this tendency are treading on dangerous ground and, as we near the end of time, speculating on these two themes will be a reason many will be led astray. Those warnings were given specifically to the leaders of the church to save the church from impending doom.

The administrative and thought leadership of the Seventh-day Adventist Church lived and worked in Battle Creek, Michigan, the home of the famous Battle Creek Sanitarium, unsurpassed in its worldwide reputation and appeal as an institution for regaining failed health. Many of these leaders fell under the charm and influence of the institution's director, Dr. John Harvey Kellogg, the world's most talented and well-known physician at that time.

The doctor wrote a book, *Living Temple,* which Ellen White warned should not be published by our publishing house because it contained deceptive pantheistic teachings. In defiance, Dr. Kellogg had his book published elsewhere and was determined to persuade the church leaders that his beliefs were correct. Being a gifted and persuasive orator, the doctor pressed his viewpoint upon those leaders and many of them accepted his interesting, yet dangerous, beliefs. God has recorded for us in the Spirit of Prophecy an inspired record of how the doctor managed to persuade these leaders of the church that his beliefs were true. Here is a brief analysis:

He used his position of authority to request those he wanted to influence to come to specially called meetings and sit before him. Having their rapt attention, he used his power of persuasion and gifted use of language to teach the principles governing his beliefs. He answered only the questions he determined would advance his cause, dismissing the rest, thus controlling the conversation. He would often intimidate the questioner and overwhelm them with his answers and explanations, finally convincing them of the truth of his theories.

Their acceptance of his teachings was frequently the result of their physical and mental exhaustion after having been made to listen to the doctor into the wee hours of the morning.

> The long night interviews which Dr. Kellogg holds are one of his most effective means of gaining his point. His *constant stream of talk confuses the minds* of those he is seeking to influence. *He misstates and misquotes words,* and places those who argue with him in so false a light that their powers of discernment are benumbed. *He takes their words, and gives them an impress which makes them seem to mean exactly the opposite of what they said.* (*Battle Creek Letters,* 109, emphasis added)

The alpha apostasy involved much more than simply spiritualistic or supernatural phenomenon and the false teachings concerning pantheism. A major component of the alpha and thus of the omega *is an abuse of power, designed to take away from God's people their freedom of choice, by control and manipulation.* Gaining control of minds, without the subject's awareness, has always been one of Satan's most successful devices in advancing his agenda.

He who said in his heart, "I will ascend into heaven, I will exalt my throne above the stars of God: I will sit also upon the mount of the congregation, in the sides of the north: I will ascend above the heights of the clouds; I will be like the most High" (Isaiah 14:13, 14 KJV), actually believes he can make this happen, but only by compulsion, for he knows that those who honor God will never willfully consent to worship him.

How could this be done? Satan had to find a way to gain control over man's power of choice. God has allowed him one way. Hence, we have the birth of spiritualism, a science over which God has allowed Satan complete control.

God is love. He does not just have love, He is love, so all He creates is the expression of love, including man. Man, in order to love God, had to be created with free will, which love demands for its existence. Without choice or the ability to decide, intelligent response to anything would be impossible—good or evil. This is why everyone's freedom of choice is so precious and needs to be honored and closely protected.

The Spirit of Prophecy contains many warnings pertaining to the abuse of power and the danger of forcing our will or ideas upon others. In God's infinitely complex plan to spread the three angels' messages throughout the entire world before Jesus returns, the Holy Spirit speaks directly to every one of God's chosen people, directing them personally in the work He would have them do. It is God who has given them gifts and talents to use according to His plan, and this work is extremely complicated and far beyond man's ability to comprehend. *This is the reason it is dangerous to interfere with the unique way in which the Lord may be leading others involved in His work.* Each one of God's children has been personally given a special and unique work by the Lord, communicated to them through His Spirit, and when the mission of that person is overruled and replaced by someone with the power to do so because of their position of authority in the church, who believes they are more in tune with God's will for that person, or because they think they have the right to decide for them, they are making a dreadful mistake and are doing the work of the enemy.

Ellen White saw this type of control as part of the "alpha" apostasy and called it *"a species of slavery."* She gives repeated warnings to those in powerful positions to never think God has placed them in those positions to decide for another how God might be influencing or leading them.

> The man-ruling power that has been coming into our ranks has no sanction in the word. Satan has stolen in to lead men to depend on men, and to make flesh their arm. …
>
> *The influence will be to destroy the God-given personality of men, and place them under human jurisdiction.* … The men, who instruct their fellowmen to look to men for guidance, are really teaching them *that when they go to the Lord for counsel and the direction of His Spirit regarding their duty, they must not follow that counsel without first going to certain men to know if this is what they must do. Thus a species of slavery is developed that will bring only weakness and inefficiency to the church of God.*
>
> Those who bring in this unhappy chapter into the experiences of our work, and willingly accept the idea that the ruler ship of other men's conscience has been given to them, need to understand that they have made a grave mistake. Their office was never intended to give to them the responsibility which they have been led to think it bestowed. The danger signal is now lifted against this evil. Never, never let men consent to stand in a position which God alone should occupy. (*Christian Leadership*, 28, emphasis added)

Men and women are not to study the science of how to take captive the minds of those who associate with them. This is the science that Satan teaches. We are to resist everything of the kind." (*Medical Ministry*, 110)

She also wrote:

So long as they refuse to heed the warnings given them, the spell that is upon them cannot be broken. God has a work that must be carried forward purely and intelligently, in his own way, entirely separated from the influence of seducing spirits that some have communion with. (*Spalding and Magan Collection*, 464)

Those leaders at Battle Creek, who would not accept the warnings in the Spirit of Prophecy, severed their connection with God, rendering them unable to discern that Dr. Kellogg was misled in many of the things he was doing. They were also unaware that they had a new master and lord, Satan; neither did most of them believe Ellen White when she told them. Brothers and sisters, neither will many of those deceived by the end-time "omega" in our time today believe, for the "omega" is the "alpha" perfected and even more able to deceive.

So what is it, in the "omega" we are looking for? We should look for supernatural manifestations of demons, counterfeiting Christianity with pantheistic and panentheistic deceptions, that sweep away the "pillars of the faith," especially Christ's heavenly ministry. There will be abusive administrative power where God's will, revealed to His servants personally, is overruled, foiling His plans for the advancement of the work and replacing them with new plans by those in authority. There will be "books of a new order" written and evangelism will be done in new and exciting ways that are especially attractive to our young people. There will be exciting music; music that was previously unacceptable to the church. Church standards will decline, with the Sabbath and Spirit of Prophecy lightly regarded. The true message of the remnant church will be more difficult to sound, and the inspired methods for its advancement ignored, countered with other plans and a softened message by those in positions of power. Remember, this is what would happen if the "omega" were to succeed and sweep through the church. I believe we all agree that some of these conditions already exist.

As frightening as some of these conditions sound, many of these things did occur in Battle Creek during the "alpha." Because a thing is hard to believe is not a very good reason not to believe it, especially if we have "a more sure word of prophecy," which tells us it's the truth.

During the threat of the alpha, immediate action had to be taken and when the church at large allowed Jesus to take the helm, the victory was won. There was, however, a warning that this "alpha of the omega" was just the first part of an ongoing threat against the remnant church, and that it would appear over and over again, and near the close of probation the "omega" of the omega would arise, having many of the same characteristics of the alpha. History would be repeated.

It has been 100 years since Ellen White wrote the warnings concerning the alpha, and the way we use certain words that she used in describing it has changed. Understanding what these words meant to her when she used them is essential to grasp the meaning of her statements concerning the alpha.

Here are a few of those warnings:

It introduces that which is nought but speculation in regard to the *personality of God and where His presence is.* No one on this earth has a right to speculate on this question. (*Selected Messages*, Book 1, 201, emphasis added)

The enemy of our souls is earnestly at work to introduce among the Lord's people pleasing speculation, and incorrect views regarding the *personality of God.*

I have seen the results of these fanciful views of God, *in apostasy, spiritualism, free-lovism.* The *free love tendencies* of these teachings were so concealed that it was difficult to present them in their real character. (*Manuscript Releases,* vol. 8, 304, emphasis added)

There is a *strain of spiritualism coming in among our people,* and it will undermine the faith of those who give place to it, *leading them to give heed to seducing spirits, and doctrines of devils.* (*Manuscript Releases,* vol. 4, 57, emphasis added)

What kind is this that will fool us?

Do Not Discuss God's Personality—Never allow yourself to be drawn into discussion regarding the *personality of God. On this subject, silence is eloquence.* (*Manuscript Releases,* vol. 11, 318, emphasis added)

The Personality of God—He (Christ) represented God *not as an essence that pervaded nature, but as a God who has a personality.* Christ was the express image of His Father's person; and He came to our world to restore in man God's moral image, in order that man, although fallen, might through obedience to God's commandments become enstamped with the divine image and character—adorned with the beauty of divine loveliness. (*Manuscript Releases*, vol. 19, 250, emphasis added)

We need not the mysticism that is in this book. Those who entertain these sophistries will soon find themselves *in a position where the enemy can talk with them*, and lead them away from God. (*Selected Messages*, Book 1, 202, emphasis added)

Here are the definitions of the key words used in these statements, as Ellen White understood them in her day. (*Webster's American Dictionary*, 1828 edition)

MYSTICISM, n. Obscurity of doctrine.

1. The doctrine of the Mystics, who profess a pure, sublime and perfect devotion, wholly disinterested, and *maintain that they hold immediate intercourse with the divine Spirit.*

MYSTICS, n. A religious sect, who *profess to have direct intercourse with the Spirit of God.*

PERSONALITY, n. *That which constitutes an individual; a distinct person or that which constitutes individuality.* The direct application or, applicability *to a person*; as the personality of a remark. (Emphasis added.)

Notice that the word "mysticism" is defined as a set of beliefs where one holds direct communication with God. So when Ellen White said, "We need not the mysticism that is in this book (Kellogg's *Living Temple*)," the subject being the "alpha" deception, she would be warning about learning methods of having direct communication with God. The reasons for this warning concerning *Living Temple* become evident when we read what she said:

We need not the mysticism that is in this book. Those who entertain these sophistries will *soon find themselves in a position where the enemy can talk with them*, and lead them away from God. (*Selected Messages*, Book 1, 202, emphasis added)

Obviously, in this "alpha" deception, people can be deceived into thinking they are in God's presence and He speaks with them, when in reality it is Satan, not God. A frightful situation indeed!

When speaking of God's "personality," she is referring to His *"personhood"* and not His behavior patterns, which is the way we use the word today. She is simply saying that God is a "person," a divine person. He is an "individual" and not an essence infiltrating all nature. She is warning us *not to try to define, explain, or speculate about His "personhood,"* also to *not speculate about His presence, where He is located.*

Do not try to explain in regard to the personality of God. You cannot give any further explanation than the Bible has given. Human theories regarding Him are good for nothing. Do not soil your minds by studying the misleading theories of the enemy. (*Counsels to Writers and Editors*, 93)

With this understanding we can come to some extremely important conclusions concerning the deceptions that will threaten our church as we near the end of time, things that will help us identify these deceptions when they occur.

The following are conclusions we can be sure of:

We are not to learn *any method* which teaches us a way to come into the presence of Jesus. Practicing such a method is not only *speculating on the location of His presence,* but is *demanding His presence* and gives you the power to control it.

We are not to learn *any method* by which we believe *God will directly communicate with us, for this is mysticism.* It is true God communicates directly with us in many ways such as Scripture, dreams, nature, thoughts, ideas, and even visions or speaking to us directly at times, but to believe we can *learn a method or technique we can use at will, resulting in His presence, according to our timing, is mysticism* and we have been warned against that kind of practice.

We are *not to participate in any teaching where God is thought of in pantheistic or panentheistic ways.* The things in this universe are not God, neither is Jesus an essence filling all nature, nor is *He personally in the hearts of all men.* It is the Holy Spirit that represents Jesus in the hearts of human beings, and exactly how this takes place is a mystery that we are counseled not to speculate about.

> It is the Spirit that causes to shine into darkened minds the bright beams of the Sun of Righteousness; that makes men's hearts burn within them with an awakened realization of the truths of eternity; that presents before the mind the great standard of righteousness, and convinces of sin; that inspires faith in Him who alone can save from sin; that works to transform character by withdrawing the affections of men from those things which are temporal and perishable, and fixing them upon the eternal inheritance. The Spirit recreates, refines, and sanctifies human beings, fitting them to become members of the royal family, children of the heavenly King. (*Sons and Daughters of God*, 28)

When we insist on following the erroneous teachings Ellen White warned against in the Spirit of Prophecy, the results are sure:

> The spiritualistic theories regarding the personality of God, followed to their logical conclusion, sweep away the whole Christian economy. They estimate as nothing the light that Christ came from heaven to give John to give to His people. They teach that the scenes just before us are not of sufficient importance to be given special attention. They make of no effect the truth of heavenly origin, and rob the people of God of their past experience, giving them instead a false science. (*Selected Messages*, Book 1, 203)

Jesus, while not restrained from traveling where He will, is our divine High Priest, and since October 22, 1844, He is in the heavenly sanctuary's Most Holy Place, performing the final work of the investigative judgment, preparing to return in all His glory. This we know and can rely on.

Now that we have taken the time for this overview and have a basic understanding of some of the dynamics of the "alpha and omega," and appreciate the impact of these characteristics, it is time to, once again, seriously consider a danger presenting itself to our beloved Seventh-day Adventist Church, God's remnant church.

It is a fact, that there is a movement spreading rapidly through the Protestant community, called the "emerging church," whose influence has reached all the way from the local congregations to the universities and leadership of our Seventh-day Adventist Church; a movement with theological beliefs and practices that are the same as those we have been warned would be those of the "alpha and omega" apostasy as explained in the paragraphs above.

A Personal Testimony

For weeks I found myself at times pondering one of the quotations above. I was convinced of its significance to the subject of this book, but could not grasp the exact application. Ellen White wrote:

> I have been instructed by the heavenly messenger that some of the reasoning in the book Living Temple is unsound, and that this reasoning would lead astray the minds of those who "are not thoroughly established on the foundation" principles of present truth. It introduces that which is naught but speculation in regard to the personality of God and where His presence is. No one on this earth has a right to speculate on this question. (*Selected Messages*, Book 1, 201)

It was Wednesday evening and I had an hour's drive to one of my churches for prayer meeting, so I asked the Lord to help me understand the significance of this statement to the subject of this book. I prayed that God would open my mind.

I began to think of how some Seventh-day Adventists were caught up in this terrible deception; how they have attended weekend Catholic and Protestant retreats, where they learned the mystical contemplative prayer, a way to pray that would eventually lead them into experiencing the "silence," an altered state of consciousness, an experience they would consider wonderful, bringing them into the "presence of God."

I recalled how easy it was for me to find warnings and reproofs as I searched the Spirit of Prophecy for counsel and how those warnings clearly spoke against attending meetings at other churches unless I was specifically led to go by the providence of God. These warnings clearly said that God must cease His protective care and have His angels retreat, leaving us vulnerable if we insisted on attending and how evil angels would then have access to our minds.

I remembered how inspiration reveals that once these evil angels gain access to our minds, they "immediately" begin to mingle their thoughts with ours. This mingling results in a form of hypnosis, placing us under their control. I recalled that these warnings were easy to find and easy to comprehend.

Then I began to think about the actual people caught up in this deception; who are they, where are they from and what kind of work do they do? As I thought about this, I realized there were no lay people that came to mind, none! Every Adventist person with whom I was able to associate this movement was a leader in the church of some sort. This thought led me to think of the "alpha" deception, which was also among those in leadership during the Kellogg era.

Why is this happening? I asked myself. What is the dynamic, the force driving it? How is it that highly educated men and women, whom the Lord has called to fill leadership positions in the church and who have dedicated their lives to giving our unique message to the world, men and women who have studied and are blessed with having available the Spirit of Prophecy, begin to practice the very things the Spirit of Prophecy specifically warns them not to practice?

It then occurred to me that this is sin. Some of these people are choosing to do something they know the Spirit of Prophecy warns against, while others, not knowing, are deceived. Either way, willful or not, it is sin.

Then I began to consider the "kind" of sin this is. Is it similar to those we all struggle with in the life-long process of sanctification, those that tempt us every day and "so easily beset us?" Can it be compared to uncontrolled anger or appetite, lust, or the love of money and power? What about laziness or smoking, lying and coveting, or cursing and gossip?

As I had these thoughts, I began to consider this sin being different. This sin does not involve any part of our fallen nature clamoring for control. There is no twisted emotion for which counseling is needed, and neither is there an overwhelming urge, desperately rising up from the depths of our fallen nature, demanding control or satisfaction. This is different. Lord, help! What is this all about?

REBELLION! What? Again, *REBELLION!*

It was unmistakable. I knew it was not my mind's voice, but the Lord's. At first I was troubled, but after a little consideration, it became clear, very clear; disturbingly clear. The decision to participate in a practice one knows to be wrong, or easily can know, is condemned in both Scripture and the Spirit of Prophecy. A practice where the decision to participate has *not* been enticed by the fallen nature overpowering better judgment is, for sure, a very different type of sin than those committed because of succumbing to temptation. With this sin there is no temptation because of any *propensity* from within the fallen nature. The "old man" is not responsible, attempting to control the power of choice. One is choosing for other selfish reasons, but is under no provocation. Neither was Satan when he sinned originally!

We cannot explain it. It is simply *the choice to disobey the inspired direction of the Holy Spirit, unexplainable,* and that is what makes it an act of "REBELLION," which Scripture claims is the same as the sin of "witchcraft," for the same reasons. Interesting!

> Those who pursue a course of rebellion against the Lord can always find false prophets who will justify them in their acts, and flatter them to their destruction. Lying words often make many friends, as is illustrated in the case of these false teachers among the Israelites. These so-called prophets, in their pretended zeal for God, found many more believers and followers than the true prophet who delivered the simple message of the Lord. (*Seventh-day Adventist Bible Commentary*, 1158)

It is an even sadder case for those of us in God's church today, for the false prophets that flatter us are not even members of the remnant church, but are the leaders of the "emerging church," sweeping the same Protestant churches of Babylon that we have been delivered from and called out of for the last 150 years.

We seem determined to lift up and put on a pedestal the leaders of this movement like George Barna, Richard Foster, and Leonard Sweet, all self-proclaimed mystics of the spiritual formation movement, by constantly inviting them to speak to our youth, our ministers, and our administrative leaders for the purpose of learning their methods of labor, in spite of the fact that the Spirit of Prophecy is filled with warnings against it.

> The different parties of professed Advent believers have each a little truth, but God has given all these truths to His children who are being prepared for the day of God. He has also given them truths that none of these parties know, neither will they understand. Things which are sealed up to them, the Lord has opened to those who will see and are ready to understand. If God has any new light to communicate, He will let His chosen and beloved understand it, without their going to have their minds enlightened by hearing those who are in darkness and error.

I was shown the necessity of those who believe that we are having the last message of mercy, being separate from those who are daily imbibing new errors. I saw that neither young nor old should attend their meetings; for it is wrong to thus encourage them while they teach error that is a deadly poison to the soul and teach for doctrines the commandments of men. ... God is displeased with us when we go to listen to error, without being obliged to go; for unless He sends us to those meetings where error is forced home to the people by the power of the will, He will not keep us." (*Early Writings*, 124)

Like Israel of old, Satan wisely brings his deceptions to the leaders of the church, knowing this is the most fruitful ground for the spreading of his false teachings.

Princes Enlisted in Rebellion.—Those men of Israel were determined to resist all evidence that would prove them to be wrong. ...Who were these? Not the weak, not the ignorant, not the unenlightened. *In that rebellion there were two hundred and fifty princes famous in the congregation, men of renown."* (*Seventh-day Adventist Bible Commentary*, 1115, emphasis added)

It was led by two hundred and fifty princes of the congregation, men of renown. Call rebellion by its right name, and apostasy by its right name, and then consider that the experience of the ancient people of God, with all its objectionable features, was faithfully chronicled to pass into history. The Scripture declares, "These things were written for our admonition, upon whom the ends of the world are come." And if men and women who have the knowledge of the truth are so far separated from their great Leader, that *they will take the great leader of apostasy, and name him Christ our Righteousness, it is because they have not sunk the shaft deep into the mines of truth. They are not able to distinguish the precious ore from the base material.*

The Lord has permitted this matter to develop as it has done, in order to show how easily His people will be misled, when they depend upon the words of men instead of searching the Scriptures for themselves, as did the noble Bereans, to see if these things are so." (*Seventh-day Adventist Bible Commentary*, 1114, emphasis added)

As we examine the words of inspiration, we see that God allowed this rebellion in ancient Israel to develop for a reason. It was for our benefit, those living at the end of the world, to show us how easy it is for God's people to be misled when they depend on men instead of searching the Scriptures for themselves, as did the Bereans.

Ellen White uses as an example Jeremiah 36:1-7, where Baruch, Jeremiah's scribe, wrote down the inspired words of Jeremiah, delivering them to King Jehoiakim, who, after listening to three or four leaves, cut them in pieces and had them thrown into a fire and destroyed. She points out that this history will be repeated in the remnant church.

> Many now despise the faithful reproof given of God in testimony. I have been shown that some in these days have even gone so far as to burn the written words of rebuke and warning, as did the wicked king of Israel. (*Testimonies for the Church*, vol. 4, 180)

It seems that many have egos that require our existence to be more mysterious and complex. There is a need for more "natural" power and "supernatural" power to explore the universe's hidden mysteries. To them, the simplicity with which we were created is humiliating, thus they strive for a more complex and powerful self-image as they search for explanations of the mysteries God has withheld from us for our own good. Consider this statement:

> There are deep mysteries in the word of God; there are unexplainable mysteries in His providences; there are mysteries in the plan of salvation that man cannot fathom. But the finite mind, strong in its desire to satisfy its curiosity and solve the problems of infinity, neglects to follow the plain course indicated by the revealed will of God and pries into the secrets hidden since the foundation of the world. Man builds his theories, loses the simplicity of true faith, becomes too self-important to believe the declarations of the Lord, and hedges himself in with his own conceits.
>
> Many who profess our faith are in this position. They are weak and powerless because they trust in their own strength. (*Testimonies for the Church*, vol. 4, 163, 164)

Many have fallen for Satan's deceptions because of their desire for power and a greater self-image. They are unhappy with the way God created them, not having the attributes that bolster their fallen egos. We know from the Spirit of Prophecy that this is the group who will not heed the warnings God gave them through divine inspiration. They are the ones with whom the king of the north has "intelligence;" the ones in the remnant church who have turned and have forsaken the holy covenant.

Consider this: As we analyze the next well-known statement from the Spirit of Prophecy, notice how it is the Protestants of America that do all the reaching. They reach over the gulf and then the abyss; first, to grasp the hand of Catholicism and then, spiritualism. She shall then "make provision for the propagation of papal falsehoods and delusions."

Friends, spiritual formation and its ancient mysticism are papal falsehoods and delusions being propagated now. It is without doubt that it is the Protestants of America that have been reaching over to Rome and incorporating these deceptions into the sisterhood of Protestant churches. This is their baby, born of St. Ignatius Loyola and the Jesuits, and handed down to the Protestants who rejected the message of the Advent awakening.

What we are about to read from the *Testimonies for the Church*, volume 5, p. 451, warns that when we see these things happening, our country is about to repudiate every principle of its constitution as a Protestant and republican form of government, that we may know it is time for the marvelous working of Satan and that we are near the end. Furthermore, the statement claims these things are a sign as were the armies surrounding Jerusalem a sign to the Christians to flee.

> When Protestantism shall stretch her hand across the gulf to grasp the hand of the Roman power, when she shall reach over the abyss to clasp hands with spiritualism, when, under the influence of this threefold union, our country shall repudiate every principle of its Constitution as a Protestant and republican government, and shall make provision for the propagation of papal falsehoods and delusions, then we may know that the time has come for the marvelous working of Satan and that the end is near.

> As the approach of the Roman armies was a sign to the disciples of the impending destruction of Jerusalem, so may this apostasy be a sign to us that the limit of God's forbearance is reached, that the measure of our nation's iniquity is full, and that the angel of mercy is about to take her flight, never to return. The people of God will then be plunged into those scenes of affliction and distress which

prophets have described as the time of Jacob's trouble." (*Testimonies for the Church*, vol. 5, 451)

Are we awake to these events, or are we like the ten virgins, fast asleep? Do we see the rapid changes in our republican form of government as the fulfillment of prophecy, or are we "neither cold nor hot," waiting to be spewed out of our rejected Savior's mouth?

To understand these implications, it is essential to establish our confidence in God's positioning of the Seventh-day Adventist Church—indeed, the remnant church of Bible prophecy identified in the book of Revelation, chapters 9 through 12—arising precisely on time, following the sixth trumpet of Revelation in chapter nine. We must be convinced that we are that movement, continued on from the Protestant Reformation, and are those people that Scripture claims keep the commandments of God and have the testimony of Jesus, the gift of prophecy.

If you have any doubt about our identity at this point I suggest you prayerfully reread chapters 4 and 5, "Who Are We Anyway?" parts I and II, remembering that it will be those who deny this truth and refuse to heed the warnings given by inspiration that will fall victim to the omega deception.

Chapter 12
Evangelizing the World

As the close of probation approaches, three powers are on a mission to reach the entire world with a spiritual message; a message each believes God has ordained them to proclaim. One of those powers, the true remnant church, proclaims the unpopular truth of the Holy Scriptures. Filled with the Spirit of the living God and under His direction, the church reaches every inhabitant of planet earth with the three angels' messages.

They live the righteousness of Christ and expose the satanic nature of the beast and its image, as well as how choosing to accept the first day of the week as their Sabbath will result in receiving the mark of the beast. The world comes to understand the sacredness God placed upon our honor of that day as a sign of our covenant relationship with Him and the reason He placed it in the very heart of the Ten Commandments, the terms of the everlasting covenant. The light shines upon every living being and it is beheld how worship is the issue in the final conflict, with the true Sabbath leading to the seal of God and the false Sabbath leading to the seal or mark of the beast.

The warning is heard by every living being, that a choice of following God's law or the beast's altered version must be made before probation closes.

There will be no compulsion or deceit used by the remnant church as they make their appeal to the entire world. They will preach the truth from the Holy Scriptures, revealing in their lives the self-abandonment of a heart filled with God's love for humanity. They will sacrifice every worldly attachment in making sure God's last message of mercy reaches every living soul on earth. All will hear the heartfelt plea of a loving God inviting them to have faith in Jesus and to keep His commandments. Then, after every person has witnessed this revelation of God's love and righteousness, after every person has made their decision, probation will close. "He who is filthy, let him be filthy still; he who is righteous, let him be righteous still" (Revelation 22:11 NKJV).

The other two powers join forces to compel and deceive the world into following their altered version of the Ten Commandments. In their edition of God's law, the Papacy changed the solemnity of the Seventh-day Sabbath of the fourth commandment to the first day of the week, a change the other power accepted.

The altered law was not the Lord's immediate focus as He called those from the Roman Catholic Church to be His remnant people. From the 11th to the 19th century, it became universally accepted among students of Scripture that papal Rome was the counterfeit church symbolized by the first beast of Revelation, chapter 13, also known as the "antichrist" and "man of sin" (1 John 2:18; 2 Thessalonians 2:3). Thus was founded the Protestant Reformation, with the mission to spread the true gospel of God's grace and forgiveness while exposing the deception of the "man of sin" to all who would hear. Then, the unthinkable occurred.

At the end of the 1,260 years in 1798, the time predicted in Bible prophecy more than any other, the Lord shed new light upon his people to continue the advancement of the reformation. This movement, called the "Great Awakening," took place in the northeastern USA during the 1820s and '30s. It was the greatest revival since apostolic times, as God opened the minds of His people to certain prophecies in Daniel and Revelation. Bible students the world over came to identify the second beast of Revelation 13:11 as Protestant America, the beast with horns like a lamb, who eventually would speak like a dragon. The "unthinkable" is what caused this power's voice to change from that of Jesus, the lamb, to Satan, the dragon: its rejection of that advanced light God shined upon them at that time, during the Great Awakening.

> God has a controversy with the churches of today. They are fulfilling the prophecy of John. "All nations have drunk of the wine of the wrath of her fornication." They have divorced themselves from God by refusing to receive His sign. They have not the spirit of God's true commandment-keeping people. And the people of the world, in giving their sanction to a false Sabbath, and in trampling under their feet the Sabbath of the Lord, have drunk of the wine of the wrath of her fornication. (*Seventh-day Adventist Bible Commentary*, vol. 7, 979)

The rejection of that light sent from God changed the way Protestant America used its power from that of a "lamb" to that of a "dragon"

(Revelation 13:11). In the world at that time, only the United States of America, with its unique Protestant heritage and Republican form of government and its potential to turn into a nation that could use its power to speak like a dragon after rejecting the first and second angels' messages, fits the characteristics of that power described in Revelation 13:15; the power that will become the image of the beast. Even more so today, since those Protestant denominations, which used to be God's remnant, have accepted Roman Catholic doctrines upholding the use of spiritualism and supernatural power. This image is established when the beast of Revelation 13:11 resorts to the use of civil power to enforce its doctrines upon the people of America.

> He had power to give life unto the image of the beast that the image of the beast should both speak and cause that as many as would not worship the image of the beast should be killed. (Revelation 13:15 KJV)

Be sure to understand that the power needed to accomplish this union of church and state in our free nation can only occur when it is empowered by its partnership with Roman Catholicism, when it becomes intoxicated with the wine (false doctrines) of Babylon. Inspiration gives a short history of this development:

> It was apostasy that led the early church to seek the aid of the civil government, and this prepared the way for the development of the papacy—the beast. Said Paul: "There" shall "come a falling away ... and that man of sin be revealed." (*The Great Controversy*, 443)

So apostasy in the church will prepare the way for the image to the beast. And the Bible declares that before the coming of the Lord there will exist a state of religious declension similar to that in the first centuries.

> In the last days perilous times shall come. For men shall be lovers of their own selves, covetous, boasters, proud ... having a form of godliness, but denying the power thereof. (2 Timothy 3:1, 5 KJV)

> Now the Spirit speaketh expressly, that in the latter times some shall depart from the faith, giving heed to seducing spirits, and doctrines of devils. (1 Timothy 4:1 KJV)

Satan will work "with all power and signs and lying wonders, and with all deceivableness of unrighteousness." And all that "received not the love of the truth, that they might be saved," will be left to accept "strong delusion, that they should believe a lie." 2 Thessalonians 2:9–11. When this state of ungodliness shall be reached, the same results will follow as in the first centuries." (The Great Controversy, 444, emphasis added)

It is the acceptance of spiritualism among the Protestant churches that opens the door. These two powers carry out their extensive missions without the knowledge that they are under the direct leadership of Satan, the prince of darkness. This frightful condition can be understood in light of Scripture revealing the rise of the papacy, also known as "the man of sin," "mystery of iniquity," "little horn" in Daniel 7, and the first beast of Revelation, chapter 13, cited above.

To recap: the image of the beast is seen to be apostate Protestant America, filling the conditions for its rise in Revelation 13:11–18. They were once the people of God but rejected the advanced light proclaimed during the 1830s and '40s in the first and second angels' messages.

Inspiration counsels us to investigate thoroughly, as these powers join forces to fight against the people of God in these last days. Now is the time for us to seek after the knowledge that will expose the mysterious workings of the "mystery of iniquity." We have the counsel to do so and have been given the Lord's knowledge of some of the workings as Satan attempts to deceive the people of God. Let us read God's instructions and revelations concerning the working of this power:

As we near the close of time, there will be greater and still greater *external parade of heathen power; heathen deities will manifest their signal power, and will exhibit themselves before the cities of the world; and this delineation has already begun to be fulfilled. By a variety of images the Lord Jesus represented to John the wicked character and seductive influence of those who have been distinguished for their persecution of God's people. All need wisdom carefully to search out the mystery of iniquity that figures so largely in the winding up of this earth's history. ...* In the very time in which we live, the Lord has called His people and has given them a message to bear. *He has called them to expose the wickedness of the man of sin who has made the Sunday law a distinctive power, who has thought to change times and laws, and to oppress the people of God who stand firmly to honor Him by keeping the only true Sabbath, the Sabbath of creation, as holy unto the Lord.* (*Testimonies to Ministers and Gospel Workers*, 117, emphasis added)

Notice our instruction to expose the wickedness of the man of sin, who will oppress the people of God once again, and note its connection with secret societies and confederations used to fight against God's law.

All need wisdom carefully to search out the mystery of iniquity that figures so largely in the winding up of this earth's history. God's presentation of the detestable works of the inhabitants of the ruling powers of the world who bind themselves into secret societies and confederacies, not honoring the law of God, should enable the people who have the light of truth to keep clear of all these evils. More and more will all false religionists of the world manifest their evil doings; for there are but two parties, those who keep the commandments of God and those who war against God's holy law. (*Manuscript Releases*, vol. 8, 322, emphasis added)

Our goal in this chapter is to gain an understanding of the principles that guide each of these powers as they attempt to reach the world with their message. This will help us see the big picture and the dangers that the remnant church will confront; dangers brought to light in the Spirit of Prophecy. We will investigate certain teachings and practices of Roman Catholicism, with origins and purposes unknown or misunderstood, such as the meaning of the liturgy, sacraments, prayers, and music. We will focus primarily on the meaning behind the liturgical structure and the various types of prayers.

Just as the papacy introduced what we call, "counter-reformation theology" in its attempt to stifle the Protestant Reformation, she is now introducing a theology that is a mystical hodgepodge of pantheism and spiritualism, artfully dressed up to appear as an acceptable Christian teaching, all for the purpose of hindering the work of reaching the world with the truth. Consider how illogical it would be to think the papacy would not use the plan of introducing false theories it used with such success in the "counter reformation" now, in this final conflict, and how unwise it would be for God's people not to investigate new theories being espoused by many in our church before beginning to practice them.

We will show how mysticism is the most important spiritual element in these new teachings, and their use is the major factor in papal plans to evangelize the whole world. We will also show how many of the Protestant churches have already accepted these teachings and are practicing them in a rapidly growing new movement called the "emerging church."

In order to influence the Seventh-day Adventist Church with these mystical teachings, Satan has wisely used the relationship we have formed with other Protestant churches, over the last twenty-five years, knowing we would be more comfortable exchanging information with them than with the papal power directly. We are at the point now where there is a regular exchange of theological ideas, teachings, theories, and evangelistic plans; a result of being enticed to mingle with them, for one reason or another, seeking their knowledge and experience, even though we have been warned not to. In doing this, we have ignored the voice of the Holy Spirit, speaking through the testimony of Jesus, saying that *if God has any new light to give to His beloved church He will give it to them and not to those churches that make up Babylon, from whom He has called us out.* A recent example of violation of this counsel is in our attendance at seminars offered by the Willow Creek Church.

Satan is in a life and death struggle, knowing his time is short, and will not hold back in the use of any means at his disposal to gain an advantage over the people of God. He is brilliant, with power, intelligence, and an understanding of the weaknesses of man far beyond what we have ever imagined. He is not sitting idly by while we proclaim the three angels' messages around the world, but is doing whatever God will allow him to do to deceive God's people. We know from the Testimonies that he has been given free rein to use the power of spiritualism as he will to deceive God's people. As we have also been warned, he is doing all he can to make the Testimonies "of none effect."

> The very last deception of Satan will be to make of none effect the testimony of the Spirit of God. (*The Faith I Live By*, 296)

He knows that all he has to do is to entice us into an attitude of indifference toward the Testimonies; that open rebellion is not required, for success is guaranteed by our simple decision to not seek after the warnings they contain.

We have been warned that Satan would present this masterpiece of deception to God's people and only those who heed the warnings in the

Spirit of Prophecy would be shielded from its deadly influence. This is his final attempt to destroy God's remnant church; we know he will do this and yet, for some reason we have turned a blind eye to these warnings, thinking those who lift up their voices about such things are misguided and extreme in their views, a reaction foretold by inspiration.

Through our unhealthy mingling with apostate Protestantism, a mingling the papal authorities know we would never have with them firsthand, she has managed to interject some of her mystical teachings into God's remnant church. We will see through the writings of the last two popes that this mingling and pulpit exchange is not accidental, but a plan that has been in the making for decades.

To more easily analyze the dynamics of the "end-time" scenario, let us consider the two powers that join forces (the beast and its image) as one, and God's remnant, the other. The mission of both is to proclaim a message that reaches every person on earth in preparation for the second coming of Jesus Christ. These two institutions, however, are directly opposed to one another, with the total success of either resulting in the utter failure of the other. This is because Satan is the leader of one power and the Lord Jesus Christ, the other.

What we are witnessing presently in the world is the beginning of the climactic battle of the great controversy, Armageddon, which has heretofore been hidden under the guise of Christian evangelization. Until Sunday legislation, the counterfeit system will not rely on compulsion, just deceit, as they forge ahead on two fronts, one being the deception of the world with false doctrine and supernatural power, the other its attempt to corrupt the remnant church with their mystical teachings. *This point is essential to understand the danger we are attempting to expose.* We repeat, there are two fronts Satan has developed in his battle to survive, one is to deceive the world at large through miracles and false teachings, and the other is the attempt to have his mystical masterpiece of deception accepted by the remnant church through our relationship with apostate Protestantism.

In the following paragraphs we will try to summarize the dynamics of how these two powers operate.

God's remnant is limited in its methods of evangelism by its faithfulness to the law of God and righteous behavior; while the other, the beast and its image, will do anything it can, even using force to win believers. It is important to understand the principles outlined below, explaining how these two opposing powers operate.

In their attempt to convince the world of the message they proclaim, the counterfeit church is aided by satanic supernatural powers who have the ability to speak directly to the minds of the people and who are not restricted by their adherence to the law of God. This lawlessness allows the use of compulsion and deceit and is the source of its power.

As the true church attempts to convince the world of the message she has to proclaim, she is aided by divinely empowered supernatural forces, who also can speak directly to the minds of the people. The choice made by heavenly beings and human beings alike to keep God's law restricts the use of compulsion or deceit, but places them on the side of divinity, the source of righteousness and infinite power.

So this final battle, called Armageddon, is a battle in which spiritual forces contend over the wills of men. On one side miracles, false teaching, and legislative power are used to deceive and force people into making a decision to worship the beast and his image, while God's people go into all the world with an offer of righteousness based on the witness of their unity and love for one another and scriptural truth, empowered in their proclamation by the Holy Spirit as they offer all men the opportunity to choose to join them in worshipping God according to His standard of righteousness. There will be no weapons of war, just Bible truth and a demonstration of divine love and righteousness against the masses of the world using compulsion, the law of the land, and false miracles to persuade men to join their ranks under the threat of imprisonment or death.

Please carefully consider this next statement.

In order for the church to remain under divine influence and protection, it must adhere to the ways of righteousness revealed in Scripture and must also heed the inspired warnings it has received in the Spirit of Prophecy. It is through this commitment, the commitment to follow the instructions given and heed the warnings given, that we maintain righteousness and the divine power needed to fulfill our mission. Without it, we will succumb to the sophistries of Satan in his last and most powerful attack on the remnant church.

As we have pointed out, in the war we are fighting against the "man of sin," he is not only proclaiming a false gospel all over the world but has also taken countermeasures against the people of God. Those countermeasures include a plan to bring in false teachings and deceive God's true workers, causing a false revival and leading God's people astray. Ellen White saw what Satan was trying to do more than 100 years ago, telling us what would have taken place at that time had God's people not stood up and met the deception head on. Here, once again, is a part of what she saw:

The enemy of souls has sought to bring in the supposition that *a great reformation was to take place among Seventh-day Adventists,* and that this reformation would consist in *giving up the doctrines which stand as the pillars of our faith, and engaging in a process of reorganization. ...* The principles of *truth that God in His wisdom has given to the remnant church would be discarded. Our religion would be changed. The fundamental principles that have sustained the work for the last fifty years would be accounted as error. A new organization would be established. Books of a new order would be written. A system of intellectual philosophy would be introduced. The founders of this system would go into the cities, and do a wonderful work. The Sabbath, of course, would be lightly regarded, as also the God who created it. Nothing would be allowed to stand in the way of the new movement.* (*Selected Messages*, 204, emphasis added).

These are some things that would have been if the church leaders did not take a stand in rejecting the "alpha" apostasy. The Lord also allowed her to see the final phase of Satan's masterpiece of deception, which she called the "omega," and whatever it was that she beheld was "startling" and made her "tremble" for the church. In her thorough analysis of this topic there are many warnings and instructions given, which imply that the conditions mentioned above will also be part of the final apostasy.

Let us now build our case for finally presenting the strategy of the enemy. Based on the counsel we have in the Spirit of Prophecy, there will be a supernatural element to Satan's final masterpiece of deception aimed at the remnant church. We know from Scripture and the Spirit of Prophecy that papal Rome fits largely into the coming conflict, and we have been counseled to learn all we can concerning her plans and strategies.

We have the testimony of this world's history to teach us her ways. As we peer back through the portals of time, we see a power that will do anything to attain her goals and to lead people away from truth. We see a power that has cloaked itself in every way with worldly beauty, things most attractive and appealing to fallen human nature. It wears a shroud of holiness and piety, concealing the wickedness of her true intentions. This is the power the Bible calls "the mystery of iniquity," and claims will attempt to deceive the entire world at the end of time.

If history is to be repeated, this power will do anything to bring down God's church, replacing the truth of the three angels' messages, with a false teaching—a teaching that will replace Christ's ministry in the sanctuary in heaven. For the last 500 years, the Jesuits, founded by Ignatius Loyola, have dedicated themselves to defending the pope and spreading Roman Catholic influence, power, and theology around the world. We should expect this deceitful organization to be directly involved in the final conflict and should consider history's evidence that they will do anything, even give their lives to succeed.

We can expect this power to attempt to reach into God's church with her teachings, winning over people in influential positions because this is the very technique history proves was used in the past. We must beware of those in God's church who would bring in false teachings learned by attending schools and seminars held by those organizations we identify as Babylon, especially teachings that present a pantheistic God and which do away with our need for Christ's ministry in the sanctuary in heaven.

Is there such a thing happening? Are there some in God's remnant church who have learned papal doctrines that undermine the foundational pillars of the Seventh-day Adventist Church, especially Christ's heavenly ministry?

There are definitely new teachings and practices that have come into our church that include mystical papal doctrines, but let it be understood that only God Himself knows who among those that have accepted these new teachings have forsaken the holy covenant. On the other hand, it is a fact beyond doubt that this is occurring and many are deceived by this new practice.

We need to point out once again that we are not saying that the papacy in any way has infiltrated our church or has spies in our church. The Lord Jesus Christ is at the head of the church and is in absolute control, able to prevent it from being taken over by any evil powers, and He does! This is not to say, however, that in His providence He would not allow the church to be threatened by false teachings, for the Testimonies reveal just such an event for the purpose of bringing revival.

Now, let us consider this scenario as a possibility: for one reason or another, some are attracted to these new discipleship programs that promise revival and excitement, along with a new spiritual experience that leaves behind the guilt of unbelief and rebellion. These are the same teachings sweeping the new revival we have identified as the "emerging church." Many of the leaders in this "emerging church," like George Barna and Richard Foster, are bringing their theories in a program called spiritual formation to Seventh-day Adventists at seminars, as well as in our classrooms.

Soon, many of our leaders will be attending seminars at institutions that have been created by the other Protestant denominations and the Roman

Catholic Church, solely for the purpose of training disciples in spiritual formation. The Shalem Institute in Maryland is one example where many of our leaders have received this training. As a part of the program they have learned a type of prayer called "contemplative," and have learned that they will eventually experience the "silence," the "quiet place," or the "stillness," where they will come into the presence of God.

They have now been to the "silence," and everything is changed. They have been in the presence of Jesus; perhaps they even heard His voice speak to them and are filled with enthusiasm and a motivation they have never known before. They have a new love for everyone, a love they had never known before. They sense the presence of God in their lives like they never did before and even feel His Spirit guiding them in every step they take, as they go forward fulfilling His mission in and through their lives.

There is something else they seem to experience beside all this; it is a connection between all people, as if they were all part of the same supernatural body, the body of Christ, all of them, everyone. They see God in all people, in all humanity, and are somehow connected; as a matter of fact, they feel connected to everything. What a wonderful loving and uniting experience, with all people and all things. This is truly an experience they never thought they would have this side of heaven.

Another aspect of their experience is that they realize how this experience has caused them to grow beyond anything they ever dreamed possible. They are convinced that this is something the church at large must have, or it will never get out of the kindergarten experience it presently has.

What I have just described is about as close as one can get to the experiences described by Roman Catholic mystics and others like Madame Guyon, Teresa of Avila, Francis de Sales, Henri Nouwen, Thomas Merton, and Richard Foster. All these are proponents of the "silence," and subscribe theologically to a pantheistic god.

It is a fact that some of our beloved church members have received training at various institutes and schools where they have learned the Roman Catholic discipline called spiritual formation, with its "contemplative/mystical prayer." Considering that a new, mystical Roman Catholic teaching, which sweeps away the efficacy of Christ's heavenly ministry, has found a foothold in the Seventh-day Adventist Church and that we have made application of a prophecy that Ellen White said would have another fulfillment in the future that predicts such an occurrence, wouldn't it be wise to investigate further into the motivations and movements of the papal power to see if we can uncover their plans?

Whatever made Ellen White tremble and fear for the safety of the church is the very thing we are talking about in this chapter, the second "front" in the war we have called the "end-time crisis."

Before looking into the plans of Roman Catholicism, let us review the meaning of what we have covered thus far. We are involved already in the Battle of Armageddon, a spiritual battle in which we have one choice to make. Will we serve God by submitting to His conditions, or not?

That's it, period. If we don't make that decision, the other is already made for us, for we are on the enemy's team and under his control.

To submit to the conditions of God means we search for and follow the warnings and admonitions given to us specifically for this occasion. We have been told that those who lose their way are those who would not heed the warnings God has given; it's as simple and as profound as that. God raised up a prophet for this cause, to lead and guide His people into the heavenly Canaan. If we refuse to study and search for understanding in the inspired writings God has given to His church, what more can God do for us? If we blindly follow new teachings such as spiritual formation's "contemplative/mystical prayer," having never sought out whether there are warnings concerning this kind of teaching, there is nothing more that can be done for our protection. It would be presumptuous to expect God to prevent us from going to Roman Catholic institutes to learn about such things when we have already been instructed not to go.

There will always be new teachings with the potential to charm and deceive us into believing we will have a more powerful experience. We need to deny such temptations and seek counsel from the testimonies God has given us. A Scripture was shown to the Lord's messenger to apply to just such temptations, and her comments follow

> Beware lest any man spoil you through philosophy and vain deceit, after the tradition of men, after the rudiments of the world, and not after Christ. For in Him dwelleth all the fullness of the Godhead bodily. And ye are complete in Him, which is the head of all principality and power. (*The Acts of the Apostles*, 473)

I am instructed to say to our people: Let us follow Christ. ... *We may safely discard all ideas that are not included in His teachings.* I appeal to our ministers to be sure that their feet are placed on the platform of eternal truth. *Beware how you follow impulse, calling it the Holy Spirit. Some are in danger in this respect.* I call upon them to be sound in the faith, able to give everyone who asks a reason of the hope that is in them. (*Counsels for the Church*, 326, emphasis added)

We are all given the power of choice, and it is essential that we choose to serve Jesus and submit to the heavenly agencies that have been ordained for our protection. Not to do so places us in a position where the beast and his image will have the power to coerce or deceive us into following them, where control by supernatural forces will take place, resulting in our complete and utter deception. We will unknowingly be deceived, believing that those warning us are the deceived ones. What a frightening condition to be in. It is necessary for us to understand the concepts outlined thus far in this chapter in order to see the danger of even tampering with new theories or attending meetings that we have been warned not to attend.

The battle is over our minds, and the fact that we have been mingling with those churches called Babylon at a level where we have sought their instructions, against the counsel we have been given, places us where Satan has had access to our minds, a dangerous place to be. With this understanding it is time to look into the plans and methods outlined by Pope John Paul II and examine apostolic letters and encyclicals he has written.

We will see the instructions given to the Catholic Church at-large, containing their strategy to win over every inhabitant of this world. We will be especially surprised to see that the use and training of spiritual formation's mystical element, contained in contemplative/mystical prayer, lies at the very heart of their strategy!

Chapter 13
The Mystery of Iniquity

As we read in the previous chapter:

All need wisdom carefully to search out the mystery of iniquity that figures so largely in the winding up of this earth's history." (*Testimonies to Ministers and Gospel Workers,* 117, emphasis added)

Why would we be thus instructed? Why not simply preach the truth instead of spending time attempting to discover the ways of Satan's ingenious counterfeit? God in His wisdom understands how we are tempted to continue down the path we are on, even when we have veered off from the straight and narrow. Pride can be a powerful adversary, driving us to ignore the quiet pleas of our conscience. The Lord knows that our knowledge of the truth alone is not enough to protect us from Satan's final work of deception, so subtle and appealing to the fallen nature that if it were possible, it would "deceive the very elect." He has exposed the enemy's plans in the Spirit of Prophecy and is telling us pointedly, the only way to victory is to have a personal knowledge of Satan's plans and activities.

I recall how often, while sharing the wonderful truth of the seventh-day Sabbath, the statement was made, "Don't tell me the rest, because then I'll be responsible for it." If we discover something that will cause us to have to commit to taking more time to study and might also result in the need to alter course in our spiritual journey, our human nature will be tempted to ignore it. In this instance, we would be making a fatal mistake. Here are some things to consider.

Satan has brainpower that far exceeds that of human beings, and after observing our race for 6,000 years he has such a grasp of how the human psyche functions that, when compared with the greatest minds on earth, earthlings would seem as little children. Add to this his supernatural power and his leadership ability, having led the angelic host now leading an army of fallen angels that rival his intelligence, and we will begin to realize that this is a force to contend with that is deadly, extremely talented, deceptive, and definitely playing for keeps. Consider also that this group of supernatural beings has had two thousand years to create the counterfeit church, and it's not difficult to realize the papal system must be the absolute ultimate in its appeal to the fallen humanity it was prepared for, and it is.

Besides being extremely logical, it is alluring, fascinating, beautifully artistic, musically excellent, captivating, mysterious, haunting and mystical, enchanting, charming, delightful, enjoyable, wonderful, pleasant, and on and on and on, and most importantly, subtle, cunning, deceptive, evil, and deadly. Our only hope in such a situation is being on the side of the infinite, all-knowing God, who can open our eyes to the danger and protect us. Does this help in seeing why we are encouraged in the Spirit of Prophecy to investigate?

Satan is using his immeasurable talents and power to the uttermost, as any living being would whose life is threatened. It would be a grave error to ignore the fact that there is a second front in this battle with Satan, a battle we have been warned about in the Testimonies. Considering all this, we can see Satan's desire that in this struggle, one of his last offensive moves would be to make of "none effect" the inspired counsels of Ellen White. He knows success lies in our ignorance of the counsels that expose his deadly plans.

Often, some use the statement from the Spirit of Prophecy that says,

We may have less to say in some lines, in regard to the Roman power and the papacy. (*Evangelism*, 577)

Here again is one of those subtle and cunning attempts to silence the voice of the remnant church in its proclamation of the three angels' messages.

Throughout history, the papacy has always adjusted her outward appearance to appear attractive to the masses, desiring to be considered the spiritual leader of the time, while remaining the same internally, never altering her evil nature or intentions. When some of those evil characteristics are exposed, she invents others to take their place. This is a part of the reason the words "in some lines" were used in that statement.

To imply, as some have, that we should no longer continue to expose the deceptions of Satan's ultimate weapon in his war against God is to aid him in this rebellion. He is intent on dragging humanity down with him to perdition, and has created a masterful deception in the counterfeit church.

To believe for the sake of political correctness that we should be silent about Roman Catholicism's false teachings is to be duped by the enemy. Carrying out our mission to warn the world of the beast and its image and calling out God's people must of necessity include giving the reasons for them to take that vital step. Why else would anyone make such an important, life-changing decision? Inspiration says:

The Roman Church is far-reaching in her plans and modes of operation. She is employing every device to extend her influence and increase her power in preparation for a fierce and determined conflict to regain control of the world, to re-establish persecution, and to undo all that Protestantism has done. (*The Great Controversy*, 565)

Men are closing their eyes to the real character of Romanism, and the dangers to be apprehended from her supremacy. The people need to be aroused to resist the advances of this most dangerous foe to civil and religious liberty. (*The Great Controversy*, 566)

After these things I saw another angel come down from heaven, having great power; and the earth was lightened with his glory. And he cried mightily with a strong voice, saying, Babylon the great is fallen, is fallen, and is become the habitation of devils, and the hold of every foul spirit, and a cage of every unclean and hateful bird, for all nations have drunk of the wine of the wrath of her fornication, and the kings of the earth have committed fornication with her, and the merchants of the earth are waxed rich through the abundance of her delicacies. And I heard another voice from heaven, saying, Come out of her, my people, that ye be not partakers of her sins, and that ye receive not of her plagues. For her sins have reached unto heaven, and God hath remembered her iniquities.

Reward her even as she rewarded you, and double unto her double according to her works in the cup which she hath filled fill to her double. How much she hath glorified herself, and lived deliciously, so much torment and sorrow give her for she saith in her heart, I sit a queen, and am no widow, and shall see no sorrow.

Therefore shall her plagues come in one day, death, and mourning, and famine; and she shall be utterly burned with fire: for strong [is] the Lord God who judgeth her. And the kings of the earth, who have committed fornication and lived deliciously with her, shall bewail her, and lament for her, when they shall see the smoke of her burning, Standing afar off for the fear of her torment, saying, Alas, alas that great city Babylon, that mighty city! for in one hour is thy judgment come. (Revelation 18:1–10 KJV)

Chapter 18 continues to expose the sins of Babylon in its illicit and materialistic relationship with the world. This is a part of the fourth angel's message, which swells to a loud cry and exposes the sins of Babylon. It is the message the world needs to hear without, however, any cutting or hurtful remarks pointed at innocent and deceived people. This is another element being addressed by Ellen White when she said we may have less to say about the papacy along certain lines. Some have always been offensive in revealing truth.

The gentleness and love of Jesus' righteous character, along with a genuine love and concern for their salvation, is needed in our striving to lead others to forgiveness and eternal life. Nothing should be said in anger, nor should there ever be bitter or condescending remarks, only a loving and active desire for their salvation, a love that can be seen. This is the love that was in Jesus' life, and is the love He showed us of the Father.

When God's people are called out from Babylon, they have every right to know and understand her sins; sins that Scripture says reached all the way to heaven. How can people be expected to make life-changing decisions without knowing why they should be made, and the facts concerning Babylon's deceptions? To think we should be silent and not expose Babylon's sins to those deceived is in itself simply another satanic deception.

With this understanding, let us now see if we can discover the subtle sophistries Satan has arranged in this system of deceptive worship. What is it that is so alluring about this system of worship that it captures the entire world? What is behind the mysterious rituals of the priest holding up the wafer and wine, or his prayers and chants as he swings the burning incense, spreading its hypnotic fragrance throughout the stunningly beautiful sanctuary? Is there special meaning to bells ringing, the lighting of candles, and the beautiful music used in worship? Is there something else hidden in these activities? *In the answers to these questions lies the secret of Satan's power over the human race! That's a powerful claim, but I believe you will agree.*

Through the extensive quoting which follows, including that of Pope John Paul II, my comments are distinguished by being enclosed in the following style of brackets [...]; all else is quoted from the papal writings identified. No corrections or changes have been made in punctuation or text, but the emphasis is mine.

Liturgy is defined in the *Encarta Dictionary for English* as a "form and arrangement of public worship laid down by a church or religion, or the order of things." In Roman Catholic tradition, the liturgy includes, among other things, the sacraments, prayers, chants and music, with the sacrament of the Eucharist being most important and at the center of every worship service (mass).

In the Protestant churches, the liturgy of worship services is meant to have the service be as spiritual as possible according to the customs and traditions of that particular people and the doctrine they believe in, bringing them into the atmosphere of worship.

In the Roman Catholic Church, the liturgy is the actual work of individual and corporate salvation. Satan has made it so, compelling all to participate in order to gain control of their minds. We must grasp this concept, for it will enable us to understand his deceptions.

The liturgy in the Roman Catholic Church is formulated to bring the worshipper into a mystical state; a level of consciousness where evil supernatural powers can speak directly to their minds, gaining hypnotic control. We will now follow the order of the references from Pope John Paul II and the new Catechism of the Roman Catholic Church.

APOSTOLIC LETTER *VICESIMUS QUINTUS ANNUS* OF THE SUPREME PONTIFF JOHN PAUL II
(b) *The self-manifestation of the Church*

9. Finally the Council *saw in the Liturgy an epiphany of the Church*: it is the Church at prayer. In celebrating Divine Worship the Church gives expression to what she is One, Holy, Catholic and Apostolic.

The Church manifests herself as one, with that unity which comes to her from the Trinity, especially when the holy people of God participates "in the one Eucharist, in one and the same prayer, at the one altar, presided over by the bishop surrounded by his presbyter-ate and his ministers." Let nothing in the celebration of the Liturgy disrupt or obscure this unity of the Church! The Church expresses the holiness that comes to her from Christ (cf. Eph 5:26–27) when, gathered in one body by the Holy Spirit who makes holy and gives life, she communicates to the faithful by means of the Eucharist and the other sacraments all the graces and blessings of the Father.

In liturgical celebration the Church expresses her catholicity, since in her the Spirit of the Lord gathers together people of all languages in the profession of the same faith and from East to West presents to God the Father the offering of Christ, and offers herself together with him.

In the Liturgy the Church manifests herself as apostolic, because the faith that she professes is founded upon the witness of the apostles; because in the celebration of the mysteries, presided over by the bishop, successor of the apostle, or by a minister ordained in the apostolic succession, she faithfully hands on what she has received from the Apostolic Tradition; and because the worship which she renders to God commits her to the mission of spreading the Gospel in the world.

Thus it is especially in the Liturgy that the Mystery of the Church is proclaimed, experienced and lived.

Catechesis and liturgy

1074 *The liturgy is the summit toward which the activity of the Church is directed; it is also the font from which all her power flows."* "It is therefore the privileged place for catechizing the People of God. Catechesis is intrinsically linked with the whole of liturgical and sacramental activity, for it is in the sacraments, especially in the Eucharist, that Christ Jesus works in fullness for the transformation of men."

1075 Liturgical catechesis aims to initiate people into the mystery of Christ *(It is "mystagogy.") by proceeding from the visible to the invis-ible, from the sign to the thing signified, from the "sacraments" to the "mysteries."* Such catechesis is to be presented by local and regional catechisms. This Catechism, which aims to serve the whole Church in all the diversity of her rites and cultures, *will present what is fundamental and common to the whole Church in the liturgy as mystery and as celebration* (Section One), and then the even sacraments and the sacramentals (Section Two).

1076   The Church was made manifest to the world on the day of Pentecost by the outpouring of the Holy Spirit. *The gift of the Spirit ushers in a new era in the "dispensation of the mystery" the age of the Church, during which Christ manifests, makes present, and communicates his work of salvation through the liturgy of his Church, "until he comes." In this age of the Church Christ now lives and acts in and with his Church, in a new way appropriate to this new age. He acts through the sacraments in what the common Tradition of the East and the West calls "the sacramental economy"; this is the communication (or "dispensation") of the fruits of Christ's Paschal mystery in the celebration of the Church's "sacramental" liturgy.*

[This last statement, in italics, is claiming that we are in a "new era," where the fruits of Christ's "paschal mystery" is a ministry where he manifests, makes present, and communicates to us through the liturgy.

How does this communication take place? Let us begin with Pope John Paul's anthropological views. They are telling!]

NOVO MILLENNIUM ineunte, section 23

Jesus is "the new man" (cf. Eph 4:24; Col 3:10), who calls redeemed humanity to **share in his divine life.** The mystery of the Incarnation lay's the foundations for an anthropology which, reaching beyond its own limitations and contradictions, **moves toward God himself, indeed toward the goal of "divinization."**

This occurs through the grafting of the redeemed on to Christ **and their admission into the intimacy of the Trinitarian life. ..."** "The Fathers have laid great stress on this soteriological dimension of the mystery of the Incarnation: it is only because the Son of God truly became man that man, in him and through him, can truly become a child of God.

[It is most significant that the pope is expressing his belief that the future of redeemed humanity is its "divinization," the moving toward the "trinitarian life," as he puts it. In other words, redeemed man becomes God.

Such agreement with the Eastern religions, plus the fact that he is a mystic, naturally results in the pope's acceptance of many of the practices of the Eastern religions. Satan has infused these religions with methods of prayer that allow entrance into altered levels of consciousness, such as spiritual formation's contemplative/mystical prayer. We will point out below the pope's use and support of the "methods" of prayer we are referring to.]

NOVO MILLENNIUM ineunte, sections 32–34

Prayer

32. This training in holiness calls for a **Christian life distinguished above all in the art of prayer.** The Jubilee Year has been a year of *more intense prayer,* both personal and communal. But we well know that prayer cannot be taken for granted. **We have to learn to pray:** . ... This reciprocity is the very substance and soul of the Christian life, and the condition of all true pastoral life. Wrought in us by the Holy Spirit, this reciprocity opens us, through Christ and in Christ, to **contemplation of the Father's face.** Learning this **Trinitarian shape of Christian prayer** and living it fully, **above all in the liturgy, the summit and source of the Church's life, but also in personal experience,** is the secret of a truly vital Christianity

33. Is it not one of the "signs of the times" that in today's world, despite widespread secularization, there is a widespread demand for spirituality, a demand which expresses itself in large part **as a renewed need for prayer**? Other religions, which are now widely present in ancient Christian lands, offer their own responses to this need, and sometimes they do so in appealing ways. But we who have received the grace of believing in Christ, the revealer of

the Father and the Savior of the world, have a duty to show to what depths the relationship with Christ can lead.

The great mystical tradition of the Church of both East and West has much to say in this regard. It shows how prayer can progress, as a genuine dialogue of love, to the point of rendering the person wholly possessed by the divine Beloved, vibrating at the Spirit's touch, resting filially within the Father's heart. This is the lived experience of Christ's promise:

"He who loves Me will be loved by My Father, and I will love him and manifest Myself to him." (John 14:21 NKJV)

It is a journey totally sustained by grace, which nonetheless demands an intense spiritual commitment and is no stranger to painful purifications (the "dark night").

But it leads, in various possible ways, to the ineffable joy experienced by the mystics as "nuptial union." How can we forget here, among the many shining examples, the teachings of Saint John of the Cross and Saint Teresa of Avila?"

[Here, Pope John Paul II is encouraging us to follow the *prayer methods* used by the mystics, St. John of the Cross and Teresa of Avila. St. John of the Cross describes in his book, *The Dark Night of the Soul*, how that low place in his life was the beginning of all his mystical experiences and is why Pope John Paul II made reference to it. These two Roman Catholic saints were friends, living in Spain during the 16th century; friends who shared in mystical experiences. Here is a quote from St. John describing the supernatural experience of "contemplative/mystical prayer."]

... an inflowing of God into the soul, which purges it from its ignorance's and imperfections, habitual, natural, and spiritual, and which is called by contemplatives infused contemplation or mystical theology. **Dark Night of the Soul, John of the Cross**

_____

[Here is a brief history of the relationship between the two:]

_____

The laxity that he found within the order disheartened him, and cooperating with his confidant and friend St. Teresa of Avila, St. John of the Cross worked for reformation of the Carmelites. Both he and St. Teresa of Avila founded other monasteries and convents and advocated disciplinary reforms. Their personal correspondence between each other is intensely mystical, describing in terms of human love the ecstasy and the agony of their struggles for personal spiritual perfection, *and specifically the mystical experience of the union of the human soul with God.* ("Mystica," online account of the mystical and the occult)

_____

[It is obvious that the pope is actually directing us to learn how to have mystical experiences. Let us continue.]

_____

Rosarium-virginis-mariae
A valid method ...

27. We should not be surprised that our relationship with Christ **makes use of a method.** God communicates himself to us respecting our human nature and **its vital rhythms.** Hence, while Christian spirituality is familiar with the most sublime forms of **mystical silence** in which images, words and gestures are all, so to speak, superseded by an intense and ineffable union with God, it normally engages the whole person in all his complex psychological, physical and relational reality.

This becomes apparent in the Liturgy. Sacraments and sacramentals are structured as a series of rites which bring into play all the dimensions of the person. The same applies to non-liturgical prayer. This is confirmed by the fact that, in the East, the most characteristic prayer of Christological meditation, centered on the words "Lord Jesus Christ, Son of God, have mercy on me, a sinner" is traditionally linked to the rhythm of breathing; while this practice favors perseverance in the prayer, it also in some way embodies the desire for Christ to become the breath, the soul and the "all" of one's life.

... which can nevertheless be improved

28. I mentioned in my Apostolic Letter *Novo Millennio Ineunte* that the **West is now experiencing a renewed demand for meditation,** which at times leads to a keen interest in aspects of other religions. Some Christians, **limited in their knowledge of the Christian contemplative tradition,** are attracted by those forms of prayer. While the latter contain many elements which are positive and at times compatible with Christian experience, they are often based on ultimately unacceptable premises. Much in vogue among these approaches are methods aimed at attaining a high level of spiritual concentration by using techniques of a psychophysical, repetitive and symbolic nature. *The Rosary is situated within this broad gamut of religious phenomena, but it is distinguished by characteristics of its own which correspond to specifically Christian requirements.*

In effect, the Rosary is simply a method of contemplation. As a method, it serves as a means to an end and cannot become an end in itself. All the same, as the fruit of centuries of experience, this method should not be undervalued. In its favor one could cite the experience of countless Saints. This is not to say, however, that the method cannot be improved. *Such is the intent of the addition of the new series of mysteria lucis to the overall cycle of mysteries and of the few suggestions which I am proposing in this Letter regarding its manner of recitation.* These suggestions, while respecting the well-established structure of this prayer, are intended to help the faithful to understand it in the richness of its symbolism and in harmony with the demands of daily life.

[I pray you have seen enough evidence from Pope John Paul II himself to verify the fact that the liturgy of the Roman Catholic Church is meant to bring the worshipper into a mystical state where they believe God infuses into them the grace needed for salvation. As the devotee enters into each of the sacraments or other aspects of the liturgy, the mind is to be directed in such a way to communicate with "the Father's face" or the "Son's face" through the power of the Holy Spirit, thus receiving the life-changing grace of God. This is how to receive the "mystery," or the hidden knowledge of salvation, but is in reality the method of Satan's hypnotic and supernatural control. As the Spirit of Prophecy has warned, Satan weaves the threads of his thoughts and ideas into their minds and they fall under his control.]

29. Announcing each mystery, and perhaps even using a suitable icon to portray it, is as it were *to open up a scenario on which to focus our attention. The words direct the imagination and the mind* toward a particular episode or moment in the life of Christ. In the Church's traditional spirituality, the veneration of icons and the many devotions appealing to the senses, *as well as the **method of prayer proposed by Saint Ignatius of Loyola in the Spiritual Exercises, make use of visual and imaginative elements (the compositio loci), judged to be of great help in concentrating the mind on the particular mystery. This is a methodology, moreover, which corresponds to the inner logic of the Incarnation: in Jesus, God wanted to take on human features. It is through his bodily reality that we are led into contact with the mystery of his divinity.** ...*

31. Listening and meditation are nourished by silence.

After the announcement of the mystery and the proclamation of the word, it is fitting to pause and focus one's attention for a suitable period of time on the mystery concerned, before moving into vocal prayer.

I have felt drawn to offer a reflection on the Rosary, as a kind of Marian complement to that Letter and an exhortation to contemplate the face of Christ in union with, and at the school of, his Most Holy Mother. To recite the Rosary is nothing other than to *contemplate with Mary the face of Christ ...*

APOSTOLIC LETTER *ROSARIUM VIRGINIS MARIAE* OF THE SUPREME PONTIFF JOHN PAUL II

A discovery of the importance of silence is one of the secrets of practicing contemplation and meditation.

[This truth is why the spread of contemplative/mystical prayer is so essential to the spreading of the gospel in the Roman Catholic Church. Consider more from Pope John Paul II.]

The Rosary, reclaimed in its full meaning, goes to the very heart of Christian life; it offers a familiar yet fruitful spiritual and educational opportunity for personal contemplation, the formation of the People of God, and the new evangelization.

[We approach now the most important aspect in carrying out the instruction from the Spirit of Prophecy: to discover and understand the way the counterfeit church will work in the final conflict. Let us once again read the plans in the Mission Statement below, from Vatican II.]

The following quotations are taken from a Vatican ll Decree, and are instructions for the Catholic Church's New Evangelization of the world. The document was distributed worldwide.

Mission of the Catholic Church
DECREE *AD GENTES*
ON THE MISSION ACTIVITY OF THE CHURCH

Note in the following quotation from this Vatican ll document, and how mysticism absolutely essential, playing the central role in church's plan to evangelize the whole world. If we will lay aside our own theories and selfish desires, and comprehend what the following quotes reveal, we will see the danger of Seventh-day Adventist involvement with Roman Catholic mysticism:

"Religious institutes, working to plant the Church, and thoroughly Imbued with mystic treasures with which the Church's religious tradition is adorned, should strive to give expression to them and to hand them on, according to the nature and the genius of each nation. Let them reflect attentively on how Christian religious life might be able to assimilate the ascetic and contemplative traditions, whose seeds were sometimes planted by God in ancient cultures already prior to the preaching of the Gospel."

Institutes of the contemplative life, by their prayers, sufferings, and works of penance have a very great importance in the conversion of souls. ... In fact, these institutes are asked to found houses in mission areas, as not a few of them have already done, so that there, living out their lives in a way accommodated to the truly religious traditions of the people, they can bear excellent witness among non-Christians to the majesty and love of God, as well as to our union in Christ. ...

Worthy of special mention are the various projects for causing the contemplative life to take root ...

Since the contemplative life belongs to the fullness of the Church's presence, let it be put into effect everywhere.

40. Religious institutes of the contemplative and of the active life, have so far played, and still do play,

the main role in the evangelization of the world.

[Again:]

... the main role in the evangelization of the world.

(Note: This ends the use of brackets to identify the author's comments.)

I pray that you have been awakened by the adrenaline racing through your bloodstream as a result of reading this last sentence. Read the following very carefully, for it will help you to understand what is presently occurring in preparation for the final crisis in this world. These things are coming together precisely as predicted in Scripture and the Spirit of Prophecy, and must occur in both the spiritual and political realms.

As referenced above from the pen of the leader of the counterfeit church on earth, identified in Scripture as the sea beast of Revelation chapter 13, the Jesuit mysticism incorporated in Ignatian spirituality, better known today as spiritual formation, is to be used as the main tool to evangelize the world in fulfillment of the prophecy in Revelation 13:3, claiming that the whole world wondered after the beast whose deadly wound was healed.

What is occurring in the political realm is telling also, although this is not the subject of this book and will not be covered in detail: a cursory examination will be helpful to gain the big picture. This same organization is the primary power working behind the scenes to create a one-world government, placing herself in a most advantageous position to be their official one-world religion, a position she has coveted ever since receiving the deadly wound in 1798.

It is a fact that the Roman Catholic Church is covertly involved in efforts to unite the nations of Europe and, indeed, the entire world. A one-world order is extremely favorable, if not essential, for the success of her plans to regain control of the world.

The Protestant churches are in great darkness, or they would discern the signs of the times. The Roman Church is far-reaching in her plans and modes of operation. She is employing every device to extend her influence and increase her power in preparation for a fierce and determined conflict to regain control of the world, to re-establish persecution, and to undo all that Protestantism has done. (*The Great Controversy*, 565)

Their efforts include the instructions that success will be dependent upon the acceptance and practice of Ignatian spirituality by the leaders of Europe's nations. Isn't this astonishing? Why would this be? What could possibly be the connection between Ignatian spirituality, and the successful effort to unite Europe and create a one-world order?

To find an answer to this interesting question, let's review our understanding of end-time events as God has revealed them to us. We know the whole world will be brought under Satan's control as they wonder after the beast whose deadly wound was healed. We know the ten kings of Revelation 17 (10 kings representing the whole world) give their "power and strength" to the beast (papacy) for a short period of time just before Jesus returns. We can conclude then that something unites the nations of the world to support fully the goal and aims of the papacy—something unites and motivates them to stand with her in these final movements on earth, albeit for only a short period of time. We know that the "something" is spiritualism, as the spirits of demons gather the kings of the earth together at the extreme end of time.

Before that finally occurs, it is logical to conclude that governments, economies, and finances will unify under one system, allowing for the control that is necessary to attempt to compel the people of God into worshipping the beast and his image. How will the world reach this point? How will Satan so control the minds of the inhabitants of earth to make the decisions necessary to carry out his plans to unite the world behind him and to destroy God's remnant church? This is his goal and only hope in his frantic attempt to save his life. One possibility is the subject of this book, for spiritual formation is without doubt a satanic means of mind control and hypnotism.

How incongruous it is that God's chosen people could be so blinded to have accepted this dangerous teaching and practice, created specifically to win the world to Roman Catholicism and to destroy God's people; a practice formulated from the supernatural and satanic revelations of the founder of the Jesuits, Ignatius Loyola. Loyola's Jesuits played a major role in bringing down God's people in the counter reformation, as spoken of in this inspired statement:

At this time, the order of the Jesuits was created, the most cruel, unscrupulous, and powerful of all the champions of popery. ... There was no crime too great for them to commit, no deception too base for them to practice, no disguise too difficult for them to assume. Vowed to perpetual poverty and humility, it was their studied aim to secure wealth and power, to be devoted to the overthrow of Protestantism, and the re-establishment of the papal supremacy. ...

It was a fundamental principle of the order that the end justifies the means. By this code, lying, theft, perjury, assassination, were not only pardonable but commendable, when they served the interests of the church. Under various disguises the Jesuits worked their way into offices of State, climbing up to be the counselors of kings, and shaping the policy of nations. They became servants, to act as spies upon their masters. They established colleges for the sons of princes and nobles, and schools for the common people; and the children of Protestant parents were drawn into an observance of popish rites. All the outward pomp and display of the Romish worship was brought to bear to confuse the mind, and dazzle and captivate the imagination; and thus the liberty for which the fathers had toiled and bled was betrayed by the sons. The Jesuits rapidly spread themselves over Europe, and wherever they went, there followed a revival of popery." (*The Great Controversy*, 1888 ed., 234, 235)

We should ask at this time, is there reason to believe that this power is not once again doing the very work she was created for 500 years ago? Is her mission the same today and is there evidence she is actively engaged in it? A resounding "yes" is the answer, and exposing her use of Spiritual Formation, as well as the inroads she has made among God's people, is the purpose of this book.

How blind modern Israel can be when ignoring the warnings and admonitions in the Spirit of Prophecy. Remember, it is Satan's plan to create a one-world order and have the whole world wonder after the beast. Ignatian spirituality is the method by which Satan can gain control of the leaders of the European nations. This instruction and information came directly from the highest office in the Roman Catholic Church, the man they believed stood in place of our Lord and Savior Himself; a man who was one of the most respected in the world, the now-deceased Pope John Paul II.

We have just outlined the strategy and plans of the Roman Catholic Church to triumph over the inhabitants of the entire planet, authored by the most renowned and beloved pope in centuries, regarded by many as the voice of conscience for the world. His writings, in the form of apostolic letters, epistles, and encyclicals, contain in detail the form of mysticism that he desires to be brought back into the mainstream of church teaching and practice, a fact clearly revealed in his own writings.

Through the use of home missions and the establishment of "religious institutes of the contemplative and of the active life the fullness of the churches presence needs to be put into effect everywhere, leading the church into the next millennium." *(Apostolic Letter Rosarium Virginis Mariae of the Supreme Pontiff John Paul II)*

Here we have the plans of the papacy to win over the entire world: the use of satanic supernatural power, deceiving all who fall into the trap of attempting to learn how to reach out to God in prayer by using the mystical traditions taught to them by the institutes and home missions they have established. The point should be made that they are not alone in this work of deception, for those Protestant churches that have joined hands with them in this work are also establishing centers where these like methods and techniques can be studied. There are literally thousands of establishments nationwide teaching spiritual formation and its methods of mystical prayer.

The following is from the pen of Pope John Paul II:

I myself wanted to make explicit the contemplative treasure of this traditional prayer that has spread far and wide among the People of God. I therefore recommended its rediscovery as a privileged path to contemplation of the Face of Christ at the school of Mary. ...

12. The Liturgy offers the deepest and most effective answer to this yearning for the encounter with God. ... Pastors must ensure that the sense of mystery penetrates consciences, making them rediscover the art of "mystagogic catechesis," so dear to the Fathers of the Church. ...

we must foster in our communities with greater commitment is the experience of silence. We need silence.

... if we are to accept in our hearts the full resonance of the voice of the Holy Spirit and to unite our personal prayer more closely to the Word of God and the public voice of the Church." ... The spread also outside Christian worship, of practices of meditation that give priority to recollection is not accidental.

Why not start with pedagogical daring a specific education in silence

within the coordinates of personal Christian experience? Let us keep before our eyes the example of Jesus, who "rose and went out to a lonely place, and there he prayed. (Mk 1:35)

The Liturgy, with its different moments and symbols, cannot ignore silence.

(Apostolic Letter Spiritus et Sponsa of the Supreme Pontiff John Paul II)

John Paul's words propose that it is necessary for all to be taught how to attain the mystical experience personally, in their own spiritual lives, separate from the experience of the worship service. This is the reason, the primary purpose, for the establishment of the many institutes and home missions. Their plan is that all people must learn to enter into silence where Satan can gain control of the life through his subtle hypnotic powers. To deny this is to deny the teachings we have just discovered in the writings of Pope John Paul II.

This is a deceptive masterpiece that Satan is presently using against the people of God. As a false revival spreads around the world and all come to wonder after the beast, it is not far-fetched to consider the possibility that spiritual formation will be a major influence in the spreading of this counterfeit religion; neither is it far-fetched to see how he can gain control of minds, the very minds which will decide to destroy God's true and faithful children.

The power Satan has, and at the level he desires to individually control humans, can only be applied by bringing them into an altered state of consciousness. In this state, he teaches, convinces, trains, and motivates. It is here that a person has the life-changing experiences such as hearing God's voice, sensing His presence, and receiving their personal mission. In short, it is here that they are hypnotized. Yes, hypnotized. This is not the hypnosis we are accustomed to, but it is hypnosis nonetheless. It is hypnosis of the masses, the result of having thoughts originated from the prince of darkness woven into their thoughts, altering their beliefs and convictions until they no longer believe as they did, but now believe as he wants.

These are the conditions outlined in the Spirit of Prophecy for the final conflict on earth; the ideal way for a massive group of people to corporately agree and decide to destroy another group of people—a people having the light of God shining from their faces and the gentle, loving character of Jesus, who they represent.

An Appeal to God's Remnant People

As God's chosen people we have acknowledged that it is reasonable to assume that we are about to witness a worldwide resurgence of papal supremacy, made a reality through the same Jesuit dedication to the pope the world witnessed in the counterreformation. This time though, they will conquer not by assassination, but by conversion as "all the world wondered after the beast" through the deception of satanic-supernatural, Ignatian Spirituality (Revelation 13:3).

Brothers and sisters, we are the Israel of God; should we not cease our courtship of the churches God has told us are fallen, never to return to Him? Should we not end our attempt to win their friendship by seeking to incorporate their teachings into our church and schools of learning? Let us begin to heed the warnings and admonitions of the Spirit of Prophecy.

It is Satan's plan to have Papal Rome regain control of the world. Scripture is clear that the nations of our world will "have one mind, and shall give their power and strength unto the beast" (Revelation 17:13 KJV), facilitating her global strategy for political and spiritual control. These are her goals, and inspiration informs us that she has not changed, but is simply waiting for vantage ground to strike. The political and spiritual conditions in the world have changed rapidly over the last 25 years, and she now has that vantage ground.

The Protestant churches have reached "over the abyss," clasping the hands of spiritualism and papal Rome, and she is striking. She is actively moving behind the scenes among the political and religious leaders of the world, using her influence to secretly attain those goals she has been patiently waiting for, and the use of Ignatian Spirituality (spiritual formation) is essential to her success as we have shown in Pope John Paul II's apostolic letters.

My dear church family, what further evidence must be revealed to expose the danger of these teachings, teachings received directly from Satan through supernatural revelations to Ignatius Loyola, founder of the Jesuits, one of the cruelest organizations in existence?

Is there some good in these teachings of Loyola? Yes, as there is in every deceptive teaching and religion. Perhaps we need to remind ourselves once again of this:

> *If God has any new light to communicate, He will let His chosen and beloved understand it, without their going to have their minds enlightened by hearing those who are in darkness and error.* (*Early Writings,* 124, emphasis added)

Let us always remember how Jesus loves His church, and that no other is the "object of His supreme regard", and that we, as His "chosen and beloved" are the ones upon whom He will shine new light. Accepting this truth compels us to reject everything of Ignatian Spirituality. If we refuse to do so, will we learn to love its false teachings? Are we apt to eventually walk away from the family of God and become their greatest enemies? We must answer "yes."

Chapter 14
Conclusion

After the second resurrection, the lost live once again and cover the face of the earth while Jesus and the redeemed dwell safely within the walls of the New Jerusalem. The unfallen worlds throughout the universe join in with them, all focusing their attention on a most remarkable event for which they have waited more than six thousand years. Every creature in God's universe witnesses in panoramic vision across the face of the sky the complete history of the great controversy between Christ and Satan. All will see the drama of the ages unfold, from Lucifer's fall and rebellion in heaven, through the creation of this world and the fall of Adam and Eve, to the redemption of Planet Earth. They will behold every act in the drama, including the part they played, either for good or for evil. There will be no escape from completely and precisely beholding the results of every decision made. They will see that God is perfectly just in His dealings with each individual and that mercy and justice truly did meet together at the cross, where Jesus, our Creator and Savior, met the demands of justice by His inconceivable act of mercy. Eternity will tell the rest of the story.

No question will be left unanswered, no mystery left unsolved and no secret thing left unexplained. The fact that God does not have love, but is love, will be understood by the lost for the very first time. There will be no deception, none led astray, nothing concealed, and no one will be able to run or hide. All truth will be revealed, with God understood and intimately known as perfect, infinite, and eternal love. Then every knee shall bow.

It will be seen that the majesty and glory of God are far beyond what fallen mortals were led to believe. Those lost because of the spiritualistic delusions of the last days will see how shameful and presumptuous it was to think they had the right to speculate concerning His person or His presence. It will be understood why the Israelites trembled and fell upon their faces when He revealed just a small portion of His glory at the pinnacle of Mt. Sinai, and why the prophets fell as "dead men" at His presence. They will see how Satan's hypnotic power overcame them, resulting in the egotistical, presumptive, and panentheistic belief that God's actual person resided in their mortal, fallen beings, to be called upon as a servant at their command.

> His grace alone can enable us to resist and subdue the tendencies of our fallen nature. This power the spiritualistic theories concerning God, make of no effect. If God is an essence pervading all nature, then He dwells in all men; and in order to attain holiness, man has only to develop the power that is within him.

> These theories, followed to their logical conclusion, sweep away the whole Christian economy. They do away with the necessity for the atonement and make man his own savior. (*Testimonies for the Church*, 291)

I am convinced that a portion of the light that illumines the dark minds of the lost on that fateful day, the light that compels the bowing of the knee, will be that which reveals how more straightforward and "childlike" they were meant to be; the light that shows worldly wisdom for what it really is—foolishness in the light of truth; that man's confidence in his own, supposed wonderful mental accomplishments was actually satanic delusion, used as bait for their selfish ambitions.

Imagine, at the beginning, Adam awakening from the eternal silent night of nonexistence. As the first new light of God's perfect creation enters his beautiful eyes, his initial sight is that of the smiling, loving face of his Creator just seconds after He breathed the breath of life into his nostrils. What love, astonishment, and gratitude must have thrilled through Adam's being as he first comprehended that his Lord and Creator had just then given him the gift of life. I wonder if words of praise broke forth before tears of thankfulness and joy ran down his rosy cheeks. Someday, as we noted, mysteries will be revealed and truth will be known.

There is a God-given simplicity to man; a simplicity we can understand when we discern the meaning of Jesus' counsel to be as little children. He said that if we don't "become as little children," we will not enter into the kingdom of God (Matthew 18:3 KJV). This is a profound remark. Obviously Jesus was not referring to the childlike characteristics of immaturity, silliness, or irresponsibility. So what characteristics were they? To understand, let's go back to the Garden of Eden and observe Eve, before and after the fall.

Precise details aside, we can logically conclude that the childlike attributes to which Jesus referred were surely a component of Eve's innocent, sinless, and pure character. The answer to this question may lie at the heart of discovering why certain people in God's remnant church will be open to the deceptions of the "omega."

Eve was perfectly contented right up to the time she chose to "stay" near the tree of the knowledge of good and evil. That choice, the choice to "stay," was her first act of disobedience. She decided to stay *after* being warned by the angels that the couple's success in the trials they would face during their time of probation would depend largely on her remaining by Adam's side as they performed their day-to-day work in the Garden of Eden.

The tree of the knowledge of good and evil was located near the tree of life. Eve inadvertently wandered away from Adam's side and found herself near the forbidden tree. She was near the tree by accident and was innocent of any wrongdoing. Startled at first, she should have fled, but her self-reliance caused her to take the next step, which was outright disobedience. *She stayed when she should have fled.* She trusted in herself instead of trusting in the counsel of God. This counsel was given to Eve indirectly through angels that God appointed to instruct and warn her concerning the trials to come. This is important for God's people to understand and is the key that unlocks the mystery of why some will fall prey to the "omega." *She did not heed the warning God gave her.*

> The omega will follow, and will be received by those who are not willing *to heed the warning God has given.* (*Selected Messages*, 200, emphasis added)

Now, this is of utmost importance. At the moment Eve decided to *stay* near the tree, the *door opened* for Satan to approach and confront her. Please understand, God's angels *had to back away,* giving Satan access. The door opened because *she chose to ignore the warning God had given.* What more could God have done? He created her with the most precious gift of "free will," and because God is love, He cannot interfere with anyone's use of that gift. Her freedom of choice, like ours, is sacred to God and He will never violate that freedom, neither will He ever compel anyone to follow Him. Loving God is only possible when there is "free will." *Without free will, love cannot exist.*

The first step in apostasy is self-reliance, which leads to *choosing to ignore the warnings God has given in the Bible and Spirit of Prophecy*. It is this difficult and this simple!

Do you see—Eve was perfect and blissful. Her downfall was first caused by self-reliance, leading to questioning God's wisdom in restricting her behavior; then she *stayed in the face of danger, though she knew she was instructed to the contrary;* and finally, *she considered what Satan was saying by conversing and reasoning with him,* thinking herself wise enough to detect any danger. She wasn't. Neither are we.

The moment Eve began to consider Satan's words, he began gaining control of her mind. She fell under his hypnotic power. His "thoughts" mingled with her thoughts, affecting her desires and created an overpowering lust for secret power, compelling her to eat the fruit in order to obtain it—and then Eve was a child of God no more.

Early on, she had *thoughts* of self-reliance that were not yet "sin," but those thoughts nurtured her decision to *stay* in the presence of danger, consider when she shouldn't have, *reason* with the devil and, finally, *rebel and sin* by believing his lies and eating the forbidden fruit that she was told by God not to eat.

Let's further consider this process. As soon as Eve decided to stay, which was the result of her self-reliant thoughts, Satan had the right to confront her. He concealed his identity and spoke to her. Why? Because he had the right to, in light of the fact that she *stayed*. She first disobeyed God's warning, allowing Satan to confront her. In listening to his voice and considering his words, she fell under his control. *This is hypnotism in the sense that Ellen White suggests*. Neither Eve, nor any human, can allow themselves to listen to Satan's words without falling under his hypnotic, supernatural power. And this is why we must not ever seriously contemplate and discuss spiritualistic theories. It gives Satan the right to confront us. Again, why? Because to do so is to reject inspired counsel against it.

When he confronts us and we consider the ideas he presents to our minds, and begin to investigate those ideas, he gains control of our minds; we, of course, don't realize that it is *his* voice and/or thoughts flooding into our minds; thoughts and ideas he has been experimenting with for 6,000 years, learning how best to gain the most complete and rapid control. When these new thoughts are beheld we are amazed at our new, inspired outlook, convinced we have been in the presence of God. "He begins to exert his power over them just as soon as they begin to investigate his theories" (*Medical Ministry*, 101).

It is presumptuous to think we can learn more of the mystery of the Almighty through any other channel than the ones He gave us: Scripture, nature, and the Spirit of Prophecy. Yes, He speaks to us in prayer through the ministry and mystery of the Holy Spirit, but when we begin to peek down pathways leading to unknown destinations, pathways that hint of being those we have been warned not to travel on, we can be sure that deception lies ahead. From the beginning, Satan has offered to man secret knowledge with the inducements of having godly power and freedom from His law. This is most attractive to the carnal nature and is his most successful deception, as revealed by the growth and popularity of spiritual movements with these two elements at their core, such as New Age and "miracle"-based Christianity.

In the context of the omega, Ellen White said,

> I knew that I must warn our brethren and sisters not to enter into controversy over the presence and personality of God. (*Selected Messages*, Book 1, 203)

Over the ages, man has been intrigued by secret mysteries and supernatural power, searching endlessly for unknown mystical concepts of God. The simple truth about God, that He is, in fact, a personal being (the meaning Ellen White was conveying in using the word personality in the statement above), a person who can sit on His throne and is the likeness in whom we have all been created, is considered by some to be too simple and lowly a concept, an ego buster.

Many have preferred to believe that they are part of some great mystery they searched out and discovered by their superior mental power, which of course placed them above the ordinary, those who just are unable to comprehend because of their limited mental capacity. Such is, at least in part, the deception by which many fall into the "omega" and other deceptions. There are concepts of spirituality whose practice is often appealing to the carnal heart's desire for Godly powers and freedom from restrictive laws. "We must be more important than merely being created as little children, made to follow and love our Creator; the truth must be more stimulating, and we must be more powerful and complex."

Many flatter their egos with the desire to have a great mystery surrounding their existence that invariably leads to believing that we will become "like God." After all, if we believe that the very person of God dwells within us, then it is a truth that I AM GOD—pantheism/panentheism at its best! And this is the philosophy the Lord told his servant, Ellen White, to "meet without delay" in Battle Creek, and is also the foundation of Roman Catholic theology, the Mystery of Iniquity.

Many seek a deeper understanding of God, more light concerning our mission, God's personhood, how to have a deeper spiritual experience, church growth, the plan of salvation, and new methods of evangelism. When we seek information on any of these subjects outside of the Lord's denominated Seventh-day Adventist Church and the inspired writings He gave to it through the gift of prophecy, *we will fall under the deceptive, hypnotic influence of the prince of darkness!* Consider this inspired statement:

> If God has *any new light to communicate, He will let His chosen and beloved understand it, without their going to have their minds enlightened by hearing those who are in darkness and error.*
>
> I was shown the necessity of those who believe that we are having the last message of mercy, *being separate from those who are daily imbibing new errors.* I saw that *neither young nor old should attend their meetings;* for it is wrong to thus encourage them while they teach error that is a deadly poison to the soul and teach for doctrines the commandments of men. ... If God has delivered us from such darkness and error, we should stand fast in the liberty wherewith He has set us free and rejoice in the truth. *God is displeased with us when we go to listen to error,* without being obliged to go; for unless He sends us to those meetings. ... *He will not keep us."* (*Early Writings* 124, emphasis added)

As soon as we begin to search outside the church, disregarding the counsel quoted above and begin to look and consider teachings we have been warned to avoid, *Satan claims us as his,* and begins the hypnotic process. Just as Eve's choice to "stay" instead of flee gave him the right to confront her, so our decision to "stay" in the presence of what we've been warned against gives him the right to confront us. We are no match for his charming, hypnotic influence, and can never expect to be able to defend ourselves, ever, no exceptions!

Remember, this is not the breed of hypnotism we are accustomed to. It is a hypnotism resulting from Satan weaving his thoughts with ours, little by little, resulting in the change of our perceptions and beliefs.

This is a secret science over which God has allowed Satan to have absolute control; it's his backyard, his territory.

Here is a channel wholly devoted to himself and under his control, and he can make the world believe what he will. The Book that is to judge him and his followers he puts back in the shade, just where he wants it. (*Early Writings*, 91, emphasis added)

He is the master artist forming his final work, the "omega," his "Mona Lisa." Our only defense—*only defense*—is the counsel given in the Bible and the Spirit of Prophecy. Ignore the warnings, and we can be sure of losing eternal life.

Satan has been perfecting this science for six thousand years and knows precisely when and how to impart it to gain control over the minds of his subjects. Adam and Eve were hypnotized by Satan because they paid attention to his words and then reasoned with him. He will quickly gain hypnotic control of anyone who listens to his words and then reasons with him. Listening to any of his ideas is automatically registered in our brains and has been calculated by him to have an immediate effect upon our ability to reason and discern truth. This is a science that is beyond normal human understanding, even though inspiration does inform us that there are always some who open themselves to his instruction. Dr. Kellogg was one example.

We are absolutely mistaken, if we think we can discern Satan's deceptions when we have ignored inspired counsel. Satan will have the advantage from the very first word spoken. It is only by the perpetual presence of the Holy Spirit and ministering angels of God that we can stay free of Satan's hypnotic power.

We may feel we are able to detect hypnotism when we see it because we are acquainted with some commonly understood forms, those we have been exposed to over the years. We've been taught to avoid the dangerous practices of particular brands of meditation or alpha mental states, of using our power of focusing the mind, concentration, or the monotone voice of the professional hypnotist. Even though some in our medical institutions are ignorantly experimenting with techniques that have their roots in the Eastern philosophies and religions, these have been detected and are generally known by astute Seventh-day Adventist Bible students and are known to be avoided.

There has been an element of this type of spiritualism in the various Protestant churches and some of these practices have, at times, threatened the Seventh-day Adventist Church, but there is an infinitely greater threat to the remnant church today.

Satan has cunningly deceived some Seventh-day Adventists into thinking they can dialogue with or study teachings of other Protestant denominations or organizations to obtain enlightened theology or better methods of evangelism. Unfortunately, some Seventh-day Adventists have done this at a *level forbidden* in the Spirit of Prophecy. While there is nothing wrong with keeping open the doors of communication with other religious bodies, there is definite counsel against *seeking to learn their methods and teachings for our own benefit*. This is exactly what some have been doing, and it has resulted in the mingling of their methods and ideas with ours, swinging the doors wide open for the spread and practice of Roman Catholic spiritualism in the form of spiritual formation and its "contemplative/mystical prayer." As we have discovered, this is in reality ancient mysticism and is sweeping evangelical Christianity today, a form of spiritualism not uncharacteristic of end-time deceptions.

Is this the subtle and dangerous deception revealed to Ellen White through the Spirit of Prophecy, which is to endanger the church just prior to the close of probation? When she beheld it, she did "tremble." Let the reader decide!

As others with like experiences, I often questioned why God allowed me to remain deceived by various satanic sciences for five years, even though I searched for the truth from the very beginning. I have a better understanding now. The type of hypnotism used as a part of this deception will be discerned by those watchmen who have been there before.

We, who have experienced mysticism, recognize Satan's science, while those deceived by it are taken by its empowering and rejuvenating effect, convinced they have learned and experienced something beneficial to their Christian experience. The other component of its delusive power is mainstream Roman Catholicism; you experience what you believe to be the wonderful mystical power of God, without repentance, or any change of heart, able to continue in your sins. This makes it very easy to accept and has always been one of the secrets of Roman Catholicism's success.

These poor deceived souls will not walk around in a trance but will be hypnotized nonetheless. There will be no outward signs when God's chosen people ignore His counsel and "refuse to heed the warnings given" (*Spalding and Magan Collection*, 464), or when they begin to investigate the theories they have been instructed not to investigate. There will be no danger signals when they seek to learn the discipline of spiritual formation and train to center their minds in "contemplative/mystical prayer." They will have what they will consider to be the most spiritual experience of their lives, growing closer to God every day, highly motivated, energized and elated with their course, yet they *will be hypnotized and under Satan's control*. As the Lord's messenger counseled the church more than a hundred years ago, when threatened by the alpha, **"MEET IT WITHOUT DELAY,"**

**NOW IS THE TIME TO MEET THE PRESENT
DANGER, "WITHOUT DELAY."**

Epilogue

Our Message
by Ellen White, Manuscript Release No. 1103
—Instruction to the Church

The Lord has given us a message for the time in which we are living. This message is to be given with clear, distinct utterance. To proclaim this message demands all the talents and capabilities that God has given us.

The fourteenth chapter of Revelation outlines the work that is to be done by God's people. The everlasting gospel is to be preached and practiced. True missionary work is to be done, not in the wisdom of men, but in the wisdom of God.

John writes, "And I saw another angel fly in the midst of heaven, having the everlasting gospel to preach unto them that dwell on the earth, and to every nation, and kindred, and tongue, and people, saying with a loud voice, Fear God and give glory to Him; for the hour of His judgment is come, and worship Him that made heaven, and earth, and the sea, and the fountains of water" (Revelation 14:6–11, 12–14).

The third angel's message increases in importance as we near the close of this earth's history. Since the beginning of the proclamation of the first angel's message, many believers have fallen asleep in Jesus. Faithful standard-bearers have laid off their armor. But the work advances. Fresh workers are brought in as those who fall are laid away to rest until the coming of the Lord.

God has presented to me the dangers that are threatening those who have been given the sacred work of proclaiming the third angel's message. They are to remember that this message is of the utmost consequence to the whole world. They need to search the Scriptures diligently, that they may learn how to guard against the mystery of iniquity, which plays so large a part in the closing scenes of this earth's history. There will be more and still more external parade by worldly powers. Under different symbols,

God presented to John the wicked character and seductive influence of those who have been distinguished for their persecution of His people. The eighteenth chapter of Revelation speaks of mystic Babylon, fallen from her high estate to become a persecuting power. Those who keep the commandments of God and have the faith of Jesus are the object of the wrath of this power.

John writes: "And after these things I saw another angel come down from heaven, having great power; and the earth was lightened with his glory. And he cried mightily with a strong voice, saying, Babylon the great is fallen, is fallen, and is become the habitation of devils, and the hold of every foul spirit, and a cage of every unclean and hateful bird. For all nations have drunk of the wine of the wrath of her fornication, and the kings of the earth have committed fornication with her, and the merchants of the earth are waxed rich through the abundance of her delicacies. And I heard another voice from heaven, saying, Come out of her, my people, that ye be not partakers of her sins, and that ye receive not of her plagues. For her sins have reached unto heaven, and God hath remembered her iniquities. Reward her even as she rewarded you, and double unto her double according to her works: in the cup which she hath filled fill to her double. How much she hath glorified herself, and lived deliciously, so much torment and sorrow give her: for she saith in her heart, I sit a queen, and am no widow, and shall see no sorrow. Therefore shall her plagues come in one day, death, and mourning, and famine; and she shall be utterly burned with fire: for strong is the Lord God who judgeth her" (Revelation 18:1–8).

This terrible picture, drawn by John to show how completely the powers of earth will give themselves over to evil, should show those who have received the truth how dangerous it is to link up with secret societies or to join themselves in any way with those who do not keep God's commandments.

"And I beheld another beast coming up out of the earth; and he had two horns like a lamb, and he spake as a dragon. And he exerciseth all the power of the first beast before him, and causeth the earth and them which dwell therein to worship the first beast, whose deadly wound was healed. And he doeth great wonders, so that he maketh fire come down from heaven on the earth in the sight of men (Revelation 13:11–13).

Religious powers, allied to heaven by profession, and claiming to have the characteristics of a lamb, will show by their acts that they have the heart of a dragon, and that they are instigated and controlled by Satan. The time is coming when God's people will feel the hand of persecution because they keep holy the seventh day. Satan has caused the change of the Sabbath in the hope of carrying out his purpose for the defeat of God's plans. He seeks to make the commands of God of less force in the world than human laws.

The man of sin, who thought to change times and laws, and who has always oppressed the people of God, will cause laws to be made enforcing the observance of the first day of the week. But God's people are to stand firm for Him. And the Lord will work in their behalf, showing plainly that He is the God of gods.

God made the world, and then on the seventh day He rested, satisfied with His work. He blessed the day of His rest and set it apart as holy; and as He did this, the morning stars sang together, and all the sons of God shouted for joy. The Sabbath is a sign between God and His people—an evidence of His love and kindness, an assurance that He will bless them in obedience. By the observance of this day they are distinguished from the disloyal, who refuse to honor God. God has taken His people into covenant relation with Himself, and has pledged Himself to fulfill His purposes for them.

On the Sabbath no servile work is to be done. God has given man six days on which to work. He claims the seventh day as His own. On this day men are to worship Him. They are to contemplate the wonderful works of the Creator, praising Him for His goodness and love. By giving them the Sabbath, it was God's design to preserve among men a clear, definite knowledge of Himself as their Creator. He declares, "It is a sign between me and you throughout your generations; that ye may know that I am the Lord that doth sanctify you" (Exodus 31:13).

Christ declared to the Pharisees, "Think not that I am come to destroy the law, or the prophets: I am not come to destroy, but to fulfill. For verily I say unto you, Till heaven and earth pass, one jot or one tittle shall in no wise pass from the law till all be fulfilled. Whosoever therefore shall break one of these least commandments, and shall teach men so, he shall be called the least in the kingdom of heaven: but whosoever shall do and teach them, the same shall be called great in the kingdom of heaven" (Matthew 5:17–19).

Thus Christ rebuked the pretentious piety of the Pharisees, and by His manner of working He corrected their erroneous ideas regarding the law of God.

From the beginning there has been opposition between the forces of good and evil. God declared, "I will put enmity between thee and the woman, and between thy seed and her seed; it shall bruise thy head, and thou shalt bruise his heel" (Genesis 3:15).

Man had vainly attempted to exalt himself by following his own way, in harmony with Satan's temptations and in opposition to the will of God. He had thus gained knowledge of evil, but he had gained it at the cost of his loyalty; and his disobedience opened the floodgates of woe upon our world. Ever since, men have been trying to exalt themselves by the same means. When will they learn that the only way to true exaltation is the path of obedience? Men's plans may seem to them to be exceedingly wise, but there is no safety in them unless they walk in accordance with a "Thus saith the Lord."

How hard it is for man to walk humbly with God, to believe His word and accept His plans. Satan's propositions appear to present great advantages, but they end in ruin. Over and over again men have found out by experience the result of refusing to walk in the path of obedience. Will not others gain wisdom from their experience? Let us think of the experience of our first parents and be afraid of any plans that are not based on obedience to God's will.

When will men learn that God is God, not man, and that He does not change? Every calamity, every death, is a witness to the power of evil and to the truth of the living God. The Word of God is life, and it will abide forever. Through all eternity it will stand fast. How can man, knowing what God is and what He has done, choose Satan's way instead of God's way? There is only one path to Paradise restored—the path of obedience.

The message given man to proclaim in these last days is not to be amalgamated with worldly opinions. In these days of peril, nothing but obedience will keep man from apostasy. God has bestowed on man great light and many blessings. But unless this light and these blessings are received, they are no security against apostasy and disobedience. When those whom God has exalted to positions of high trust turn from Him to human wisdom, their light becomes darkness; and how great is that darkness. Their entrusted capabilities are a snare to them. They become an offense to God. There can be no mockery of God without the sure result. There always has been, and till the conflict is ended there always will be, a departing from God. Sins have a close connection. One act of disobedience, unless repented of, leads to another. He who justifies himself in sin is led on step by step in deception, till at length he sins with impunity.

Often the professed followers of Christ are found with hearts hardened and eyes blinded, because they do not obey the truth. Selfish motives and purposes take possession of the mind. In their self-confidence they suppose that their way is the way of wisdom. They are not particular to follow the path that God has marked out. They declare that circumstances alter cases, and when Satan tempts them to follow worldly principles, they yield, and, making crooked paths for their feet, they lead others astray. The inexperienced follow where they go, supposing that the judgment of Christians so experienced must be wise. Those in positions of responsibility who follow their own way are held responsible for the mistakes of those who are led astray by their example. "Shall I not judge for these things?" God asks.

It is a departure from the ways of the Lord that brings perversity that will not be humbled or corrected. Many, when reproved for their wrong course, harden their hearts and continue to follow wrong principles. Holding fast their own wisdom as precious, they sullenly pursue their own way. This is the reason that the Holy Spirit is not manifested with greater power in our churches. If those who have been corrected by the Spirit of God would humble themselves before the Lord, and gladly reform, Christ would bestow upon them rich gifts, answering their contrite prayers and helping them to understand themselves. There are those who think that they can improve upon the plan that God has made, that they can mark out for themselves a course better than the course He has marked out for them. Such ones, choosing the things that be of men, harden their hearts against God's leading, and follow their own way. Unless they repent, the time will come when they will look upon the utter failure of their life work. Man's wisdom, exercised without Christ's guidance, is a dangerous element.

Any recognition or exaltation gained apart from God is worthless, for it is not honored in heaven. To have the approval of men does not win God's approval. Those who would be acknowledged by God in the day of judgment must here listen to His counsels and be governed by His will. Only thus can they receive the rich blessings that will fit them to receive His commendation. They must hold fast to the truth until the end, refusing to be drawn from their allegiance by ambitious projects. They must put away from them every vestige of prevarication, because God will acknowledge no falsehood.

The Message in Revelation, by Ellen White, Manuscript Release No. 1305 —The Message in Revelation

I am not able to sleep past one o'clock. Things are presented to me that keep me wide-awake.

There are dangers before us that we are to avoid. Christ has laid down for His church great principles that are to be made known to the world in good works. His instruction on this point is given with authority. The principles to be maintained are valid for all time, shedding from age to age a clear, definite, steady light to be regarded by every tempest-tossed church that shall exist in our world. These principles are not to be confused with worldly-policy plans, but are to stand free from any binding about of God's people.

In endeavoring to harmonize with worldly sentiments, Dr. Kellogg does not discern the influences that are exercised upon the commandment-keeping people of God. His spiritual eyesight is not clear. Not all of his work is approved by God. No one who has had the light of truth before him for years, and has not yielded to its influence, can be expected to be sensitive to the clear, gospel sentiments of the truth. There is constant danger that the obedient and the disobedient in the world and in the nominal churches will become so amalgamated that the line of demarcation between him that serveth God and him that serveth Him not will become confused and indistinct.

The exaltation of a so-called medical missionary work, while the character of true medical missionary work has not been understood, has dishonored and displeased God. There is danger that the church, instead of being built upon the foundation, Jesus Christ, will be marred by the introduction of objectionable, base material; that worldly-policy principles will steal in as a supposed necessity in order to maintain influence with unbelievers; that wood, hay, and stubble will take the place of gold, silver, and precious stones, representations of heavenly principles that abide through time and through eternity.

Dr. Kellogg has not magnified the holy principles God would present to His people. The Lord does not acknowledge the methods that he has brought into the medical missionary work. These methods are confusing to the minds of God's people. Let Dr. Kellogg step from between his fellow physicians and the light of heaven for this time, then they will be able to see with anointed eyes how closely the medical missionary work is to be bound up with the proclamation of the message of this time.

The Lord has presented before me the dangers that are threatening His people who have the sacred work of proclaiming the third angel's message with clearness and distinctness. God's people must beware lest they be ensnared by unsanctified propositions. Our young people must not be placed where they will be misled by wrong sentiments. The truth is not to be blanketed. The message for these last days is to be given in no indistinct utterance.

"And I looked, and lo, a Lamb stood on the Mount Zion, and with Him an hundred and forty and four thousand, having His Father's name written in their foreheads. And I heard a voice from heaven, as the voice of many waters, and as the voice of a great thunder: and I heard the voice of harpers harping with their harps: and they sung as it were a new song before the throne, and before the four beasts, and the elders: and no man could learn that song but the hundred and forty and four thousand, which were redeemed from the earth. These are they which were not defiled with women; for they are virgins. These are they which follow the Lamb whithersoever He goeth. These were redeemed from among men, being the first fruits unto God and to the Lamb. And in their mouth was found no guile: for they are without fault before the throne of God" [Revelation 14:1–5].

This Scripture represents the character of the people of God for these last days. The everlasting gospel is to be preached, and it is to be practiced in true missionary work carried forward not after the wisdom that men may devise, but after the wisdom of God. All who walk in safe paths are to understand that the third angel's message is of consequence to the whole world, and must be carried to the world in clear, straight lines, and in its distinctive features, as Christ revealed it to John.

"And I saw another angel fly in the midst of heaven, having the everlasting gospel to preach unto them that dwell on the earth, and to every nation, and kindred, and tongue, and people, Saying with a loud voice, Fear God, and give glory to him; for the hour of his judgment is come: and worship him that made heaven, and earth, and the sea, and the fountains of waters. And there followed another angel, saying, Babylon is fallen, is fallen, that great city, because she made all nations drink of the wine of the wrath of her fornication. And the third angel followed them, saying with a loud voice, If any man worship the beast and his image, and receive his mark in his forehead, or in his hand, The same shall drink of the wine of the wrath of God, which is poured out without mixture into the cup of his indignation; and he shall be tormented with fire and brimstone in the presence of the holy angels, and in the presence of the Lamb: And the smoke of their torment ascendeth up for ever and ever: and they have no rest day nor night, who worship the beast and his image, and whosoever receiveth the mark of his name. Here is the patience of the saints: here are they that keep the commandments of God, and the faith of Jesus" (Revelation 14:6–12).

This is the message we have to bear; this is the work we have to do. This is the message God has kept before the Seventh-day Adventist people. The truth of this message will not decrease, but will increase in force and importance as we are brought down to the close of the work of God on earth. We have no time to lose.

"And I heard a voice from heaven saying unto me, Write, Blessed are the dead which die in the Lord from henceforth: Yea, saith the Spirit, that they may rest from their labors; and their works do follow them" [Revelation 14:14]. Since the proclamation of the first, second, and third angel's messages, many standard bearers have fallen asleep in Jesus; they have laid off their armor, but their works do follow them. The work advances, and the faithful ones hold the beginning of their confidence firm unto the end. This vision that Christ presented to John, presenting the commandments of God and the faith of Jesus, is to be definitely proclaimed to all nations, peoples, and tongues. The churches, represented by Babylon, are represented as having fallen from their spiritual state to become a persecuting power against those who keep the commandments of God and have the testimony of Jesus Christ. To John this persecuting power is represented as having horns like a lamb, but as speaking like a dragon.

"And I beheld another beast coming up out of the earth; and he had two horns like a lamb, and he spake as a dragon. And he exerciseth all the power of the first beast before him, and causeth the earth and them which dwell therein to worship the first beast, whose deadly wound was healed. And he doeth great wonders, so that he maketh fire come down from heaven on the earth in the sight of men, and deceiveth them that dwell on the earth by the means of those miracles which he had power to do in the sight of the beast; saying to them that dwell on the earth, that they should make an image to the beast, which had the wound by a sword, and did live. And he had power to give life unto the image of the beast, that the image of the beast should both speak, and cause that as many as would not worship the image of the beast should be killed. And he causeth all, both small and great, rich and poor, free and bond, to receive a mark in the right hand, or in their foreheads: and that no man might buy or sell, save he that had the mark, or the name of the beast, of the number of his name" (Revelation 13:11–17).

As we near the close of time, there will be greater and still greater external parade of heathen power; heathen deities will manifest their signal power, and will exhibit themselves before the cities of the world, and this delineation has already begun to be fulfilled.

By a variety of images the Lord Jesus represented to John the wicked character and seductive influence of those who have been distinguished for their persecution of God's people. All need wisdom carefully to search out the mystery of iniquity that figures so largely in the winding up of this earth's history. God's presentation of the detestable works of the inhabitants of the ruling powers of the world who bind themselves into secret societies and confederacies, not honoring the law of God, should enable the people who have the light of truth to keep clear of all these evils. More and more will all false religionists of the world manifest their evil doings; for there are but two parties—those who keep the commandments of God and those who war against God's holy law. One of the marked characteristics of these false religious powers in that while they profess to have the character and features of a lamb, while they profess to be allied to heaven, they reveal by their actions that they have the heart of a dragon, that they are instigated by and united with satanic power, the same power that created war in heaven when Satan sought the supremacy and was expelled from heaven.

Now, in these last days of this earth's history, the commandment-keeping people of God by keeping His law are to make earnest efforts to exalt the Lord God of heaven. The Word of God is specific, marking to a certainty the opposing influences against the seventh-day Sabbath, which is the sign of God and by which the loyalty of His people is tested. "And the Lord spake unto Moses, saying, Speak thou also unto the children of Israel, saying, Verily My Sabbaths ye shall keep: for it is a sign between Me and you throughout your generations; that ye may know that I am the Lord that doth sanctify you.

"Ye shall keep the Sabbath therefore; for it is holy unto you: every one that defileth it shall surely be put to death: for whosoever doeth any work therein, that soul shall be cut off from among his people. Six days may work be done; but in the seventh is the Sabbath of rest, holy to the Lord: whosoever doeth any work in the Sabbath day, he shall surely be put to death. Wherefore the children of Israel shall keep the Sabbath, to observe the Sabbath throughout their generations, for a perpetual covenant. It is a sign between Me and the children of Israel for ever: for in six days the Lord made heaven and earth, and on the seventh day He rested, and was refreshed" [Exodus 31:14–17].

The Sabbath was God's sign between Him and His people, and evidence of His kindness, mercy, and love, a token by which His people are distinguished from all false religionists of the world. And God has pledged Himself that He will bless them in their obedience, showing Himself that He is their God, and has taken them into covenant relation with Himself, and that He will fulfill His promise to all that are obedient. Not upon the first day, but upon the seventh day, God rested and was refreshed—satisfied with His work of creation. Then "the morning stars sang together, and all the sons of God shouted for joy," and now man's observance of the Lord's day of rest will again cause joy among the angels of heaven.

The time in which we live is a time when the church militant will realize the oppressive power of persecution, because they keep the Sabbath of creation which God has sanctified and blessed. The observance of the Sabbath is a line of demarcation between him that serveth God and him that serveth Him not. It is God's great memorial of the fact that in six days He created the heavens and the earth, and "on the seventh day He rested, and was refreshed." It is His memorial to preserve among the nations a clear, definite, unmistakable knowledge of the only true God, an evidence that He is a God above all gods.

For this reason He set apart the day on which He rested after creating the world, a day in which no common work should be done. God has given men six days in the week in which to labor and do all their work; the one day wherein He rested after creating the world and all things that are therein was to be His own holy day, when men should worship Him, the Creator of the heavens and the earth. This portion of time is especially set apart for rest and for worship, that men may look upon the heavens and the earth, and honor, worship, praise, and exalt the God who created all things by Jesus Christ. By observing the Sabbath day wherein God rested, the knowledge of God would be preserved. It is a "sign between Me and you ... that ye may know that I am the Lord that doth sanctify you." Those who keep the Sabbath holy as the Lord has specified, reveal that they are His peculiar people, and that He who made the heavens and the earth is their God.

In His ministerial labors Christ declared to the Pharisees and to the Sadducees and to all the Gentile world, "Think not that I am come to destroy the law, or the prophets: I am not come to destroy, but to fulfill. For verily I say unto you, Till heaven and earth pass, one jot or one tittle shall in no wise pass from the law, till all be fulfilled. Whosoever therefore shall break one of these least commandments, and shall teach men so, he shall be called the least in the kingdom of heaven: but whosoever shall do and teach them, the same shall be called great in the kingdom of heaven" [Matthew 5:17–19]. Thus did He rebuke the pretentious piety of the Pharisees, and thus did He correct their erroneous ideas of the law of God.

In the very time in which we live, the Lord has called His people and has given them a message to bear. He has called them to expose the wickedness of the man of sin who has made the Sunday law a distinctive power, who has thought to change times and laws, and to oppress the people of God who stand firmly to honor Him by keeping the only true Sabbath, the Sabbath of creation, as holy unto the Lord. He has called them to bear the sign of God, to exalt the Lord in keeping holy His law; for it is a transcript of His character. No part of the law of God and their covenant obligation to keep that law holy is to lose its binding claims upon all the world. Those who have had the light upon keeping the law of Jehovah are to stand firmly in the faith, and to make that light shine forth in clear, distinct rays.

The thirteenth chapter of Revelation presents a power that is to be made prominent in these last days. Let all understand that it is Christ, the Captain of the Lord's host, who gave these visions to John. Christ came in person to the lonely isle of Patmos, and showed John the things that must be, [things] that were of the highest importance to His people. Through the person of His highest angels. He had veiled His own glory.) This message is to come to God's people, straight, sharp, and clean from all mixture of human wisdom and tradition.

The enmity between the seed of the woman and the serpent is clearly defined by the Lord. "And I will put enmity between thee and the woman, and between thy seed and her seed; it shall bruise thy head, and thou shalt bruise his heel." "And unto Adam He said, Because thou hast hearkened unto the voice of thy wife, and hast eaten of the tree, of which I command-ed thee, saying, Thou shalt not eat of it: cursed is the ground for thy sake; in sorrow shalt thou eat of it all the days of thy life; thorns also and thistles shall it bring forth to thee; and thou shalt eat of the herb of the field; in the sweat of thy face shalt thou eat bread, till thou return unto the ground; for out of it wast thou taken: for dust thou art, and unto dust shalt thou return."

By following his own way, by acting in harmony with Satan's temptations and in opposition to the known will of God, man vainly attempted to elevate and bless himself. Thus he gained an experimental knowledge of disobedience to God's commandments. Thus he knew good and evil; thus he lost his fidelity and loyalty to God and opened the floodgates of evil and suffering to the whole human family. How many today are making the same experiment! When will man learn that the only means for his safety is through a full confidence in a "thus saith the Lord?"

Satan is seeking to intrude his own inventions upon the children of God through human methods. He is seeking to be received as God, or even to be placed above God.

In changing the Sabbath to the first day of the week, he leads men to disbelieve God's declarations, and so to regard their own ways and plans that they appear exceeding wise in their own eyes and in their perverted judgment. Through human policy he leads men to regard the expressed commandments of God as of less force than human tradition, and to regard a deviation from that law which is always holy and just and good, as of little account. He sees that by thus preventing human agencies from walking as obedient children in harmony with God, he can hinder the accomplishment of God's work in our world.

But Satan's connivings with human agencies who stand in responsible positions are just as much to be feared and shunned now after the experiment of sin has been tried, as it was in the case of our first parents. I am instructed to say that the men who are placed in positions of responsibility in the work of God have overestimated their right to control others. The position a man occupies does not change his character. Some have seemed to feel that they must devise for churches and for sanitariums and that there was to be no questioning of their judgment. Let them learn of Jesus at every step. He should be the chief authority for every man.

The One who has often been our Instructor says, "How hard it is for man to walk humbly with his God, in a contrite spirit taking God's way and rejecting Satan's propositions which seem to present great worldly advantages." The influence of man's having his own way in the place of firmly standing on the solid foundation that God alone has laid, has been repeated over and over again. Refusing to walk in the straight paths that God has signified will bring them to confusion and will not teach wisdom to others who have the same test and trial. When will man learn that God is God, and not a man that He should change?

Some who have departed from the right way have been in a continual fever to grasp responsibilities that God has not laid upon them. God calls upon every minister and every physician to maintain the simplicity of the truth. The Son of God who is revealed in both the Old and New Testaments is the Savior of our world today. From Him every medical missionary is to receive his training. Unless he shall separate himself from the prince of the power of the air, he will mislead souls who have confidence in him. Let all beware of men who are so educated and uplifted that their plans cannot be understood by the common people.

The intrigues of sin surpass infinite conception. Every calamity, every suffering and death, is an evidence not only of the power of evil but of the truth of the living God. Having known the truth, the word of the living God, which abideth forever, and which through obedience gives life, man's weakness in conforming to Satan's ingenuity is surpassingly strange. All who are taught of God recognize Christ as His Son. All who disbelieve the known declarations of God demonstrate the popularity of sin, and are not working on the side of life and immortality which are brought to light through perfect sanctification of the truth. Unless they make a change in character, in words, and in spirit, souls will be lost.

There is no middle path to Paradise restored. The message given to man for these last days is not to become amalgamated with human devising. We are not to lean upon the policy of worldly lawyers. We must be humble men of prayer, not acting like those who are blinded by Satan's agencies.

Many have a faith, but not a faith that works by love and purifies the soul. Saving faith is not simply a mere belief of the truth. "The devils also believe, and tremble." The inspiration of the Spirit of God gives to men a faith that is an impelling power that molds character, and leads men higher than mere formal actions. The words, the actions, and the spirit are to bear testimony to the fact that we are followers of Christ.

The greatest light and blessing that God has bestowed is not a security against transgression and apostasy in these last days. Those whom God has exalted to high positions of trust may turn from heaven's light to human wisdom. Their light will then become darkness, their God-entrusted capabilities a snare, their character an offense to God. God will not be mocked. A departure from Him has been and always will be followed by its sure results. The commission of acts that displease God will, unless decidedly repented of and forsaken, instead of seeking to justify them, lead the evildoer on step by step in deception till many sins are committed with impunity. All who would possess a character that would make them laborers together with God and receive the commendation of God, must separate themselves from the enemies of God, and maintain the truth which Christ gave to John to give to the world.

"I was in the Spirit on the Lord's day, and heard behind me a great voice, as of a trumpet, Saying, I am Alpha and Omega, the first and the last: and, What thou seest, write in a book, and send it unto the seven churches which are in Asia; unto Ephesus, and unto Smyrna, and unto Pergamos, and unto Thyatira, and unto Sardis, and unto Philadelphia, and unto Laodicea. And I turned to see the voice that spake with me. And being turned, I saw seven golden candlesticks; And in the midst of the seven candlesticks one like unto the Son of man, clothed with a garment down to the foot, and girt about the paps with a golden girdle. His head and his hairs were white like wool, as white as snow; and his eyes were as a flame of fire; And his feet like unto fine brass, as if they burned in a furnace; and his voice as the sound of many waters. And he had in his right hand seven stars: and out of his mouth went a sharp twoedged sword: and his countenance was as the sun shineth in his strength. And when I saw him, I fell at his feet as dead. And he laid his right hand upon me, saying unto me, Fear not; I am the first and the last: I am he that liveth, and was dead; and, behold, I am alive for evermore, Amen; and have the keys of hell and of death. Write the things which thou hast seen, and the things which are, and the things which shall be hereafter; The mystery of the seven stars which thou sawest in my right hand, and the seven golden candlesticks. The seven stars are the angels of the seven churches: and the seven candlesticks which thou sawest are the seven churches" (Revelation 1:10–20).

The revelation of Christ to John is a wonderful, dignified, exalted, solemn message. To present this message with decided emphasis demands all the talents of capabilities that God has given to man. When John received it, he was worked by the Holy Spirit, for Christ Himself came from heaven and told him what to write.

Those who claim to be disciples of Christ often express hardness of heart and blindness of mind, because they do not choose and practice God's way instead of their own. Selfish motives come in and take possession of mind and character, and in their self-confidence they suppose their own way to be full of wisdom. They are not particular to follow the ways and words of God. Circumstances, they say, alter cases. Worldly policy comes in and they are tempted and drawn away. They move according to their own unsanctified desires, making crooked paths for their own feet and for the feet of others to tread in. The lame and weak suppose them to be led by God, and therefore think that their judgment must be right. Thus many follow in false paths that are not cast up for the ransomed of the Lord to walk in.

The leaders are responsible not only for their own unsanctified mistakes, but for the mistakes of those who follow their example. When reproved for bringing in wrong principles they manifest a perverse spirit, a spirit that will not be corrected or humbled. "Shall I not judge for these things, saith the Lord of hosts?" Their own wisdom and their own judgment they hold fast as a precious possession, and sullenly pursue their own ways. This is the reason that the Holy Spirit of God is not manifest in our churches.

If those who have had the blessings of being corrected would humble themselves before God, and gladly take the Lord's way, reforming their own ways, Jesus Christ would bestow upon them rich gifts and grant answers to humble, contrite prayers.

By walking in the light given, they would better understand their own individual character. Those who think they can improve upon God's plan, that some other course would be better than that which Christ has laid down in His Word, savor not the things that be of God, but those that be of men. They harden their hearts and close their eyes in regard to the ways of the Lord, and prefer their own ways. Unless these are transformed in every respect—in thought, in word, and in deed—they will be requested to take the lowest seat.

If men only knew that their own wisdom exercised without Christ is a dangerous element that will mislead! If those who occupy positions of trust would be benefited by the intercession of Christ, and receive the rich blessings of His commendation, if they would be owned of God in the judgment, they must hear His counsels and be governed by His will; they must hold their confidence firm unto the end, never deviating from a plain "thus saith the Lord." Prevarication, even in the slightest shadow, must not be seen; every jot and tittle of this must be put away, because no falsehood can honor God.

There is no man who works in obedience to Christ's life in this world, who does all in Christ's name and to His glory, but will be honored. Those who hope to gain worldly recognition, who desire to be the highest in authority, and yet refuse to maintain Bible principles, principles of unselfish character in the service of God, however they may be exalted by those who themselves have not wisdom to obey God in keeping all His commandments, such exaltation and honor is of no value, for it is not recognized or endorsed in the heavenly courts. Seeking to stand as supreme in wisdom by securing the approval of men does not exalt them one tittle with God.

"Every good gift and every perfect gift is from above, and cometh down from the Father of lights, with whom is no variableness, neither shadow of turning." But few in our churches are true Christians. But few are bright and shining lights amid the moral darkness of this world. Were those who occupy positions as teachers worked by the Holy Spirit, Satan could not take possession of their hearts and minds.

We call for a decided, earnest seeking of God. Satan has come down in great power to our world, and is working with all deceivableness of unrighteousness in them that perish.

There is hope for our churches if they will heed the message given to the Laodiceans. Sabbath after Sabbath they meet together, and with effort sing the songs that are assigned, but that do not come from the heart. The joy of Christ in the heart will make songs to come from inspired lips and warm, thankful hearts.

The Lord would be much better glorified if His people possessed the spirit of meekness and humility. Personal labor is needed in our churches. Men and women inspired with an evangelistic spirit should go forth and invigorate others with the hope of the gospel.

Let all our assemblies be stirred by the old heart-searching truths of the gospel. These truths will bring conviction to souls. Say to those assembled, "'When the Son of man cometh, shall He find faith on the earth?' Be warned, be entreated to arise from lethargy, and remove this self-complacent spirit." When true faith is exercised, the Spirit of God will mold and fashion the soul that it may become a pure and holy place, a dwelling place for God. When Christ is "formed within, the hope of glory," a new life is imparted.

Satan is busily at work in our crowded cities. His working is to be seen in the confusion, the strife, and discord between labor and capital, and the hypocrisy that has come into the churches. That men may not take time to meditate, Satan leads them into a round of gaiety and pleasure-seeking, of eating and drinking. He fills them with ambition to make an exhibition that will exalt self. Step by step the world is reaching the conditions that existed in the days of Noah. Every conceivable crime is committed. The lust of the flesh, the pride of the eyes, the display of selfishness, the misuse of power, the cruelty, and the force used to cause men to unite with confederacies and unions—binding themselves up in bundles for the burning of the great fires of the last days—all these are the working of satanic agencies. This round of crime and folly men call "life."

Death, eternal death, will soon be the portion of all who reject Christ. All heaven is looking on to see what is being done by those who know the truth. Many are in the condition that Christ speaks of as "neither cold nor hot." The works of such testify against them that they are not walking, and working, and praying, and teaching the word of life.

The world, who act as though there were no God, absorbed in selfish pursuits, will soon experience sudden destruction, and shall not escape. Many continue in the careless gratification of self until they become so disgusted with life that they kill themselves. Dancing and carousing, drinking and smoking, indulging their animal passions, they go as an ox to the slaughter. Satan is working with all his art and enchantments to keep men marching blindly onward, until the Lord arises out of His place to punish the inhabitants of earth for their iniquities, when the earth "shall disclose her blood, and shall no more cover her slain." The whole world appears to be in the march to death.

Will the message to the Laodicean church now be heeded? Christ represents Himself as being disgusted with the churches of today. He cannot endure their taste; but yet He offers for them a word of hope. "As many as I love, I rebuke and chasten: be zealous therefore, and repent." Let every one heed the words that come to the people of God today, "Arise, shine; for thy light is come, and the glory of the Lord is risen upon thee." Shall we by confessing our sins, seek the Lord before the terrible spirit from beneath becomes the sole ruling power in our lives?"